W9-BXL-017

The PSYCHOLOGY of ANXIETY

EUGENE E. LEVITT is Chief of the Section of Psychology, Department of Psychiatry, Indiana University Medical Center, and Professor of Clinical Psychology at Indiana University School of Medicine.

The PSYCHOLOGY of ANXIETY

Eugene E. Levitt

The BOBBS-MERRILL Company, Inc.
A Subsidiary of Howard W. Sams & Co., Inc.
Publishers • Indianapolis • New York • Kansas City

TO MY MOTHER

who never made me any more anxious than she had to.

Printed in the United States of America
Library of Congress Catalog Card Number 67-19654
First Printing

In all ages, everything changes. Manners, customs, speech, views on life, even morals—all change. But fear is the same. Only fear is the same.

Carter Dickson, 1956

FOREWORD

We are living in an age of anxiety. The causes for contemporary anxiety are complex: two world wars within our century, and a cold war persisting since the last one; enormous mobility of peoples, geographically and economically, disturbing the sense of rootedness; shifting values, so that we are uncertain about child-rearing practices, about moral standards, about religious beliefs. Whatever the causes, the signs of anxiety lie around us, in part through social disaffection and delinquency, alienation and anomie, alcoholism, drug addiction, divorce, and mental illness. When, then, a book attempts to give a sober introduction to what we know about anxiety, it is dealing with a problem of central importance to our times. In this book Dr. Levitt has attempted to point out both what we know and what we do not know. Much of the evidence is fragmentary, and the conclusions from research tenuous; this is the state of our knowledge, and Dr. Levitt has not tried to distort what we know to make a case for some particular interpretation. At the same time, he has not hesitated to point to the directions in which present research is taking us.

Ernest R. Hilgard

Stanford University
April 1966

ACKNOWLEDGMENTS

The author of a book like this one needs a great deal of assistance ranging from incentive through clerical skills to expert advice. I have had a full share of helping hands and heads. I am indebted to Ernest R. Hilgard, Clayton E. Ladd, Jean McKeithen, Sidney Ochs, and Charles D. Spielberger for many criticisms and suggestions for improving the organization and content of the book; to Luciano L'Abate who kindly provided me with his unpublished bibliography of anxiety studies, and Janet Foy who abstracted many of the articles listed therein; to the authors and publishers who allowed me to reproduce copyrighted materials; to Carol Arden, Elizabeth Dailey, and Vivian Eldridge, who faithfully typed the many drafts which preceded these printed pages, and Barbara Cancel, who edited the final one; and to the publishers for suggesting that a book like this one could actually be written.

Despite this formidable succorance, nothing publishable would ever have emerged without the prolonged forbearance of the six Levitts who lived with me while I drafted and redrafted, and the unfailing encouragement and support of my friend and colleague, John I. Nurnberger, chairman of the Department of Psychiatry, Indiana University School of Medicine.

Eugene E. Levitt

Indianapolis, Indiana
November 1966

CONTENTS

LIST OF TABLES xii

LIST OF FIGURES xiv

1. INTRODUCTION 1

Why a Book on Anxiety? 1
The Approach to the Subject 3

2. THE TERMINOLOGY OF ANXIETY 5

The Problem of Definition 5
Anxiety, Fear, and Phobia 7
Anxiety and Stress 11
Tension 12
Kinds of Anxiety 13
Summary 15

3. THEORIES OF THE BASIS OF ANXIETY 17

The Purpose of a Theory 17
Freud's Psychoanalytic Theory 18
Neo-Freudian Theory 23
Learning Theory and Experimental Psychology 26
Summary 32

4. DEFENSES AGAINST ANXIETY 34

Defense Mechanisms 35
Coping Mechanisms of Everyday Life 50
Summary 53

5. THE EXPERIMENTAL MEASUREMENT OF ANXIETY 55

Measuring Anxiety Objectively 55
Physiological Measures 56

Psychological Measures 57
Sources of Anxiety in Experimental Studies 77
Validity of Artificially Induced Anxiety 79
Experimental Design in Anxiety Studies 82
Sampling Variations 84
Extraneous Personal Factors Affecting Anxiety Experiments 85
Summary 89

6. THE PHYSIOLOGY OF ANXIETY 91

Physiological Reactions to Emotional Stimulation 91
Theories of the Neurophysiology of Emotion 92
Endocrinology of Anxiety 97
Does Mental Illness Have a Physiological Cause? 103
Summary 107

7. ANXIETY AND LEARNING 108

A Definition of Learning 108
Measuring Learning in the Laboratory 110
Theories of the Effect of Anxiety on Learning 112
Some Factors Affecting the Relationship Between Anxiety and Learning 120
Learning and Muscle Tension 132
Summary 136

8. ANXIETY AND COGNITIVE PROCESSES 139

Problem-Solving 139
Incidental Learning 144
Verbal Communication 145
Mode of Responding 148
Intelligence Test Performance 149
Summary 152

9. ANXIETY AND PERSONALITY 153

Is There an "Anxious Personality"? 154
Anxiety and Personality Styles 158
Summary 166

10. THE ANXIETIES OF EVERYDAY LIFE 167

Illness 168
Surgery 171
Dental Treatment 174
Death 175
The Social Psychology of Anxiety 177
Summary 184

11. ANXIETY: A BRIEF OVERVIEW 186

Methodological Problems 186
The Origin of Anxiety 192
The Concept of Anxiety 194
Anxiety as a State of General Arousal 196
Intracranial Stimulation as Psychotherapy 198
The Social Value of Anxiety 199

REFERENCES 201

SELECTED SUGGESTIONS FOR ADVANCED READING 214

INDEX 215

LIST OF TABLES

I. Sample Items from Taylor's Manifest Anxiety Scale 61
II. Sample Items from the IPAT Anxiety Scale 63
III. Sample Items and Sample Responses from the S-R Inventory of Anxiousness 65
IV. Sample Items from the Assimilation Scale, Adult Male Form 66
V. The Affect Adjective Check List 68
VI. The Subjective Stress Scale 69
VII. Sample Items from the Freeman Manifest Anxiety Test 70
VIII. Sample Items from the State-Trait Anxiety Inventory 72
IX. Sample Items from the Test Anxiety Questionnaire 73
X. Sample Items from the Achievement Anxiety Test 76
XI. WAIS Digit Span Scores as a Function of Reported Stress 81
XII. Original Tabulation of Results in the Mednick Experiment: Average Number of Incorrect Responses by Anxiety Level Subgroups 87
XIII. Breakdown of the Data in Table XII According to Time of Participation 88
XIV. Examples of Actions of the Autonomic Nervous System 92
XV. Increases in Physiological Measures as a Function of Induced Anxiety and Anger: Data from Three Experiments 99

XVI. Average Performance and Muscle Tension Under Varying Conditions of Motivation 119

XVII. Average Number of Nonsense Syllables Learned as a Function of Anxiety and Task Difficulty 125

XVIII. Effect of Reassurance on the Relationship Between Anxiety and Verbal Learning 131

XIX. Number of Anagrams Solved as a Function of Anxiety-Proneness 141

XX. Effect of Anxiety on Timed and Untimed Measures of Intelligence 151

XXI. Theoretical Relationships Between Defense Mechanisms and Personality Traits 158

LIST OF FIGURES

1. The Gradient of Stimulus Generalization as a Function of Strength of Fear Evoked by the Original Stimulus 28
2. Types of Conflict Situations Schematized 31
3. The Original Finding of the U-Shaped Curve Relating Drive Level and Learning 118
4. Anxiety Proneness and Learning 121
5. Learning and Muscle Tension 133
6. Performance, Induced Tension, and Heart Rate 136
7. Effect of Naturalistic Stress on Problem-Solving 143
8. Temporal Course of Anxiety in Various Groups of Surgery Patients 172
9. Postoperative Emotional Disturbance as a Function of Preoperative Anxiety Level 173

1

INTRODUCTION

Why a Book on Anxiety?

We are not aware of any systematic conception of personality, particularly with regard to its development, which does not give the concept of anxiety a role of great, if not of central, significance (Sarason, *et al.*, 1960).

Anxiety is one of the most important concepts in psychoanalytic theory. It plays an important role in the development of personality as well as in the dynamics of personality functioning. Moreover, it is of central significance in Freud's theory of the neuroses and psychoses and in the treatment of these pathological conditions . . . (Hall, 1954).

If anxiety could be controlled by biological or social means, fundamental alterations in the organization of our civilization would ensue and the probability of individual happiness would be greatly enhanced. . . . Anxiety is the most pervasive psychological phenomenon of our time . . . (Hoch and Zubin, 1950).

Anxiety is the official emotion of our age (Schlesinger, 1948).

It is difficult to dispute the contention that anxiety is a "pervasive psychological phenomenon" of modern society. The world seems literally to drip with it. It begins in infancy with a fear [1] of the unknown and the yet unexperienced of life, winds its way painfully through countless occurrences, large and small, and concludes with a fear of that unknown which is death. It is not that the emotion itself is of recent origin, or that it is somehow of greater significance today than it has been in the past. Surely fear is as old as human existence and belongs to no particular era or culture.

[1] For the absence of distinction between anxiety and fear, see Chapter Two, pp. 7–11.

The capacity to experience fear is an inheritance from our infrahuman ancestors. Among organisms with meager intelligence, it is necessary for survival. If an animal were incapable of fearing the larger, stronger, or more heavily armed predator, or the forest fire, it might never realize the need for disengagement and flight until death was imminent. Emotional experience cues an immediate reaction; in the forest and jungle, there is often no time for deliberation even if the organism were capable of it.

The utility of fear as a survival mechanism decreases as intelligence increases. The need for emotion as a quick trigger for behavior is inversely related to reasoning ability. In the pinnacle of phylogeny—in the maximum in cerebral efficiency, man—fear has lost most of its survival value and has become instead the most serious problem of his existence.

Man no longer urgently needs fear as a protective device, but its strength, its ability to motivate behavior, is no less in us than in unreasoning organisms. This has been perennially recognized by human society, which uses fear in shaping the behavior of its members, especially the young. The trouble is that we do not yet know *how* to use fear without producing distortion and malignancy. Anxiety is a sort of cunning, malicious *golem,* which seems to serve us well, at least for a time, but eventually turns and threatens to destroy its creators.

Anxiety is timeless; but only in recent years, with the growth of sophistication in the mental health professions and the behavioral sciences, have we begun to realize its enormous impact on human life. The list of phenomena in which it has been claimed that anxiety plays a role is imposing. Nearly every identifiable form of pathology—psychological, physical, and social—is included. Almost every corner of human endeavor is thought to be affected somehow by anxiety. Thousands of papers and reports of experiments are devoted to it each year in learned journals. Anxiety is not only our official emotion; it is the primary focus of a concerted effort aimed at the improvement, and perhaps the perpetuation, of human life.

The Approach to the Subject

A group of medieval monks, the story goes, were diligently engaged in learned contention about the number of teeth in the mouth of the horse. Finally, one of the monks, doubtless young and unseasoned in the ways of theological disputation, suggested that the argument might be resolved by procuring the nearest horse and examining its mouth. The others were horrified. It is not certain whether they banished the offender from the monastery, turned him over to the Inquisition as a heretic, or simply hushed him up. In any event, it is quite certain that the monks totally rejected the idea of discovering any answers by *empirical* means.

"Empirical" literally means "by observation," especially as it refers to natural phenomena. Nowadays, hardly anyone seeks information about nature in venerable books or religious writings, as medieval monks would have done. We moderns obtain our knowledge "from the horse's mouth."

Naturalistic observation, while undoubtedly superior to unsupported opinion, even the opinion of an expert, also has its shortcomings. Horses are not all alike, and counting the teeth in the mouth of a single horse would not demonstrate that *all* horses had the same number. Furthermore, the human eye, ear, and brain, the instruments of observation, are notoriously fallible.

Naturalistic observation, though still the primary data-gathering technique of a few disciplines like astronomy and anthropology, has in turn given way to a superior procedure: scientific method. The word "empirical," in a parallel fashion, has undergone a transformation of meaning and is now considered to be practically synonymous with "scientific" or "experimental."

All this is by way of introduction to the statement that this book is an empirical account of anxiety, not a philosophical treatise. Most of the inferences and conclusions about anxiety that will be encountered are derived from scientific experimentation, not from mere observation or expert opinion. This renders the exposition credible, but it does *not* mean that subsequent pages are crammed full of ultimate, unchallengeable facts. Quite the contrary—behavioral science, a category that includes psychology, sociology, and experimental education, among others, is barely out of its infancy. Its journals abound with reports of experiments that are conflicting, confusing, ambiguous, or difficult to interpret, to say nothing of some which are badly done. Very little about human behavior has been established conclusively. No final words have as yet been written. Some findings are reported more often than others; some appear more logical or reasonable than others; there are many promising trends, and avenues yet to be fully explored.

The Psychology of Anxiety is based upon these findings. A comprehensive collation of all the experiments dealing with anxiety would be of inestimable value to a few scientists, and a hodgepodge of confusion to everyone else. The reader should keep in mind that I have exercised my private discretion in selecting certain ideas and works for inclusion, and in not presenting others. I am unimpressed by some experimental reports frequently cited by my colleagues; I have made much of findings that many of them would, perhaps, regard as trivial. My approach is, I think, properly characterized as scientific, but the book is nonetheless not without a subjective bias.

2

THE TERMINOLOGY OF ANXIETY

The Problem of Definition

In science, states like emotions and most of the words used to describe human personality are *constructs*. A construct is a broad abstraction, a hypothetical entity which has no actual physical existence, but which has proven useful in explaining observable phenomena. It is distinguished from something that has definite physical properties, like a table or a highway, or from an observable act that can be described by such a statement as "He ran down the street."

These "somethings" are directly manifest; an emotion like anxiety is not. One can dissect a human body and find a heart or brain, but one cannot locate objects which are properly called anxiety, or extraversion, or intelligence.

Constructs are used to explain behavior. We say that a person runs away because he has fear, or that his face reddens because he is angry. We also infer the existence of the emotion itself from these observable manifestations.

Constructs are popularly (but not scientifically) regarded as "things" that are amenable to purely verbal or vernacular definition. Various verbal definitions of anxiety sound very much alike:

> A painful uneasiness of mind over an impending or anticipated ill . . . (Webster, 1956).

> A danger signal felt and perceived by the conscious portion of the personality. It is produced by a threat from within the personality . . . with or without stimulation from . . . external situations . . . (APA, 1952).

> An unpleasant emotional state in which a present and continuing strong desire or drive seems likely to miss its goal; a fusion of fear with the anticipation of future evil; marked and continuous fear of low intensity; a feeling of threat, especially of a fearsome threat, without the person's being able to say what he thinks threatens . . . (English and English, 1958).

> Almost everyone agrees that anxiety is an unpleasant-feeling state, clearly distinguishable from other emotional states and having physiological concomitants. In addition to this common core of meaning, however, the term takes on other nuances and shadings of meaning, depending upon the particular theoretical orientation and operational criteria employed by individual researchers (Ruebush, 1963).

Apparently, we can say simply that anxiety is very much like fear and thus establish the "common core of the meaning," a general idea of what is meant by the construct, anxiety. Fear is a universal, personal experience; each of us has an awareness of fear deriving from our own existence. Or we could say, roughly speaking, that it is a complex state characterized by a subjective feeling of apprehension and heightened physiological reactivity.

We all understand the meaning of anxiety in this broad, vague sense, but it will not suffice for the purposes of science. Scientific definitions must be precise, objective, and quantifiable. Vernacular definitions of anxiety are themselves full of abstract constructs requiring definition. Exactly what is meant by "painful uneasiness," or "danger signal," or "unpleasant"? If we attempt to define each of these words, we find ourselves merely adding further constructs, each of which also requires defining.

> We could go on forever in this absurd fashion, adding word after word and phrase after phrase in a vain attempt to define the original, single-word construct. Even if the volume of verbiage becomes infinite, we shall not have added much more clear meaning to the word with which we began . . . (Levitt, 1961).

To be scientifically useful, a construct must be defined in terms of *acts*, not words alone. These acts are what Ruebush calls "operational criteria." In the experimental situation, anxiety is defined by a response or class of reactions by individuals to a particular stimulus or experimental situation. The experimenter threatens to shock the subject with electricity; the subject begins to sweat and his pulse rate increases. The threat of shock, the sweating, and the pulse rate together constitute a definition of anxiety. Or the experimenter may ask each subject the standard question, "Are you afraid?" The question and the response, "Yes," constitute another definition of anxiety.

The range of possible definitions is, in principle, unlimited, and, in practice, very broad. All of them are reasonably encompassed by the abstract, purely verbal definitions of anxiety. No one of these *operational definitions* is the ultimate definition. Rather, each is a partial definition, a *paradigm* or typical instance of anxiety. Each experimenter selects his own definition, guided by a "particular theoretical orientation," or by hunch, whim, previous research, common sense, or personal experience. The important consideration is whether the definition will eventually predict human behavior, and whether it is found to be related to other partial definitions.

If all the partial definitions actually define a single construct, then we should expect to find that they are correlated in the experimental situation. The individual who admits to being afraid should also manifest the physiological signs. When partial definitions turn out to be uncorrelated, some doubt is cast on the usefulness of the construct (although, of course, in an individual instance it may be the partial definition that is invalid). In such a case, we must conclude that what we have called anxiety is not a unitary phenomenon and perhaps ought to be fractionated. Perhaps we ought to distinguish between a psychological anxiety and a physiological anxiety and not try to group them under a single construct heading. Viewed in this light, anxiety is hypothetical, as well as a construct, for we are not yet sure that it does actually "exist" in the scientific sense.

Anxiety, Fear, and Phobia

The idea that anxiety is not a unitary phenomenon is not new. Many clinicians and theorists contend, for instance, that *fear* ought to be distinguished from anxiety. Two lines of argument support this decision.

Source

Various theorists have proposed that the term "anxiety" should be reserved for fear stemming from a source that is unknown to the stricken individual. It occurs "without stimulation from . . . external situations." When a person is aware of a threatening object or situation, we should speak of fear rather than of anxiety.

This difference between specific and "free-floating" proves difficult to maintain either in theory or in practice. It is obviously true that the person who steps from the curb and looks up to find a speeding car bearing down on him is afraid of a specific eventuality. But not much of significance in our lives is determined by this kind of fear. Nor do we tend to experience unpleasant emotion when we have to cross the street.

The person who is beset by free-floating anxiety is afraid that "something terrible is going to happen," but he does not know what it is. Such anxiety is seen in psychiatric patients suffering from anxiety states, but it is uncommon in the general population. Between the specific and the diffuse apprehension lie most anxiety reactions. They are neither highly specific nor completely diffuse. The mother who worries incessantly about her children's welfare is afraid of a multitude of occurrences. A man may be afraid that he will be injured in any one of a large number of different mishaps. At any particular moment, the fearsome stimulus is specific; in general, it is diffuse.

It has been suggested that free-floating anxiety is a relatively infrequent occurrence because anxiety does not remain for very long in a free state. To be afraid is painful; not to know why you are afraid can be catastrophic because you are then deprived of any avenue of escape from the threatening danger. To forestall a complete emotional collapse, the regulatory mechanisms of the personality are thought to attach the free anxiety to some object or event which then comes to be feared. A usual characteristic of this object or event is that it can be avoided without seriously impairing the person's general functioning (most of us can do very well even if we never take an airplane trip). There will ordinarily be a small kernel of reality to the fear (one *could* fall from a high place), but the fear is greatly exaggerated in proportion to the actual fearsome aspect of the stimulus. Such a state is called a *phobia*.

Phobia

A phobia is an exaggerated fear of a specific object or event when the probability of harm to the individual is very small. Phobias do exist, but the idea that they represent the investment of free-floating anxiety is not easy to verify. There is a kind of logic to the connection; one asks how a fear could become greatly exaggerated if it did not have an unclassified reservoir of anxiety to feed it. But logic, no matter how impeccable, cannot substitute for empirical verification. (The concept of stimulus generalization, discussed on pages 27–30 and represented graphically in Figure 1, is an alternative explanation of the development of phobia.)

The idea of a relationship between free-floating anxiety and phobia originated with Freud. Early psychoanalysts were very much concerned with the problem of identifying and treating phobias. Fifty years ago, a learned psychologist (Hall, 1914) compiled a list of 135 phobias, assigning to each the customary Greek derivative name, like *claustrophobia* (fear of enclosed places), *algophobia* (fear of pain), and *taphophobia* (fear of being buried alive).

Contemporary mental health practitioners are little concerned with phobia, though it is still conventional to refer to any anxiety not thought to be free-floating as "phobic." Interest in phobia has declined because it is usually difficult to determine when a fear is specific enough to be called a phobia. Obviously, peccatophobia (fear of committing a sin) is a common and partly idiosyncratic phenomenon. It is a rare person who will not avoid pain if he can; at what point should we refer to an algophobia? Instances in which the fear is clearly a phobia seldom occur.

The distinction between anxiety and fear based on a specific source holds up only at extremes. It is appropriate for the relatively rare occasions in which the emotion is provoked by a sharply delineated object or situation, and for the state of the psychiatric patient who cannot ascribe a reason for his feelings; it is difficult to apply to a multitude of states which fall in the midrange.

Proportionality

Another suggested distinction is that fear is proportionate to a perceived, objective danger, whereas anxiety is a disproportionately intense reaction. Suppose, for example, that a person finds himself living in an epidemic area in which as many as one out of every four people is contracting a very serious disease. Manifestations of fear in the form of prophylactic measures that cause inconvenience, discomfort, pain, hardship, and loss of pleasure would not be regarded as disproportionate. Now suppose that the incidence of the disease was one in 100,000 of the local population. The probability that any one person will contract the illness is so infinitesimal that extreme behavior would reflect an exaggerated fear.

This example is unusual. In many instances, it is no simple matter to determine the reality of the situation except, perhaps, in rather crude terms. For example, there is always *some* danger that something untoward will happen to a child who is permitted to go downtown by himself. Obviously, one does not allow this license to a four-year-old. At what age or stage of development, or under what circumstances, should a child be allowed to undertake this venture? At what point does parental anxiety cease being reality-oriented and become disproportionate? The determination is complex and difficult to make apart from a specific child and a specific circumstance.

The proportionality argument is very much like the matter of source. It can be maintained only at the extreme, but is otherwise lacking in applied value.

Finally, it should be noted that no difference between anxiety and fear, no matter how they are conceptualized in theory, is reflected in physiological concomitants. The human body reacts in much the same fashion whether the anxiety is considered to be specific, diffuse, exaggerated, or realistic.

The distinction between anxiety and fear is no more than theoretical, at least at present. Experimentalists consider the terms to be interchangeable, with perhaps different minor shadings of meaning. This position governs succeeding discussions in this book.

Anxiety and Stress

The word *stress* is used constantly in connection with emotional states; it appears almost as often in discussions of anxiety as does the word "anxiety" itself. The expression seems to be employed in a number of different ways, usually without a specific explanation of the user's intent. This usage has resulted in a fair amount of confusion, and suggests that there is no consensus on its meaning. But the word is so well implanted in the scientific literature on emotion that it cannot be ignored in any systematic treatment of anxiety.

Stress is a construct which psychology and medicine have taken over from the physical sciences. Physical stress is force exerted on a structure or system which, if increased beyond a certain intensity, will result in deformity of the structure or system. Hans Selye, the great proponent of stress as a factor in medicine, sought to apply the construct to dysfunction of the human body.[1] Despite its salience in his philosophy of medicine, Selye (1956) is none too clear about what he means by stress. At one point he says that stress is purely an abstraction, something like the mathematician's $\sqrt{-1}$ which is operationally useful but cannot have an actual existence. At another point, he refers to stress as a condition of the organism measured in terms of its reactions. And again, he calls it something which is brought about by a "stressor."

This confusion is carried on in the psychological literature. Varying contexts indicate that stress, to different experimenters and theorists, means:

1. A particular stimulus situation, without reference to the reactions of the subject;
2. A particular reaction or set of reactions of the individual, without reference to the situation;
3. A particular situation *and* a particular response or group of responses; or

[1] See Chapter Six, pp. 104–105.

4. A state of the individual which brings about a particular set of reactions.

The multiplicity of uses of the word very much resembles the employment of the word "anxiety" itself. The inference is that stress is being used approximately synonymously with anxiety, or with any other emotional state with which the experimenter or theorist is dealing. Anxiety and stress are "homomorphisms," as one theorist (Aiken, 1961) puts it. The value of a word like stress appears to be that its syntactical properties permit the writer to employ more graceful phrasings, that is, "stressful" rather than "anxiety-evoking," or "stressed" instead of "subjected to an anxiety-evoking stimulus."

To avoid any possible misunderstanding, I will indicate the specific terms under which stress will be used, in this book, to refer to anxiety.

1. A "stress" or "stressful" situation is one containing stimuli or circumstances calculated to arouse anxiety in the individual.
2. "Under stress" or "stressed" refer to an individual who is faced by, or in the midst of, a stress situation.
3. A "stress reaction" is an alteration of the individual's condition or performance which comes about presumably as a result of being under stress.

Essentially, this is the position advocated by Lazarus (1966):

> It seems wise to use "stress" as a generic term for the whole area of problems that includes the stimuli producing stress reactions, the reactions themselves and the various intervening processes. . . . Stress is . . . a collective term for an area of study. . . . As used here, it will be nothing more than a general label like motivation or cognition. It defines a large, complex, amorphous interdisciplinary area of interest and study.

Tension

Tension is another physical concept closely allied to stress. Literally, something that is tensed is stretched taut or distended by pressure or stress. If the stress continues past a certain point, the taut object will break.

In an analogous fashion, psychological tension refers to a state of the organism created by stress. The appropriateness of the concept is enhanced by the fact that an actual tensing of the musculature of the body is an ordinary concomitant of emotional arousal. Tension is also conceptualized more broadly as a state of disequilibrium brought about by some psychological need, leading to behavior that tends to satisfy the need and thereby restore equilibrium. In this sense, the tension of anxiety can be thought of as the result of a need to behave in a manner calculated to reduce the anxious feeling. Often, the anxiety is not experienced consciously because of the buffering effect of the defense mechanisms discussed in Chapter Four. The subsequent feeling is popularly known as "nervous tension."

Tension thus may have two meanings with reference to anxiety and stress. Less commonly, it refers to a condition of the musculature which accompanies anxiety, or which may be an anxiety residual. More often, tension means a vague feeling of disquiet, a restlessness, a diffuse, unidentified wanting to do *something* that is a consequence of anxiety occurring at a level below conscious awareness. In this sense, tension is an *intervening variable,* a state which links unconscious anxiety to manifest behavior.

Kinds of Anxiety

When the psychologist says that a person is anxious, the statement may be interpreted in either of two ways. It may mean that the individual is anxious *at the moment,* or it may mean that he is an *anxious person.* The two interpretations are quite different. The former refers to an immediate and probably ephemeral state, whereas the latter is a constant condition without a time limitation. The interpretations are usually differentiated by applying the adjectives *acute* and *chronic,* words commonly used to describe states of human pathology. "Acute" means of high intensity and relatively short duration; "chronic" means of relatively low intensity and indefinite duration.

"Acute," as a descriptive term, applies reasonably well to pathological anxiety states. The "acute anxiety attack" that brings a person to the psychiatrist's office seldom lasts very long, at least not in its initial, intense form. This high level of intensity is rarely encountered in experimental situations in which anxiety is being studied. The stressed laboratory subject often experiences an upsurge of anxiety, but it hardly ever achieves the proportions seen in naturally occurring psychopathology. We might therefore distinguish between *acute* as referring to the psychiatric patient, and *situational,* or *transient,* as describing the noticeable, but lesser, anxiety of the stressed subject.

Following general usage, chronic anxiety should mean a continuing state of relatively low anxiety. This conception is in conflict with the available facts. The acutely anxious person is characterized by a horrible awareness of his feelings, though he may not always be able to identify the feeling as anxiety. Continuous anxiety of *low* intensity is simply never reported. In theory, most of us may be characterized by a constant, low level of anxiety, of which we are ordinarily unaware. The individual who is regarded as chronically anxious, the "worrier," is identified not by a degree of anxiety but by a *high frequency of occurrences and objects* that evoke a detectable degree of anxiety in him.

"Chronic," in the sense of constant or continual, is misleading when applied to an emotional state like anxiety. What is actually meant is a high *proneness* or *predisposition* to experience anxiety. The anxiety-prone individual is one who has a noticeable upsurge of feelings of anxiety on a relatively large number of occasions, under more circumstances and in a larger number of different situations than do his peers.

The distinction between acute or situational anxiety and anxiety-proneness or predisposition has been delineated by Cattell and Scheier (1961), Lazarus (1966), and Spielberger (1966). Situational anxiety is a transitory *state* which is ephemeral, occurs in response to a stimulus and is likely to vary in intensity as a function of the stimulus, and is characterized by a variety of associated physiological reactions. Anxiety-proneness is a relatively unfluctuating condition of the individual which exerts a constant influence on his behavior. Such conditions of the individual are usually regarded as personality *traits* (see the introduction to Chapter Nine).

Spielberger (1966) has pointed out that anxiety-prone individuals—those who are high on "A-trait"—will experience "A-state" more frequently than those who are low on A-trait, but they will not necessarily experience A-state more intensely. In any given situation, the anxiety-prone individual is more likely to experience anxiety, but the intensity of his feeling will be a function of the nature of the situation as well as of his personal characteristics. Since we do not expect a perfect correlation between trait and state, it is invariably important to know which of the two meanings is intended by an experimenter or theorist when he employs the terms "anxiety" or "anxious." Meaning is determined by the operational criterion of anxiety, the instrument or device that is used to measure it in the experiment. The point will be clearer after the reader has been exposed to the heterogeneity of measurement techniques displayed in Chapter Five.

Summary

Anxiety and its allied concepts are, like many of the phenomena with which behavioral science deals, constructs. They are inventions of the scientist, so to speak, which are used to explain observable behavior, but have no clear physical existence themselves. Theoretical distinctions among anxiety, fear, and phobia are based on the degree to which the emotion is specific to a stimulus, or its appropriateness to a situation. These criteria are difficult to maintain pragmatically except for occasional extreme instances. For all practical and experimental purposes, anxiety and fear are indistinguishable.

The terms "stress" and "tension" are used frequently with reference to anxiety. The former appears to be a kind of operator word which is applied in connection with emotion-evoking situations and reactions. Analysis suggests that it is customarily employed in a more or less synonymous fashion with the particular emotion under investigation.

Tension may refer either to a condition of the musculature of the body which indicates the presence of anxiety, or to a vague feeling of restlessness which suggests the presence of anxiety at a level below conscious awareness.

The terms "acute" and "chronic" do not appear to be suitable for describing anxiety. For experimental purposes, the appropriate adjective to describe a temporary upsurge of anxiety is "situational." The individual to whom the word "chronic" is commonly applied might better be described as a person with a high predisposition or proneness to experience anxiety.

Constructs like anxiety and fear may be defined purely in vernacular terms for purely theoretical purposes. In the scientific investigation, constructs are defined in terms of operations and responses. Operational definitions are seen as partial definitions of the construct. An eventual demonstration of relationships among various partial definitions would verify the existence of a unitary construct. In this sense, behavioral science has not yet demonstrated that "anxiety" actually does exist.

3

THEORIES OF THE BASIS OF ANXIETY

The Purpose of a Theory

Most people know that the purpose of a theory is to explain the existence of an observable phenomenon whose cause is not yet fully known. If there were no other restrictions on theorizing, a theory would be indistinguishable from an opinion, a belief, or sheer fancy. A theory in science must be more than just a belief. It must also have certain properties:

1. The phenomenon being explained must be capable of being measured objectively;
2. The theoretical statement must be based on some already known facts and must encompass these facts in a logical manner; and,
3. The theory must permit the deduction of new hypotheses (subsections of a theory) which can be tested experimentally.

It is not necessary that a theory be true or correct in an absolute sense. A number of different theories can be advanced to explain the same phenomenon. Obviously, they cannot all be absolutely correct, but they can all be "true" *temporarily* if only they conform to the three conditions stated above, simply because none of them has as yet been proven inadequate. Many theories about all sorts of things have been "true" at one time but are now "false" because new facts have been discovered which the particular theory cannot explain.

A scientific theory is a means to an end, not an end in itself. Scientists are more concerned with the usefulness of a theory than with its accuracy. The major criterion of usefulness is the extent to which a theory gives rise to testable hypotheses. A useful theory is a powerful stimulus for research, for the uncovering of facts.

Usefulness is largely a function of the degree to which a theory is based on established facts rather than on speculation, though there will always be some "inferential bridges." These unsupported assumptions are themselves suitable subjects for experimental testing. But no theory can have more facts underlying it than are currently available to theorists. Because experimental work in the behavioral sciences is in a rather rudimentary state at present, the accumulated body of hard facts is small. The paucity of data sometimes forces the theorist to state even the primary phenomenon of his theory in looser terms than would ordinarily be permissible. This is true of theories of the origin of human anxiety.

The three theories which will be presented in subsequent pages are the most satisfactory of those that have been proposed, but no one of them is really adequate. Their shortcomings do not, however, render them unworthy of consideration.

Freud's Psychoanalytic Theory [1]

Sigmund Freud was a keen observer and a vastly imaginative thinker, but his genius was insufficiently tempered by regard for scientific method. Although the basic structure of his theory of personality development remained relatively constant over some fifty productive years, many aspects of it, some of them important, were never set down precisely. Freud does not seem to have been strongly impelled to keep his views logically consistent with one another, as long as they were consistent with the basic underpinning of his theory. He was a prolific writer, and his position on particular points changed from decade to decade, some-

[1] An exposition of psychoanalytic theories of the origins of anxiety necessarily makes references to the concept of the defense mechanism. The reader may wish to read the discussion of this phenomenon in Chapter Four before continuing.

times without reference to an earlier stand, or to other facets of the total structure. Thus the master's intentions are not always perfectly clear, and his followers have been left room for interpretation, occasionally with embellishments of their own.

Freud's concept of anxiety development is one of those which is not clearly formulated. Possibly the ambiguities result from the fact that Freud's position on anxiety underwent a drastic alteration some thirty years after the establishment of psychoanalysis. In the beginning, Freud regarded anxiety as a purely physiological reaction to the chronic inability to reach an orgasm in sexual relations. The process was considered to transpire on a neurophysiological-chemical level, and was not thought to be a truly psychological disturbance. It could (presumably) be completely alleviated simply by appropriate adjustments in the patient's sexual technique.

It seems incredible that not until much later did Freud recognize the crucial importance of anxiety for a theory of personality development. The change in his viewpoint was announced in a little book called *The Problem of Anxiety* (1923). Anxiety, he now said, is "a specific state of unpleasure accompanied by motor discharge along definite pathways . . . a signal of danger. . . . Symptoms are created in order to remove . . . the situation of danger. . . . Anxiety would be the fundamental phenomenon and the central problem of neurosis."

He went on to distinguish three types of anxiety differing with respect to provocation. *Reality anxiety* has a clearly identifiable, warranted source in the external world and is proportionate to the threat posed by the feared object or situation. To have reality anxiety is sensible and adaptive.

Neurotic and *moral anxiety* are the troublemakers. Their sources must be discussed within the framework of Freud's well-known tripartite concept of basic personality structure.

Freud conceptualized the human personality as being composed of three parts: the *id,* the *ego,* and the *superego.* The id represents the biological or "instinctual" drives, including sex, aggression, hunger, thirst, elimination, and needs involved in sensory processes, like the need for warmth or coolness.

Freud was always much impressed with the strength of biological drives. He saw the id as an unreasonable, animal-like entity that constantly seeks immediate and complete gratification, totally without reference to other consequences for the organism.

The ego is the aspect of the personality which is attuned to reality. It perceives the world external to the organism and controls its voluntary behavior. It assimilates information from the environment, reasons, thinks, and solves problems. In other words, the ego is as typically human as the id is animal.

One might say that id and ego are naturally occurring entities whose existences are inevitable. The superego—roughly synonymous with "conscience"—is strictly a social creation. Its development is a consequence of conflict between the id and ego.

All human societies impose limitations on the expression of id impulses. Failure to conform can bring punishment in different forms from the environment. In the early years of life, the ego is too weak to deal directly with the powerful id. Superego develops in an effort to assist the ego in controlling the id.

The superego has its beginnings in restrictions and punishments imposed upon the small child by the all-powerful parent. Eventually, the lessons originally imposed from without become unconsciously internalized by the individual and are transformed into moral and ethical tenets, which the individual regards as part of his own philosophy of life.

Freud's concept of the superego differs considerably from the philosopher's idea of a moral conscience. The superego is as arbitrary, unreasonable, and rigid in imposing limitations as is the id in demanding immediate gratification. Both id and superego are unaffected by external reality, nor can they compromise with each other in their constant struggle. The tendency of the id is to feel, to want, to do, regardless of circumstances. The countertendency of the superego is to block any behavior initiated by the id, also regardless of circumstances. Superego is conscience, in the popular sense, only when it is reality-directed by the ego; id is controlled to the benefit of the individual only when control is exercised by an ego-directed superego.

According to Freud, the first experience of anxiety in human life occurs at birth, simply as a consequence of the neonate's precipitate exodus from the calm, sheltered uterine environment into a barrage of unfamiliar stimulation. Physiological needs are no longer gratified automatically as they were *in utero*. Nor is the infant capable of obtaining gratification through its own efforts. A diffuse tension arises which is a consequence of the infant's vague awareness that his id needs may be frustrated because he is helpless to satisfy them by himself. He perceives dimly that he cannot survive without the attention of his mother. Cries of discomfort attest to this realization.

Freud goes on to say that "the perception of the absence of the mother now becomes the danger at the appearance of which the infant gives the signal of anxiety . . ."[2] (Freud, 1923). This *primary anxiety,* arising from a circumstance which is a basic threat to the survival of the organism, sets the pattern for all subsequent anxiety reactions.

Primary anxiety is peculiar to the first months of life when the human being lacks both ego and superego, and during which all his id needs are gratified as completely as possible. Ego development begins late in the first year of life, largely as a function of normal maturation. With it comes the first, externally imposed limitations on the expression and gratification of id needs.

Every society imposes such restrictions through its current generation of parents. Without curtailment of id, such an institution as society would be impossible. Parents enforce restrictions by means of threats of loss of love and support, which the very young child interprets as potential deprivation of basic physiological needs.

A new kind of anxiety now arises. It is a direct consequence of the fact that the id still dominates the child's existence. Both ego and superego are relatively weak, though the former is sufficiently well developed to perceive the new threat. For the id is constantly threatening to overwhelm the ego and thereby to bring about deprivation of needs in the form of punishment. With id-inspired greediness, the child wants the cookies which

[2] Of course, the only "signal of anxiety" that is within the behavioral repertory of the infant is crying or perhaps diffuse body movement. It is evident that the accuracy of the interpretation cannot be verified.

are forbidden to him between meals. The drive is strong, but the child who acts to gratify it faces the fearful prospect of parental discipline. The situation recalls, unconsciously, the primary anxiety of the early months of life and is similarly interpreted as a "signal of danger."

In later life, the id is brought under the control of ego and superego and seldom presents a conscious threat. However, it may be unconsciously threatening, for there are still circumstances that provoke id impulse. These are primarily instigations to sexual and aggressive behavior, such as the attractive or seductive neighbor's wife, or the unpleasant but powerful employer. Such instigations may not be perceived directly by the ego. Rather, they are experienced unconsciously as anxiety against which the ego must be defended and about which it must actively do something. This is the experience of neurotic anxiety, the threat of the id to overwhelm the ego with consequent acting-out of socially unacceptable sexual or aggressive impulses.

The superego—the ego's early ally in controlling the id—may also become a recalcitrant over which the ego may lose control. The superego may then threaten severe punishment, not only for the overt expression of id needs when they are inappropriate, but also for id expression at any time, or even the thought of id-directed behavior. This threat leads to Freud's "moral anxiety." It is experienced not as a fear reaction but as guilt or shame. For example, a hostile expression or act toward a bully, or the fantasy of a sexual approach to the neighbor's wife, may call forth a moral anxiety reaction.

The primary function of the ego is to maintain the individual's emotional stability by preventing the conscious experience of anxiety arising from id and superego threats. For this purpose, the ego develops the defense mechanisms and personality characteristics discussed in Chapters Four and Nine. The successful ego uses these to transform the energy of anxiety into socially acceptable, useful behavior. But when anxiety becomes so strong, for whatever reason, that the defenses are overwhelmed, psychopathological symptoms develop in an effort to cope with the surging anxiety.

Neo-Freudian Theory

Neo-Freudianism was a movement that sprang up during the 1930's and 1940's (see, for example, Thompson, 1950). Its leaders were the psychiatrist Harry Stack Sullivan, the analyst Karen Horney, and Erich Fromm, a social psychologist. To summarize neo-Freudianism in one sentence, we might say that it changed the orientation of psychoanalysis from the biological and instinctual to the cultural and environmental. The movement obtained much impetus from the work of the psychoanalyst-anthropologist Abram Kardiner. Kardiner's psychoanalytic examinations of primitive cultures derived from an effort to demonstrate that Freud's biological-instinctual theory was correct. Kardiner found exactly the opposite. Instead of an immutable, basic pattern of personality development, which would be expected according to Freudian theory, he discovered that personality development and characteristics varied widely around the world, in much the same way that social patterns, customs, and cultures vary.

The neo-Freudians accept much of orthodox theory and freely acknowledge a debt to Freud. Their deviations from the orthodoxy of Freudian psychoanalysis may be viewed as merely a matter of differential emphasis, but they have resulted in elaboration of points barely touched upon by Freud, to the extent that we may reasonably speak of new ideas.

The neo-Freudians regard human personality development as largely a product of social influence in which biological drives play a relatively minor role. They do not consider that biological impulses are inherently threatening to the organism; they scarcely make use of the word "id," though they retain "ego" and "superego."

They do not credit the Freudian concept of primary anxiety. Anxiety cannot arise before the ego has reached a minimum stage of development—that is, before the organism has some awareness of its environment. What the neo-Freudians view as primary anxiety comes about early in life—probably before the end of the first year. It comes after the young child realizes, however dimly, that he is relatively helpless and heavily dependent upon influential adults, primarily his parents, not only for gratification of his basic physiological needs, but also for protection and support in the constantly appearing new situations with which he feels that he cannot cope alone. The threat of frustration of physiological needs is regarded as unimportant. It is the possibility of loss of protection and security, the frustration of *dependency needs,* which is anxiety-arousing. Dependency needs arise as a consequence of the child's realizing his helplessness and his need for support by those who are more powerful.

The process of socialization begins as soon as the minimum amount of ego has developed (that is to say, as soon as the child can understand his parents' wishes). The parents enforce the social mores and customs, with their inevitable restrictions on expression of impulse, by means of punishment and threats of withdrawal of affection and support. This threat to dependency needs evokes anxiety and impels the child to conform to the parents' expectations in order to avoid it.

If the process went no further, adult anxiety would be much less a problem. But restriction on the expression of basic impulses is frustrating, and the natural response of mammals to frustration is an outburst of hostility directed against the frustrating agency. The neo-Freudians are much more impressed by the developmental importance of aggression as a drive than the Freudians. Frustration itself is a relatively minor influence; the consequent hostility creates the difficulties.

All human society places definite limitations on the expression of aggression, regardless of its origin. In Western civilizations, childhood aggression is likely to be met by severe parental disapproval. This is most often true when hostility is directed toward the parents themselves. Disapproval may take the form of physical punishment, coercion, or threats of loss of support—in short, all the kinds of pressures that arouse primary anxiety in the child. He must learn, therefore, to handle his aggressive feelings in some way other than direct expression against the parents. The defense mechanisms, primarily repression, serve this purpose. Repression is a kind of automatic, immediate forgetting of a feeling or thought which takes place without the awareness of the individual.

In later life situations in which the person's anger is provoked, the original connection—perhaps long forgotten—between parental disapproval and expression of hostility may cause an upsurge of anxiety to be experienced. This *secondary anxiety,* anxiety arising as a consequence of the very defenses employed against primary anxiety, is a new concept contributed by the neo-Freudians. Most human anxiety, they point out, is secondary. The individual personality comprises defense mechanisms and traits that were developed to defend against primary anxiety.[3] Once developed, they tend to become stable and somewhat rigid. The individual must adjust to new demands made by the environment, to new threats, without disturbing his basic defensive system. A severe threat to the defensive system is likely to evoke a fresh secondary-anxiety reaction which in turn may require harsh intensification of an existing defense, or the employment of a new defense.

Suppose, for example, that the individual has developed compulsivity—a strong need to be neat and methodical, to arrange his environment in an orderly fashion—as a defense against primary anxiety. He finds himself in the midst of a disordered, chaotic circumstance which he cannot rectify and from which he cannot extricate himself. He is likely to find such a situation anxiety-producing. He may now defend himself against this anxiety by means of denial—that is, by a new defense, one that distorts reality by insisting that the disorder does not, in fact, actually exist.

Original defenses that are basically sound are not easily threatened by new situations. If they are weak, or become weak because of prolonged stress, a vicious cycle may ensue in which fresh anxiety requires a new defense, which causes further anxiety, and so on. This "pyramiding of defenses" is the burden under which psychopathological illness develops.

[3] See the discussion of this theoretical point in Chapter Nine, pp. 157–158.

Learning Theory and Experimental Psychology

Psychoanalytic theory is based largely on observational data obtained from psychiatric patients. It is almost entirely clinical, unlike theories of science for which data are derived from experimentation. Although psychoanalytic theory should not be ignored or lightly cast aside, to accept it uncritically would be unwise, no matter how logical it may seem or how much it appears to agree with one's own thinking or experiences.

Psychoanalytic theory, despite the looseness of its formulation and the absence of empirical foundation, has served the primary purpose of all theory; it has given rise to testable hypotheses. A considerable amount of scientific research has been done in an effort to investigate various components of psychoanalytic theory. A major effort in this direction has been made by psychologists John Dollard and Neal Miller (1950).[4] The form of their theory of the origin and development of anxiety is typically that of the experimental psychologist who works in the area of learning, but its content parallels psychoanalytic theory.

In order to understand the Dollard-Miller conception, we must start with a few basic concepts of learning theory. Motivating forces are called *drives*. The primary characteristic of a drive is that it energizes the organism to seek some method to reduce the degree or intensity of the drive. The *primary* drives are those with which the organism is innately endowed, like hunger, thirst, and sex—the components of Freud's id. These are limited in number. The more important and influential drives are *secondary*, or acquired during the existence of the organism through the learning process. The number of such possible drives is literally unlimited. The acquiring of drives is mediated by reward and punishment, in the broadest sense of these terms. A reward or punishment which affects or brings about behavior is called a *reinforcement*.

[4] Dollard and Miller draw heavily upon the theories of Clark L. Hull, one of the outstanding leaders of experimental psychology. Hull's position is outlined in detail in his book, *Principles of Behavior* (1943).

According to Dollard and Miller, anxiety is a powerful secondary drive.[5] Their theory suggests how anxiety is learned and how it becomes associated with objects and events.

Dollard and Miller begin with the implicit postulation of a primary drive to avoid physical pain. Indeed, one can hardly question the idea that pain avoidance is an innate motivation, for without it an organism would be likely to perish early in its existence. An organism must learn to fear whatever produces pain in order to survive. Pain, then, is the reinforcer for the secondary drive, anxiety, or fear.

The strength of a drive can be shown to depend primarily upon the number of reinforcements—that is, the number of occasions upon which the feared object or condition is accompanied by pain—and upon the intensity of the reinforcement. The greater the number of associated experiences and the more intense the pain, the stronger will be the fear. Pain as a reinforcer of anxiety applies equally, in principle, to a hot stove and to the parental hand.

Anxiety would surely not be the pervasive phenomenon that it is if the organism could learn to fear only the isolated stimulus which evokes pain at a particular moment. The fear reaction is extended—is *generalized*—in two ways. The organism may learn to fear not only the stimulus itself but also things associated with the stimulus and the circumstances within which it is experienced. These associated phenomena are called *cues*. For example, if the spankings which young John receives from his father are invariably accompanied or preceded by a scolding in a loud voice, scolding may then become a cue and John will fear it as he does the spanking. The extent to which the emotion generalizes to cues is a function of its strength. If John's fear of parental punishment is strong enough, he may come to fear any loud voice even if it is not finding fault with him.

A second way in which anxiety is extended is through *stimulus generalization*. The organism learns to fear objects or conditions that are descriptively similar to the original, fearsome stimulus.

[5] In laboratory animals, learning impelled by fear (or by pain, to be more precise) is faster and more resistant to change than learning motivated in any other fashion.

Little John was bitten by a fox terrier named Rover and is now afraid of Rover. Possibly he is also afraid of all fox terriers, or all dogs, or even cats or other four-legged animals. This *gradient of generalization* depends on two factors: the degree of similarity of objects or conditions to the original, fear-evoking stimulus, and the strength of the fear drive. Fear of the original stimulus will always be strongest; fear will decrease as the objects which resemble it become less similar to it. John's fear of fox terriers other than Rover will be stronger than his fear of other breeds of dog, which will in turn be stronger than his fear of four-legged animals which are not dogs. The generalization gradient is illustrated in Figure 1.

Stimulus similarity can follow dimensions other than the

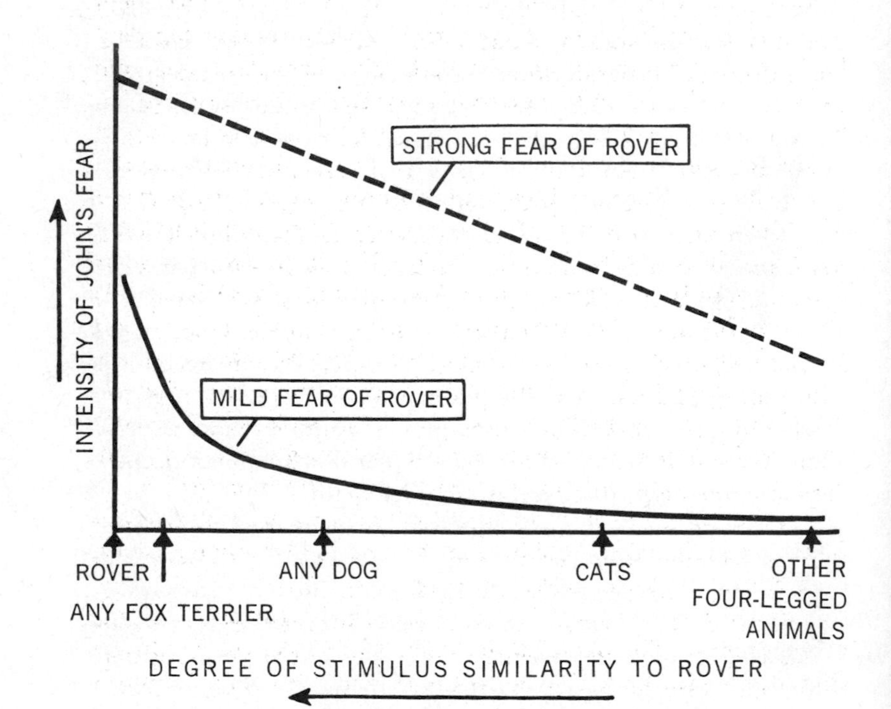

Figure 1. The gradient of stimulus generalization as a function of strength of fear evoked by the original stimulus.

purely physical. Any dimension can be meaningful provided that the organism is aware of the similarity and that it is associated with anxiety. Even a verbal description of objects that are totally dissimilar in structure can mediate generalization. If John fears the stove that burned him, he may also fear a lighted match because both stove and match are labeled "hot." It is evident that language enormously extends the potential of stimulus generalization.

Generalization also applies to cues that have become fear stimuli through association. Suppose John is badly beaten by the school bully and has in consequence developed a fear of his school (the cue). This fear may be extended to another school, or to schools in general. John's refusal to go to school will not be altered much by a change of schools.

When fear is weak, generalization may not occur. However, some degree of generalization is common and not unexpected; it usually follows the steep gradient depicted by the solid line of Figure 1. When the fear is strong, generalization is enhanced; the curve of the gradient flattens out and is raised, as in the dotted line of Figure 1. The interpretation of the curves of Figure 1 is that when the fear drive is weak or moderate, a stimulus must be very similar to the original one in order to evoke a marked fear response. Stimuli which are relatively dissimilar will have little effect on the organism. When fear is strong, the fear reaction will be marked even when the stimulus is relatively dissimilar. Another interpretation of these gradients is that when fear is relatively mild, perceptual discrimination of stimuli is more accurate than when it is strong. This view is parallel to the concept of *response stereotypy* discussed in Chapter Eight.

Generalization of anxiety does not, in principle, have malignant effects on the organism. On the contrary, its consequences may be regarded as adaptive. Fear-producing cues permit the organism to avoid dangerous situations. Stimulus generalization is involved in the comprehending of abstract concepts; it is obviously useful for a child to know that there is a *class* of objects labeled "hot" or "sharp" that should be avoided or handled carefully. In popular terminology, learning by generalization is "profiting from one's experience."

The distinction between fear as adaptive and fear as disruptive is a function of its intensity. A strong fear impairs the organism's ability to discriminate among stimuli and cues and thereby leads to excessive and unrealistic generalization. If John is spanked briefly and moderately for occasional extreme behavior, his fear will tend to be restricted to the spanking itself and (his parents hope) to the behavior that provoked it. But if John is spanked frequently, harshly, and unreasonably, he will fear not only the spanking but also his father, and perhaps other male authority figures. To make matters worse, John may be aware, somewhat later in life, why he dislikes his father, but he is likely to be unaware of the reason for his reaction to other authority figures. Similarly, John's fear of the school bully was so intense that he was unable to discriminate among cues. Schools in which the fear-producing stimulus was not found became indistinguishable from the one school in which it was located.

Another way in which anxiety arises is through *conflict*. Conflict occurs when the organism is motivated simultaneously by two strong, competing drives. The drives involved may be either primary, learned, or both, provided only that they are of equal or nearly equal strength at the moment that the organism is motivated. In addition to situations in which fear itself is one of the two conflicting drives, fear is heavily involved in conflict. First, a number of complex learned drives, such as guilt, shame, and conformity, contain an aspect of anxiety. Secondly, conflicts having serious consequences for the organism seldom arise unless fear is involved. Finally, anxiety is a key factor determining the resolution of conflict.

Dollard and Miller conceptualize conflict as deriving from two tendencies: *approach* and *avoidance*. Approach is the tendency to do something, to seek something, to go toward something, in general, to behave. Avoidance is the antipodal tendency: not to go toward something, not to do something, in general, not to behave.

When the organism is motivated simultaneously to pursue two desirable but incompatible goals, this is called *approach-approach* conflict. Such conflicts do not ordinarily give rise to anxiety and rarely have serious consequences for the organism. Anx-

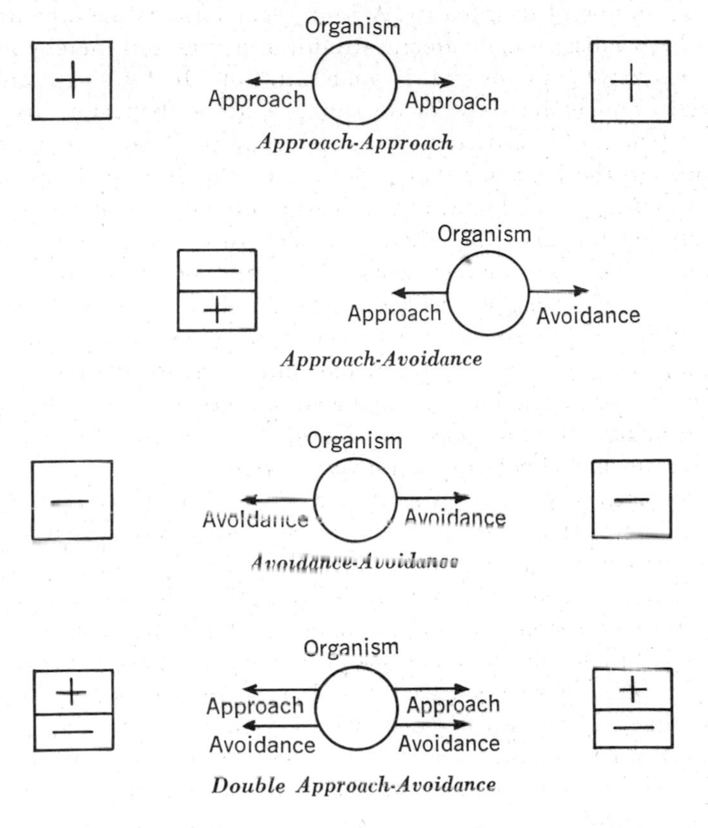

Figure 2. Types of conflict situations schematized. *Reproduced from Underwood (1949) by permission of Appleton-Century-Crofts, Inc.*

iety-evoking conflicts invariably involve avoidance. *Approach-avoidance* conflict occurs when the organism simultaneously wishes to approach and to avoid a goal. It is represented, for instance, by sex-anxiety and anger-anxiety conflicts, and by many conflicts involving competing, complex learned drives like "honesty" and "tact."

A third type of conflict is *avoidance-avoidance*. It occurs in situations in which the organism must choose between two undesirable goals or behaviors. The conflict situation is like that of the movie hero who finds that he must risk a dangerous leap across the chasm or be caught by his enemies.

Probably the most common type of conflict among humans is *double approach-avoidance*. In this situation, each of the counterposed alternatives has both desirable and undesirable aspects. Such conflicts are represented in life by the decisions involved in choosing a husband or wife, buying a house, embarking on a career, hiring an employee, seeking a new job, and the like. The clinician refers to double approach-avoidance conflictual feelings as *ambivalence*.

Emotional conflict, as Dollard and Miller point out, is no novelty in human existence. It is "the constant accompaniment of life at every age and social level." The basis of psychopathological anxiety seems to be strong conflict occurring early in life, but the circumstances under which the relationship applies have not been determined to the satisfaction of the experimental psychologist. The requisite knowledge, as yet unavailable, comes under the rubric of a "science of child rearing," as Dollard and Miller call it. We know very little about how most complex, learned drives are acquired, or about those factors that permit one person to easily and adequately resolve a conflict, while another is plunged into a painful emotional state. Lacking these vital data, the experimental psychologist feels unable to extend his theoretical conception of the relationship between conflict and anxiety.

Summary

Theories of the origin of anxiety in the human organism are in a relatively rudimentary state because the available core of definitely established facts is quite small. Theories of the origin of anxiety have come primarily from two sources: the psychoanalyst and the learning theorist. Freud believed that anxiety arises originally in the infant as a result of sudden, diffuse stimulation occurring at birth. This is followed closely by a fresh source of danger, the possibility of deprivation of physiological needs. Later, the feeling of anxiety may become attached to actions on the part of influential adults which implicitly carry a threat of physiological deprivation, and thus give rise to a threat reminiscent of the primary anxiety.

The neo-Freudians abandoned the notion of a primary anxiety occurring in the first months of life. They believe that anxiety originates in the social process and that it therefore cannot arise before the child develops an awareness of its status relative to the environment. Anxiety begins when the young child realizes his own helplessness, and the degree to which he is dependent upon others for protection and survival. The growth of anxiety is a consequence of restriction, threat, and punishment which is used to control the behavior of the young organism. The threat is not one of physiological deprivation, but of frustration of dependency needs, of the need for protection and support. An important complication is the fact that the natural reaction to frustration is hostility aimed at the frustrating agent. This leads to further coercive action by the environment so that hostility feelings themselves become invested with anxiety. Finally, the neo-Freudians suggest that most of adult anxiety is secondary, that is, a consequence of threats against the defenses—the adaptive behaviors—which keep primary anxiety from coming to consciousness.

Experimental psychology regards anxiety as a learned drive based upon an innate tendency to avoid pain. Anxiety begins with the attachment of pain to a particular stimulus. If the fear reaction is strong enough, it may become extended to objects or situations which are similar to the original fearsome stimulus. Individuals who have been exposed in early life to intense fears are thus more likely to manifest a high predisposition to anxiety in later life.

Anxiety is also a function of conflict, which is seen to occur when the individual is simultaneously motivated by two competing drives. Anxiety-proneness is also believed to be a consequence of intense conflicts which occur early in life.

4

DEFENSES AGAINST ANXIETY

The human body has a host of internal processes that must be continually regulated in order to maintain health and life. Body temperature, blood pressure, heart rate, and levels and balances of many chemicals in the blood and tissue must be maintained at an optimal level. When the regulation process fails, the individual becomes ill. The level of hydrogen in the blood, for instance, is so crucial that any variation beyond narrow limits results in death.

The maintenance of physiological equilibrium is carried out autonomically, without conscious effort or awareness on the part of the individual. The physiologist calls it *homeostasis.*

The principle of homeostasis is also found in the psychological sphere. The person who is overwhelmed by anxiety is in a state of psychological disequilibrium. All or any of his behaviors may be adversely affected. His functioning is disrupted, impaired, and, in extreme instances, comes to a complete halt.

The prevention of these dire effects—the maintenance of emotional stability—is a function of psychological homeostasis. Psychological homeostasis refers to the capacity of the human "psyche," the "mental apparatus" as Freud called it, *to keep the feeling of anxiety from coming into consciousness,* or to preclude awareness of thoughts or impulses that would be anxiety-evoking. The "mental apparatus" maintains homeostasis through various processes which Freud called *defenses against anxiety,* or *defense mechanisms.* Other theorists refer to them as mental dynamisms, security operations, or character defenses.

Defense Mechanisms

The existence of defense mechanisms is consensually acknowledged by psychiatrists and psychologists. Beyond this consensus there is considerable disagreement, if not confusion. The problem is that defense mechanisms are constructs. Their existence is inferred from observations of behavior and assessment of personality. A bit of behavior may be termed a consequence of different defense mechanisms according to different viewpoints. Or different behaviors may be subsumed under the same construct heading depending upon the theorist's orientation and background.

The number of defense mechanisms varies considerably. Freud originally proposed nine, but the list has been expanded by his followers and by other psychiatrists and psychologists so that a perusal of the literature currently discloses about two dozen. Some are overlapping, or even identical despite different construct labels. Some have a degree of experimental backing whereas others not only lack this touch of respectability but are in principle incapable of scientific evaluation.

Orthodox Freudians conceive of most defense mechanisms as ways of dealing with anxiety that are irrational because they distort or deny reality and thereby impede the attainment of emotional maturity. Among the majority of mental health professionals, defenses against anxiety are currently viewed as necessary, adaptive functions common to all of us. It is doubtful that anyone could develop into a productive, socialized adult without them. White (1952) sums up the case for the majority position:

> One is certainly not justified in asserting that people without neuroses are free from residues of childhood anxiety and defense. No one can get through childhood without anxiety, and no one is likely to be wholly free from the patterns of defense that served him in his early crises. It is perhaps reasonable to suppose that when childhood anxieties are less severe, the defenses will be less primitive, less indiscriminate, less likely to interfere with important directions of new learning. . . . Case studies of relatively healthy people show that problems of anxiety and defense are part of the universal stuff of development.

The functioning of defenses against anxiety is very much like that of the body's physiological defenses against disease. In normal, effective functioning, homeostasis is maintained without effort or awareness on the part of the individual. The mobilization of physiological homeostatic mechanisms to combat a seriously threatening condition results in clinical symptoms. Analogously, when severe anxiety threatens to break into consciousness, the stiffening of the defense mechanism, and its increased intensification and greater impingement on the individual's behavior, expresses itself in psychopathological symptoms like excessive irritability, withdrawal, depression, or somatic complaints.

A comprehensive accounting of all the defenses ever proposed would be little more than an exercise in semantics. Because it is difficult to grasp the concept of defense without a description of various defense mechanisms, a handful of these constructs is outlined in subsequent pages. They represent mostly those that have some demonstrated basis in experimental research. A few, though not clearly experimentally based, are accepted by most clinical practitioners in the mental health professions, and seem to square logically with pragmatic observation and common sense.

Avoidance

One of the simplest, most common methods of defending against anxiety is simply to *avoid* stimuli and circumstances that arouse it. A person who is afraid of airplanes travels by train. One who is made uneasy by horror movies does not watch them. Someone who becomes anxious at the prospect of losing impulse control may avoid cocktail parties or refuse to drink liquor.

Avoidance may be employed consciously and deliberately when the individual acknowledges the anxiety-invoking properties of the stimulus or situation. This is apt to be the case when the anxiety itself is socially acceptable, as in the instance of airplane phobia. Avoidance may also be used unconsciously; the individual is then aware of the avoidance but does not realize its actual significance. This is most likely to occur when the true precipitant of the avoidance is socially unacceptable. The person who shuns cocktail parties is probably not able to state that he fears that the disinhibiting influence of alcohol is likely to make him quarrelsome or lustful.

Social adjustment is not seriously impaired by avoiding airplanes, movies, or alcohol. Anxiety may, however, be so intense and pervasive that avoidance as a defense becomes seriously maladaptive—as in the case of the person who is literally afraid to go out of his house and must therefore avoid streets, the market place, unfamiliar people, and any occupation which would require that he leave his home. Such an individual is severely emotionally ill. This is the simplest exposition of the difference between a defense mechanism that is a normal, ubiquitous phenomenon and one that is a disabling, psychopathological symptom.

Denial

Avoidance as a defense functions within a fairly limited scope. When the anxiety-provoking stimulus arises internally—like a thought, belief, or feeling—or when the external circumstances are inescapable, avoidance is impossible. A threatened individual may then resort to *denial,* a disavowal of the reality of a thought, feeling, or situation which is then reflected in the individual's behavior. Denial is often an unconscious process, or at least largely so. Usually the individual is not aware that he is denying anything, although sometimes he has some awareness of it. In any case, denial is still distinguishable from deliberate falsification.

In order to understand denial, let us admit that the world is, in a certain manner of conceptualization, a dangerous place. Each of us faces the prospect of being cut down by debilitating or fatal diseases, by natural catastrophes like floods, tornadoes, and lightning, and by automobile accidents, fire, train wrecks, thieves, murderers, and war. Disaster might strike not only the self but also those whom one loves. To be sure, the probability of a catastrophe during any limited time period in a person's life is quite small. Yet, if one continually considered all the possible disastrous occurrences, one would probably be in a constant state of anxiety.

Denial is a common, garden-variety mechanism for dealing

with such anxiety. The individual ignores the environmental dangers. Others may be victimized but "it can't happen to me." This is not usually a conscious procedure; the individual does not amass incidence statistics and compute therefrom that the probability of a tragic occurrence befalling him is only one in 40,000. He implicitly acknowledges the dangers by taking out life insurance or by installing safety belts in his car. He simply does not experience anxiety as an unpleasant emotion, though he is unable to tell you why he does not.

Denial and avoidance may sometimes function as co-defenses. For example, the individual denies the possibility that he may be physically ill, insists that he is as healthy as ever despite the encroachments of age, and avoids an annual medical checkup lest his denial defense be assailed.

Whereas more generalized instances of denial of danger are common and normal, denial that leads to failure to take necessary precautions inclines toward the pathological. Dodging the doctor because one denies the possibility of physical illness, or failing to install seatbelts because one denies any possibility of an accident, are unhealthy manifestations. To minimize an environmental danger is one thing; to deny categorically that it exists is quite another.

Denial of an actual, impending danger—one that has a high probability of occurrence—is most clearly pathological. As Janis (1958) puts it, "When a situation approaches that of clear and present danger . . . denial behavior becomes a serious deviation in the sense that it is essentially delusional in character and suggestive of a psychotic break with reality."

Repression

The individual who is beset by acute anxiety is frequently urged by well-intentioned relatives or friends, or even by his family physician, to "forget all about it; it's just in your mind." The implication that the condition is trivial because it is psychological rather than physical is unjustified, and the advice, though sensible, is futile. It is almost impossible to escape strong feelings of anxiety by conscious effort.

As we have seen, defenses against anxiety usually do not function on the level of conscious awareness. One of Freud's observations was that people do seem to use the "forget it" mechanism, but on a totally unconscious level. An event, a feeling, or a memory that would evoke anxiety, or the anxious feeling itself, is *actively* forgotten. Freud called this process *repression.*

Repression, in its theoretical conceptualization, is sharply distinguished from normal forgetting, or even from selective memory. No one can possibly recall every stimulus or situation to which he has been exposed, and the amount of recall decreases with the passage of time. There is considerable evidence that most of us tend to remember occurrences which we considered pleasant rather than those which were unpleasant. None of this forgetting is clearly repression, according to the Freudian conception. In theory, the recollection which is repressed is forced back into unconsciousness in a very short time, perhaps almost immediately, even if no other events are competing for the individual's mnemonic retention capacity. The process is dynamic; the force involved is the urgent need to defend against awareness of anxiety. This seems to be especially true of very frightening experiences occurring in childhood, such as an attack by an animal or being locked in a dark place.

Repressed material, though it is below the level of awareness, is considered to continue to be functional. It constantly seeks expression in some indirect form. It may simply cause tension in the individual in certain situations or in the presence of certain stimuli, even though anxiety is not consciously experienced. It may bring about preferences, choices, and decisions or structure attitudes and beliefs. It may necessitate the employment of other defense mechanisms in order to maintain itself and prevent anxiety from coming to consciousness.

Most laboratory studies of repression are unconvincing because the experimental procedures do not clearly follow the theoretical structure of the construct, thereby leaving the significance of the results in doubt. There is, however, a certain artificially induced phenomenon whose very occurrence suggests some degree of validity for the concept of repression. It is called *hypnotically induced amnesia.*

A small number of people spontaneously fail to recall anything that happens under hypnosis, and a substantially larger number can be induced to forget, to one degree or another, by the intervention of the hypnotist. Hypnotically induced amnesia resembles repression because it is actively brought about in a very short time and does not appear to happen because other recollections compete for space in the person's memory.

A study employing hypnotically induced amnesia (Levitt, *et al.*, 1961) suggests a simple demonstration of the operation of repression. Normal subjects were hypnotically made to forget a period of severe anxiety that had also been experimentally induced by means of hypnosis. These same subjects were later asked to participate in a second study, which, they were told, would be similar to the first (which they could not remember). Almost all the subjects volunteered for the second study, at the beginning of which various measurements of anxiety, including plasma levels of hydrocortisone, a hormone associated with anxiety, were made.

All the anxiety measurements indicated higher levels of anxiety in the second experiment than in the first. More to the point, the levels recorded just before the second study were unanimously higher than those recorded before the first study. In fact, the average plasma hydrocortisone level taken *at the beginning* of the second experiment was higher than the level attained *during anxiety* in the first experiment!

If the subjects actually did not remember the first experiment (and there is no reason to doubt this), what explanation can there be for the manifestations of increased anxiety at the outset of the second study? An explanation which recommends itself is that the subjects were aware of the painful earlier experience at a level below conscious awareness. This unconscious recollection provoked tension in the individual as he anticipated another, similar situation. This is clearly comparable to one of the hypothesized, indirect effects of repression.

Because of its far-reaching consequences and its links with other defense mechanisms, repression is considered by orthodox analysts to be the cornerstone of the defenses. It is thought that everyone uses repression to some extent, and that it is especially characteristic of the early years of life, though some people may continue to use it extensively in adulthood. Its functioning in childhood is generally regarded as normal; extensive repression in the later years is associated with various forms of psychopathology. It is thought to be at the root of free-floating anxiety and to be etiological in psychosomatic motor and sensory defects.

Projection

In order to maintain a reasonable emotional adjustment, a person must be at least minimally satisfied with himself—his appearance, his characteristics, traits, abilities, and so forth. A person's actual self-concept is rarely identical with the ideal self that he might imagine; probably there is no one who would not want to be stronger, or more beautiful, or wiser, or able to do things that are beyond his actual capacity. Within limits, the difference between the self-concept and the ideal concept is tolerable and may, in fact, lead to desirable self-improvement. If the discrepancy is too great, however, it becomes threatening to the individual and can cause chronic discontent, unwholesome personality patterns, and even psychopathological symptoms.

To escape the anxiety evoked by a threatening self-concept, the individual may employ a defense mechanism which Freud called *projection*. Projection is the ascribing of characteristics of the self, including thoughts, feelings, beliefs, and traits, to other people. In Freud's original conception, the individual is made anxious by the incipient awareness of his own undesirable impulses. To defend against the anxiety, he projects his feelings outwardly, much as if he were unconsciously thinking, "I have no desire to be sexually promiscuous, but the world is full of lustful people, and immoral practices are rampant." Or, "I am not a hostile person, but the world is a jungle in which every man's hand is poised to strike." Thus the perceived source of anxiety is transferred from the perceiver to the environment.

Freud's preoccupation with sex and aggression, together with the fact that his theories were derived primarily from observations of psychiatric patients, led him to this limited view of projection. Attribution of one's own undesirable impulses to others appears to be characteristic primarily of the emotionally disturbed person. Campbell and his associates (1964) have demonstrated that among normal people, projection functions to attribute *contrasting* characteristics to others. Within the distorted milieu, the individual can perceive his own undesirable trait as rational and not exaggerated. For example, the person who is overly suspicious views others as gullible; a stingy person regards his fellows as spendthrift. Thus one is able to maintain a desirable self-concept without distorting the perception of the self.

It is not surprising to learn that people who tend to employ projection are unaware that they possess undesirable traits themselves (Sears, 1936); the very purpose of projection is to prevent such insight. While we know that lack of insight into the self and attribution of undesirable characteristics to others are correlated, the direction of the relationship is unclear. It is logical to infer that projection blocks insight, but it is no less logical to conclude that projection can be employed as a defense only by those who lack introceptive capacity.

The effect of projection is pointedly illustrated in a study by Friedman (1955). To understand Friedman's results, we must assume—on fairly safe grounds—that a normally functioning person is reasonably well satisfied with himself. His view of himself is fairly close to what he would like, ideally, to be. The self-concept and the ideal concept are close together. The neurotic, tormented by anxiety but unable to escape reality, has a poor opinion of himself. His self-concept and his ideal concept are far apart. An anxious person who has broken with reality and who is prone to use projection as a defense mechanism is likely to distort reality in the interest of improving his self-concept. The psychiatric patient group which is considered to fit this latter category is that of the paranoid schizophrenic.

Friedman's investigation showed that a substantial, positive correlation existed between self and ideal concepts among normal people, but no relationship at all among neurotics. Among paranoid schizophrenics, the correlation was almost as high as it was for the normal group. Evidently, the paranoid individual, by distorting his view of himself or of his environment, is able to establish a relationship between self-concept and ideal concept which resembles that of normal individuals who have no need for such distortion.

Projection resembles other defense mechanisms in that the intensity and extent of its functioning differentiates normal utilization from psychopathological symptom. A girl who is reasonably well adjusted to reality may suspect that her suitor's motivation is primarily sexual; only the psychotic woman, who cannot accept her own sexual impulses, believes that all men are interested in her for sexual reasons alone, or that the world is heavily peopled by rapists, or that many men follow her on the street with intent to violate her chastity. It would be unrealistic to deny that hostile and unscrupulous individuals exist in the community, but there is a strong odor of psychosis about the person who claims that there is a widespread plot to kill him.

Regression and Fixation

As a person advances from infancy through childhood and adolescence to maturity, personal autonomy, privilege, and scope of activity increase. These desirable accompaniments are balanced by greater responsibility, especially for the consequences of one's own behavior, and greater need to exercise control over one's emotions and impulses. These aspects of maturation tend to produce some anxiety, the degree depending upon many personal and developmental factors. Regardless of reality, most of us look back upon the earlier phases of our existence as less stressful than our current stage of development.

Assuming that physical and psychological development have been within normal limits, the desirable adjuncts of maturation ordinarily outweigh those that are anxiety-producing. In times of acute stress, a person may unconsciously seek to return to an earlier developmental period as a way of escaping the current anxiety. He may then begin to behave in ways which characterized an earlier period and which usually reflect less responsibility and greater dependency. This defense is called *regression*.

Regression is a dynamism that is most typical of the early years of life and appears then in its most dramatic and easily identifiable forms. Its prototype is the toilet-trained preschooler whose security is greatly threatened by the advent of a sibling. In consequence, the youngster may regress to an earlier stage in which he did not practice bowel and bladder continence. It is almost as if he were attempting to regain the uncritical parental nurturance of a period in his life when he was not expected to behave responsibly with respect to eliminatory functions. He seems to be urgently requesting that his parents once more treat him as an infant so that he can escape from his current anxiety.

All emotionally abnormal behavior could be regarded as regressive in the sense that it is less acceptable in adults than in children. But such a conceptualization has not been especially fruitful either in formulating theories of personality or personality development, or in devising treatment procedures. One reason is that distinguishing between regression and what Freud called *fixation* is often difficult. Fixation is a stunting of some aspect of the personality so that the individual can avoid the anxiety which is seen to accompany further development. He attains chronological adulthood with characteristics or behaviors that are immature. He does not regress from an advanced point of development; he simply never reaches it.

Probably all of us have some fixated characteristics. In psychopathology, fixations are seen primarily in personality trait disorders, a neurotic type of illness. Regressions are found in more serious illnesses, such as hebephrenic schizophrenia, which may be characterized by a loss of bowel and bladder control or inability to feed or dress oneself. The mental health professional generally regards regression as indicating greater emotional disturbance than does fixation. However, a great deal depends upon the nature of the regressed behavior itself. Certainly no one would equate the hebephrenic with the person who bites his fingernails when under stress.

A temporal aspect must also be considered. A regression that has become firmly established may be a symptom warranting professional attention. On the other hand, ephemeral regressions occurring at occasional peaks of stress in a person's life are not likely to be cause for alarm. In fact, some psychiatrists maintain that the ability to regress under stress is healthy and desirable. Tyler (1964), for example, believes that mental health depends upon "the ability to use the regression to dependency . . . as a temporary adaptive mechanism which can be given up or used in direct relationship to the realistic stress the individual faces." The distinction between normal and pathological regression, according to Tyler, is "the rate of recoverability to the type of relationship existing prior to the time the stress was perceived." In other words, we may, when very anxious, temporarily assume a dependent relationship with another human which resembles that of a child and an adult. When the stress is past, the original relationship, whatever it may have been, is smoothly reassumed.

Somatization

One of the very first of Freud's brilliant insights was the observation that emotional reactions may be reflected in physical symptoms. To be sure, the temporary physiological concomitants of anxiety—increased heart rate, breathing, and so forth—have been observed for centuries. But Freud demonstrated that seemingly permanent physical afflictions such as blindness and paralyses of the limbs may be primarily emotional in origin. He theorized that malignant emotions like anxiety, in order to avoid coming to consciousness, were converted into physiological symptoms.

The intervening process by which anxiety becomes "bound" in physical symptoms is unclear, but it is certain that some physical symptoms cannot have an organic basis. The so-called glove paralysis of the hand is accompanied by a loss of cutaneous sensitivity which ends in a straight line at the wrist. The nerves in the area do not, however, form such a neat structure; a true organic paralysis of the hand would be accompanied by skin numbness that terminated in an irregular fashion.

Freud observed that these physiological concomitants characterized patients who were afflicted with an emotional illness once called *anxiety hysteria;* hence he referred to the converting of anxiety into somatic symptoms as *conversion hysteria.* A defensive aspect of this kind of symptom is sometimes immediately discernible. An example is the classic case of the young woman of puritanical background whose powerful sexual impulses were leading her to fear, unconsciously, that she would become a prostitute. The consequent psychogenic paralysis of her legs evidently served to defend against this anxiety; one cannot become a streetwalker if one cannot walk. This purposefulness of the conversion of anxiety has led a psychiatrist (Dunbar, 1947) to call it "the beloved symptom," one to which the patient will cling desperately no matter how painful or disabling it may be.

That emotional illness is frequently accompanied by minor somatic manifestations is now generally recognized, and Freud's diagnostic label has fallen into disuse. It is reserved almost entirely for the relatively rare case of dramatic loss of motor or sensory function.

The relationship between the psychological and the physical is the main reason that many emotionally disturbed people seek help first from the nonpsychiatric physician. One survey (Tyler, 1960) indicates that nearly 40 per cent of the patients of physicians in general medical practice are considered to have emotional disorders either as a primary diagnosis or as a complication of organic disease. Manifestations range from simple phenomena like headache and back pain to gastrointestinal ulcers and skin diseases.

The association between emotional and physical symptoms does not of itself demonstrate that the latter serve as defenses against anxiety. That successful treatment of the emotional component often relieves the somatic is suggestive. A causal connection is more strongly suggested by the relative ease with which many physical symptoms can be manipulated by hypnosis, a purely psychological approach. A striking finding is that a physical symptom which has been relieved by hypnosis is frequently replaced in short order by another physical symptom or by an emotional state. Monroe (1960) once described a patient in whom a sequence of symptom-substitution began with a paralysis that was followed in order by acute claustrophobia, tachycardia (rapid heart beat), and a severe skin disease.

Conversion hysteria is a serious illness. Whenever the converting of anxiety into physical symptoms results in severe impairment of functioning or acute pain, we cannot avoid the inference that the individual is very ill. The "beloved symptom" may also be the temporary defense of a person who is not emotionally ill. It is not at all uncommon for people under stress to suddenly develop minor symptoms, like headache, acute fatigue, or a running nose, which distract them from threatening awareness of anxiety and, at the same time, provide them with an excuse for withdrawing from a stressful situation.

Counterbehavior

Prominent among Freud's original classification of defenses is a mechanism he called *reaction formation.* An unacceptable impulse like hostility is repressed in the interest of avoiding punishment or threat of punishment. In the presence of a stimulus that is capable of evoking hostile behavior, the individual experiences anxiety lest he behave in accordance with the unacceptable impulse. To avoid this eventuality, he is unconsciously led to adopt a completely opposing position. He feels affection, love, or need for affiliation—acceptable feelings—instead of hostility. Taking refuge in this antipodal stance, the individual minimizes the possibility of expressing the unacceptable impulse.

Reaction formation is one of the defenses that is difficult to pin down experimentally. Most clinicians accept it and can cite instances of its functioning among their patients. A classic example is the paranoid schizophrenic who insists, perhaps as a matter of religious scruple, that he loves everyone, including those who are plotting against him, or have railroaded him into the hospital for some malicious reason, or are otherwise appropriate targets of hostility and aggressive action. The extreme contrast of feelings, together with the apparent conjunctive use of projection as a defense, certainly suggests a reaction formation.

The existence of this type of countertendency among normal people and others who are not psychotic is questionable. Clinical case histories and accounts of diagnostic conferences appear to indicate that the concept of reaction formation is overused in clinical circles. It is postulated to explain away inconsistencies in the psychiatrist's or psychologist's formulation of the patient's personality structure or dynamics. It is used to explain why the patient does not behave in accordance with his motivation as the mental health professional has diagnosed it. This requires the assumption that the diagnosis is correct, an unsafe assumption in many cases.

A special instance of reaction formation, considered by some theorists to warrant a classification of its own, is called *counterphobia.* It is usually thought to occur less frequently than reaction formation, but the evidence for its existence is ordinarily more definite and less subject to question.

Suppose that a person has an irrational, exaggerated fear of an identifiable object or of performing an act. Common sense suggests that the fear will be dispelled if the person will approach the object or perform the act and be convinced thereby that his fear is unjustified. Adults often urge such an approach on the fearful child, with inconsistent success.

Counterphobic behavior seems to be impelled from within the individual, reflecting a drive to conquer anxiety by defying it. The individual has somehow become more afraid of being afraid than he is of the fearsome stimulus.

The "process of ruthlessly marching over an anxiety," as Horney (1937) summarizes counterphobia, can become a desirable end in itself, perhaps because successful thwarting of anxiety enhances self-esteem in addition to relieving psychic pain.

> . . . instead of being avoided and run away from, danger is eagerly sought and even produced. One sees it in a childish form in the defiance of feared danger, "whistling in the graveyard." This symptom is of particular social importance in adolescents when the temptation to overcome fear by bravado is uncontrolled by mature judgment, with the result that the laws of reality and of the community are apt to be flouted, not so much in contempt of law as in fear of cowardice (Menninger, *et al.,* 1963).

Counterphobia need not have malignant consequences. To face one's anxieties and attempt to overcome them is not inherently pathological. There is nothing basically maladaptive in the man who becomes a herpetologist as a counterreaction to a childhood phobia of snakes, or in the career in the public limelight that is a consequence of an awkward, painfully shy, and retiring early adolescence. Counterbehavior becomes psychopathological when, as Menninger suggests, it drives the individual to fly in the face of reality by eschewing good judgment or by assuming a role for which he is unfitted because of insufficient intelligence, aptitude, or physical capacity, or when the counter-behavior becomes so exaggerated that it seriously impairs general functioning.

Compulsivity

Childhood is a time of purity and innocence when man is closest to God. Or it is a stage during which man's base inheritance from lower animals must be hammered out of him by a corrective society. It depends on one's point of view. But no one can deny that, compared to adults, children are messy, careless, unmethodical, profligate, irresponsible, and maladroit. The task of parent and teacher is to inculcate in the developing organism inclinations that will lead to neatness, cleanliness, precision, responsibility, and competence. A high premium is placed on the appropriate behaviors. Neatness and achievement are rewarded; sloppiness and incompetence are punished.

The behaviors of childhood incompetence, because they are negatively reinforced, tend to arouse anxiety in the child. By learning to overcome his incompetence, the child avoids the anxiety associated with impending punishment and gains in its stead desirable approval. Eventually, social values are internalized, and the adult accepts them as his own personal views. Yet, the heritage of childhood training is never completely lost. An adult may find that he becomes tense and irritable if circumstances prevent him from behaving responsibly or from being neat and methodical. At the conscious level, he explains his feelings on the basis of his values. Unconsciously, he seems to anticipate the punishment that followed incompetent behavior in his childhood.

The behaviors counter to childhood incompetence may therefore come to have anti-anxiety properties. Awareness of anxiety is avoided by behaving in a manner that is associated with approval—as if the person unconsciously reasons, "I am beginning to feel afraid. Some danger is imminent. I am probably going to be punished for my sloppiness, irresponsibility, and lack of precision. Therefore, I shall behave responsibly, competently, and so forth, and I will thus be praised intead of punished."

The anti-childhood-incompetence syndrome as a defense against anxiety is known as *compulsivity,* or the *obsessive-compulsive* defense mechanism. It seems to be fairly common in its benign form, in which it leads to personality characteristics and behaviors that are obviously adaptive and useful.

Some people seem to be able to compartmentalize a strong compulsive defense mechanism so that it is used intensively in a particular situation—one in which it is useful—and intrudes less on the remainder of the person's life. This is exemplified by the craftsman who works at tasks requiring great precision.

In people highly predisposed to anxiety, or in those threatened by acute anxiety, the clinician discovers peculiar compulsive behaviors. These range from phobic reactions to dirt and insects, tension accompanying the perception of anything out of its customary place (like the person who simply *must* straighten the askew picture on the wall), inordinate emphasis on punctuality (always a half-hour early for appointments), and frugality carried to the point of miserliness, to bizarre behaviors in which the individual washes his hands several dozen times a day, or systematically engages in meaningless ritual activity like turning around in place three times every few minutes.

Compulsivity is the best example of a defense mechanism which serves the individual and the community well when it is employed within limits, but which reduces the individual to a futile mechanical man when it gets out of hand.

Coping Mechanisms of Everyday Life

Defense mechanisms are a liability as well as a necessity. In most normal people, the maintenance of the defenses in good repair requires a constant, unconscious vigilance. The more defenses are threatened either chronically or intermittently, the greater is the strain brought about by the need to maintain them.

The neo-Freudians suggest an explanation of this strain. Using a defense mechanism necessarily entails a certain amount of rigidifying of the personality, a restriction of the scope or the clarity (or both) of perception of reality. To keep defenses intact, the individual must distort reality to some extent so that it is perceived as consistent with the defense mechanism. For example, the compulsive individual—who cannot help being compulsive because this is a defensive effort—has to find reasons for his compulsivity, even when an objective assessment of reality indicates that compulsive behavior is unwarranted.

A second source of strain on the defense mechanisms is the realistically perceived stress of everyday living. Man, points out Menninger,

> . . . tries to survive, with minimal pain and maximal pleasure, including the pleasures of achievement, of pride, and of loyalty to principle. All this requires an infinitude of doing, of trying and failing, of trying and succeeding, of trying and partially succeeding and having to compromise. It involves going ahead, stepping aside, stepping back, perhaps even running away. It involves fights and embraces, bargains and donations, gestures and conversations, working and playing, reproaches, rewards and retrenchments. . . . The series of "one damned thing after another" which is said to constitute life refers to those successive irritations, changes, traumata, and emergencies which have been successively met with varying degrees of success in the course of one's development (Menninger, *et al.*, 1963).

Minor stressful occurrences test defenses either because they threaten to evoke anxiety that must be defended against, or because they subtract from the total of psychic energy available to maintain the defenses. In this latter category are fear-evoking experiences which considerations of reality dictate must be permitted to come to conscious awareness.

The pressures involved in maintaining the defenses, together with the stressful occurrences of life, result in tension—a kind of diffuse restlessness, a vague feeling that something must be done without awareness of why the feeling comes about or of what needs to be done. Every one of us experiences this tension, no matter how effective our defenses may be. It is an integral part of living, as Menninger suggests.

The ability to tolerate tension varies considerably among individuals, but each of us has his limit. Regardless of individual personality or environmental circumstances, at some time or other tension accumulates to the point where it must be relieved in order to maintain psychological equilibrium.

People can resort to many behaviors in order to obtain temporary relief from tension. These are called *coping mechanisms.* They are, as Menninger and his colleagues point out, not symptoms, not marks of psychopathology. Most of them are common recourses, considered to be within the range of normal behavior or, at worst, to be eccentricities. The coping mechanism is used transiently until tension has declined and then discontinued until the need for it arises again. When it is not used transiently, as in the case of chronic alcoholism or drug addiction, then we no longer speak of a coping mechanism.

Theoretically, a coping mechanism is considered to be a consequence of the use of defenses, not a defense itself or part of a defensive operation. The draining off of tension is, in theory, different from preventing an awareness of anxiety. The latter functions totally on the unconscious level, whereas the individual may be aware, to varying degrees, of the tension-relieving properties of coping behavior. In examining instances of actual behavior, however, the distinction is not always so clear. In some instances coping mechanisms appear to support defenses like avoidance and denial that otherwise could not be successfully maintained. The functioning of avoidance and denial is evidently enhanced by daydreaming or alcoholic intoxication. Coping behavior probably appears more frequently when it is directly involved with a defense mechanism and should not be considered as a separate entity in such cases.

The number and variety of coping mechanisms is practically limitless, depending largely upon the forms of behavior regarded as acceptable by a society or subculture. Human motivation is so complex that no one can say exactly when a behavior is used exclusively or even primarily for the reduction of tension. Many behaviors have more than a single purpose. Some, in common use, appear clearly to be coping mechanisms. The following partial list is adapted from Menninger's exposition (Menninger, *et al.,* 1963).

1. Reassurances of touch, rhythm, and sound; pleasant sensations which perhaps unconsciously recall the comfortings of infancy.
2. Eating and other oral behaviors like smoking and chewing gum.
3. Ingestion of alcoholic beverages and drugs.
4. Laughing, crying, and cursing.
5. Sleeping.
6. Talking out; discussing one's problems with a sympathetic listener, or even just excessive verbalization.
7. Working off, as in direct physical exercise.
8. Pointless overactivity, such as walking up and down, scratching, finger-tapping, and hand-rubbing.
9. Retreating into fantasy and daydreaming, especially fantasies in which one's problems are solved or do not exist.

When these minor stabilizers fail, psychological homeostasis becomes seriously threatened. New defenses against anxiety are erected. Old ones are extended and intensified. All this is symptomatic of emotional disturbance which may culminate in a failure of defenses, a "nervous breakdown." The expression, though technically incorrect, is a dramatic analogy with the taut structure that breaks under excessive physical tension.

Summary

The concept of the defense mechanism is one of the most significant of Freud's insights. The experience of anxiety is often extremely painful; when it becomes intense and pervasive, the functioning of the organism becomes seriously impaired and may break down entirely.

The purpose of defense mechanisms is to prevent this dire occurrence, to maintain a basic, psychological homeostasis. The defense mechanism operates at a level below conscious awareness, in a manner somewhat analogous to the autonomic mechanisms which maintain physiological homeostasis.

Employment of defense mechanisms usually involves some distortion of reality. Nevertheless, their functioning is seen as necessary to normal development and functioning. For many of us, the distortions are not serious ones, and are overcompensated by the diminution of psychic pain. However, when the intensity level of anxiety rises sharply, the defenses tend to rigidify and to extend their influence over the individual's behavioral repertory. It is at this point that we begin to speak of psychopathology.

The employment of defenses, the effort to keep anxiety from awareness, brings with it a degree of tension. This is incremented by the actual stresses of everyday living. These tensions add to the burden of the defenses. To drain off tension, the normal individual makes use of coping mechanisms. These cover a wide range of actual behaviors depending upon what is acceptable in particular societies.

5

THE EXPERIMENTAL MEASUREMENT OF ANXIETY

The preceding chapters were largely theoretical and speculative, with a strong clinical orientation. They emphasized concepts and ideas that are supported by a sprinkling of experimental findings. This imbalance will be remedied in subsequent chapters, in which inferences and conclusions will be based primarily on research, most of it carried out in psychologists' laboratories.

This chapter introduces the experimentally oriented discussions that follow it. It skims the surface of research methodology, briefly presenting measuring instruments, procedures, and problems of methodology. Its purpose is to provide a background for the understanding of experiments on anxiety. The reader will, it is hoped, also derive an appreciation of the difficulties involved in the scientific investigation of human emotion.

Measuring Anxiety Objectively

As explained in Chapter Two, anxiety is a hypothetical construct that must be defined operationally for experimental purposes. The definition is essentially the instrument or technique that is used to measure anxiety in the experiment. The investigator's first task is therefore to adopt or devise a measuring procedure.

The potential supply of operational definitions of anxiety is very large because so much of human behavior is thought to be affected by this emotion. Cattell and Scheier (1958) located more than three hundred proposed definitions of the construct. The present context precludes a comprehensive presentation of anxiety measures. This chapter will be limited to discussion of the two classes of measures that are most frequently used by experimenters: physiological manifestations of autonomic nervous system action, and psychological tests.

Physiological Measures

The validity of a subjective report of feelings of anxiety is sometimes doubtful because of the common use of denial as a defense against awareness of anxiety. Autonomic nervous system reactions can seldom be controlled voluntarily and are thus immune from denial. This consideration especially has led to the use of many physiological reactions as operational definitions of situational or state anxiety.

The results, viewed as a whole, are disappointing. The four most frequently used physiological measures—blood pressure, heart rate, respiration rate, and electrical skin resistance [1]—are components of the *polygraph* or "lie detector," a device that enjoys an unwarranted popularity among law enforcement departments and other investigative agencies. There are really no acceptable scientific data that support its use (Levitt, 1955). This statement applies generally to physiological systems as sources for the experimental measurement of anxiety, as will be suggested by the discussions in Chapter Six. Physiological measures are seldom found to be related either to each other, or to psychological indexes of anxiety, or to the intensity of stress. The best that we can surmise is that patterns of physiological reactivity to anxiety are idiosyncratic, a circumstance which renders them unsuitable for use at the current stage of research on anxiety as a construct.

[1] A common sympathetic effect of anxiety is sweating. A moist skin is a more efficient conductor of electricity than a dry one. This electrodermal change, known as the *galvanic skin reflex*, or GSR, has been a favorite among physiological measures of anxiety, primarily because it is simple and easy to administer. It has proven, however, to be a relatively unreliable index, possibly because sweating can be the result of a number of factors other than anxiety.

Furthermore, physiological measures are administratively disadvantageous. In most cases rather expensive equipment, and sometimes highly specialized analytic procedures, are needed. Measurements invariably must be made individually; physiological measures are not suitable for the economical procedure of group administration. Many of the measures are notoriously labile, rising and falling rapidly, subject to diurnal variations that are not entirely understood, and easily affected by conditions of the experiment other than the experimental treatment itself. Lability may actually be an alternate explanation for what is presumed to be individuality of response.

Psychological Measures

Projective Techniques

The most important instruments used by the psychologist in clinical evaluation are projective techniques. Briefly, these are devices in which unstructured or partly structured stimuli are presented to the patient; he must add structure in order to respond, thereby revealing aspects of his personality. The best known projective technique is the Rorschach ink-blot test. There are any number of ways in which to analyze an individual's response to the ten ink-blots that make up the test. Some of these ways of analyzing responses are generally considered to yield indexes of anxiety.

An advantage of the projective test is that the subject rarely has any idea of the interpretation of his responses. He cannot "fake good," as the clinical psychologist puts it, meaning that he cannot know how to deny or otherwise conceal his anxiety. However, as experimental measures of anxiety, projective tests also have disadvantages, some of them quite serious. The difficulties involve interpretation of responses, quantification of data, and administration. Both administration and interpretation require a specially trained examiner, a qualified clinical psychologist. The significance of many responses to projective test stimuli are idiosyncratic. Their true meaning is revealed only in the context of a detailed study of the respondent's status and background. Many factors obtained from projective test protocols can be quantified, but it is not certain how these numbers should be treated mathematically. The psychological significance of four responses of a certain type may not be simply one more than three. In terms of anxiety, six might be much more than twice as much as three. While projective tests can be adapted for group administration, a considerable amount of their diagnostic value is lost. These considerations make projective tests poor instruments for experimental measuring.

The Inventory

By far the most popular device for the measurement of anxiety in experimental situations is the *inventory,* sometimes called a "scale" or "questionnaire" though ordinarily neither of these terms is precisely correct. An inventory consists of a series of items—statements or words—that are descriptive of the way in which an individual may feel or think about himself or his environment. The subject responds by assigning a degree of truth or falseness, or agreement or disagreement, to the items, each of which contributes one or more points to his total score, depending upon the arrangement for responding. The total score is considered to be a direct, quantitative account of the individual's anxiety level. Some examples of typical items are listed in Tables I–X in this chapter.

The popularity of the inventory is a function of its outstanding research advantages. It can be administered and scored quickly and easily by almost anyone, and it presents no difficulties in group administration. Its reliability is greater than that of physiological measures or projective tests, meaning that it is less affected by extraneous or trivial factors in the experimental situation.

Most psychologists would probably agree that the advantages of the inventory outweigh its disadvantages, but the latter should nevertheless be considered. Inventories that use the true-false or agree-disagree method of keying responses are subject to *response set,* the tendency of a considerable number of people to choose one response category (usually the positive, "true" or "agree") with apparent disregard for the content of items. For example, a surprising number of people will respond "true" to such directly conflicting statements as "Human nature being what it is, there will always be war" and "Wiping out international war is simply a matter of getting the right people into high places in government."

The tendency to agree, usually called *acquiescence set,* can be partly controlled simply by wording items in the inventory so that the "true" or "agree" response is not always one that adds to the subject's score. Preparing the items so that an equal number of "yes" and "no" responses contribute to the subject's total score on the inventory helps to eliminate acquiescence set.

Inventories which measure attitudes and beliefs are more susceptible to response sets than those which deal with emotional states. In the measurement of anxiety, or of any other undesirable phenomenon, response set is of less consequence than is the effect of *social desirability*. People want to think of themselves as possessing socially desirable motives, feelings, and behavior patterns. They tend to deny, either deliberately or without actual awareness, their socially undesirable qualities. Many people might very well respond, "false," to the item, "I sometimes feel like killing somebody," no matter how they really felt.

The effect of response sets and social desirability on inventory responses is a function of the nature of the subject group and the purpose for which the inventory is administered. A patient who has come voluntarily to a mental health clinic is likely to be least affected by the social desirability factor. A job applicant, or anyone who has something to gain by a low score, will probably be most affected. A person who responds anonymously will be less influenced than one who signs his name to the inventory.

Extraneous influences on inventory responses are probably only minimally influential in the experimental measurement of anxiety. To begin with, an emotion is being measured, not an attitude or belief. The subject ordinarily becomes aware early in the study that its intent is to provoke anxiety in him, or to measure a naturally occurring anxiety. In either instance, the admission of untoward feelings or behavior tendencies is less apt to be perceived as socially undesirable than in most other situations.

Test constructors resort to several techniques in an effort to overcome extraneous influences affecting inventory scores. Some inventories include a "lie scale" comprising self-evaluations which are socially undesirable but which almost no one can honestly deny. Some examples are, "I do not always tell the truth" and "I get angry sometimes." The subject who attempts to deny these behaviors is probably strongly affected by the social desirability factor, and his inventory score should be suspect.

A method of circumventing both the social desirability factor and response sets is the use of the *forced-choice* item. Statements that have been determined to be of comparable social desirability, one of which is a measure of the particular construct and the other not, are paired. The subject must choose which of the two statements best describes himself.

The development of the first anxiety inventories (Taylor, 1951; Mandler and Sarason, 1952) actually was the initial impetus behind a sharp increase in experimentation with the construct. As Levy (1961) has shown, the volume of reports of anxiety studies appearing in psychology journals rose sharply in the five-year period following 1952.[2]

Taylor's Manifest Anxiety Scale. The first anxiety inventory to come into general use was developed by Taylor (1951) and published two years later (Taylor, 1953). The Manifest Anxiety Scale (MAS) is one of a number of inventories of different kinds taken from the 550 items of the Minnesota Multiphasic Personality Inventory. The MMPI, whose purpose is to identify psychopathological tendencies, is itself the most widely used inventory of all time.

Taylor was interested in developing a measure of general drive in accordance with Spence's theory (see Chapter Seven, pages 112–114), not a measure of clinical anxiety per se. Nevertheless, the 50 items of the MAS were selected originally on the basis of their ability to detect clinical anxiety, as determined by the

[2] Most of the currently available anxiety inventories are discussed briefly in this chapter. A comprehensive discussion of findings with each inventory is beyond the scope of this book. For some further information, see Sarason's review (1960).

Table I

Sample Items from Taylor's Manifest Anxiety Scale

I frequently find myself worrying about something.	TRUE	FALSE
I always have enough energy when faced with difficulty.	TRUE	FALSE
I am usually calm and not easily upset.	TRUE	FALSE
I have diarrhea once a month or more.	TRUE	FALSE

judgments of expert clinicians. Some characteristic items from Taylor's scale are shown in Table I. The subject's score is the number of items to which he has given the anxious response, which may be either true or false depending on the item.

Inspection of the items in the inventory suggests several characteristics of the MAS. First, it measures a predisposition to anxiety, not an immediate state. Most items in the scale call for a self-report of a general condition, as evidenced by such phrasings as "frequently," "often," "usually," "hardly ever," and so forth. None of the items requires an estimate of the respondent's emotional state at the moment of responding.

It has been well demonstrated that the MAS distinguishes nicely between normal groups and samples of psychiatric patients. The former obtain an average of about 15, and the latter, about 28.

There is also a 20-item short form of the Manifest Anxiety Scale (Bendig, 1956) which comprises those items that seem to be most successful "in predicting clinical criteria of manifest anxiety."

In a forced-choice (FC) form of the MAS (Heineman, 1953), each of its 50 items is grouped with two other items: one that is determined to be of equal social desirability, and one that differs greatly. For example:

A. I have strong political opinions. (*Nonanxiety item, unmatched.*)

B. I sometimes tease animals. (*Nonanxiety item, matched with MAS item for social desirability.*)

C. I am a high-strung person. (*MAS item.*)

The subject is instructed to mark the item in each triad that is most descriptive of him, and the one that is least descriptive. The scoring key allows for the same range as the MAS, 0 to 50.

Scores on the FC form are highly correlated with scores on the regular MAS form. However, the average score is considerably higher, about 22 compared with 15. The variabilities are much the same. This may illustrate the effect of social desirability on the MAS.

Christie and Budnitzky (1957) propose that Bendig's 20 items as they appear in Heineman's FC form would be a maximally effective version of the MAS.

The MAS is also available in a special 42-item form for use with elementary school children (Castaneda, McCandless, and Palermo, 1956). It yields an average of between 13 and 18 for normal children, and around 20 for child guidance clinic patients. A short, 10-item form of the CMAS has been suggested by Levy (1958).

Other MMPI Anxiety Measures. The Manifest Anxiety Scale is one of a number of proposed measures of anxiety composed of MMPI items. Modlin (1947) suggested the use of the combined score of MMPI's Hypochondriasis (Hs), Hysteria (Hy), and Depression (D) scales, a total of 124 items with the scale overlap removed. A modification by Purcell and his associates (1952) substitutes the Psychasthenia (Pt) scale for Hy, reducing the item count to 120.

Welsh has proposed two anxiety measures. One, the so-called A factor (Dahlstrom and Welsh, 1960), consists of 39 items taken mostly from the Pt and Schizophrenia (Sc) scales. The Anxiety Index (Welsh, 1952) employs a differential weighting of the Hs, Hy, D, and Pt scales, as indicated in its formula form:

$$AI = \left[\frac{Hs + D + Hy}{3} + (D + Pt) - (Hs + Hy)\right]$$

The AI has a total of 159 items yielding an average score of about 50 for normal groups and between 80 and 95 for various samples of psychiatric patients.

Scores on the various inventories composed of MMPI items are usually found to be highly intercorrelated. Some of the coefficients, such as those between the MAS and a few MMPI scales, especially Pt, have been reported to be as high as .92 (Eriksen and Davids, 1955).

IPAT Anxiety Scale. The anxiety inventory developed by the Institute for Personality and Ability Testing derives from a more general attempt to measure human personality using the inventory approach. By means of a complex statistical technique called *factor analysis,* the IPAT investigators identified 16 personality traits. A number of these trait measures contained items which appeared to be measuring anxiety. Furthermore, it could be shown (Cattell and Scheier, 1961) that these items formed a "cluster" (that is, were all related to each other statistically to a significant degree) and also were related to psychiatric evaluation of anxiety in individuals. Forty of these items constitute the IPAT Self-Analysis Form, more commonly called the Anxiety Scale. Some examples of the items and the keying system are shown in Table II.

Table II

Sample Items from the IPAT Anxiety Scale

Item			
I need my friends more than they seem to need me.			
	RARELY	SOMETIMES	OFTEN
I always have enough energy when faced with difficulties.			
	YES	IN BETWEEN	NO
I sometimes feel compelled to count things for no particular reason.			
	TRUE	UNCERTAIN	FALSE

The developers of the IPAT Scale believe that it measures "free-floating, manifest" anxiety, by which they evidently mean anxiety-proneness. The IPAT items, like those of the MAS, clearly refer to a continuing, not a momentary state, as is shown by use of the words, "often," "always," and the like.

Values assigned to different responses range from 0 to 3; the possible score range is 0 to 80. Normal subject groups obtain average scores of between 25 and 30, while psychiatric patient samples average between 30 and 40.

IPAT has also developed a Questionnaire Measurement of Trait Anxiety in Children which is derived from a more general personality inventory for adolescents called the High School Personality Questionnaire (Cattell and Scheier, 1961).

S-R Inventory of Anxiousness. Of all anxiety inventories, the S-R (stimulus-response) Inventory (Endler, *et. al.,* 1962) is most clearly an attempt to measure proneness. The core of the inventory comprises brief descriptions of eleven situations that are likely to produce some anxiety in most people. Fourteen response tendencies, of which seven are physiological, are listed. The subject responds by indicating on a five-point scale the intensity with which he experiences each of the response tendencies in each of the eleven basic situations.

The S-R Inventory thus provides an index of a number of situations in which anxiety is experienced, the number of anxious responses to each situation, and the intensity of each response.

The maximum possible score on the S-R Inventory is 770 (5 × 14 × 11), or 70 if the score is taken as an average for the eleven basic situations. Normal subjects average from 330 to 360, or 33 to about 36.

Some of the basic situations and the responses are shown in Table III.

The S-R Inventory is obviously designed for the college student population from which subjects for many psychological experiments are drawn, as is clearly indicated by the inclusion of basic situations such as "You are going to meet a new date," "You are going into a psychological experiment," and "You are entering a final examination in an important course." Some other of the situations are not aimed so directly at the college student, but are experiences that many subjects are likely never to have faced, such as "You are starting out in a sailboat onto a rough sea." To the unimaginative person, such situations may have little significance, and his attempt to evaluate his responses to them would have questionable meaning.

Table III

Sample Items and Sample Responses
from the S-R Inventory of Anxiousness

Basic situations
You are going to meet a new date.
You are alone in the woods at night.
You are entering a final examination in an important course.

Responses	*Not at all*				*Very much*
Heart beats faster.	1	2	3	4	5
Emotions disrupt action.	1	2	3	4	5
Want to avoid situation.	1	2	3	4	5
Enjoy the challenge.	1	2	3	4	5
Experience nausea.	1	2	3	4	5

Another drawback of the S-R Inventory is that it requires a total of 154 responses, the largest number of any general anxiety measure. It is therefore more time consuming both to administer and to score.

A short form of the S-R Inventory has been suggested by Perkins (1966). It employs three of the original S-R situations and an original one, "You are being tested by a psychologist concerning your emotional stability." The number of symptoms is 10 instead of 14. The total number of required responses is thus reduced to 40, with a maximum possible score of 200. A reported mean for a student sample is 103.

Despite these limitations, the S-R Inventory represents a methodological advance over earlier anxiety inventories. The nature of the basic situations presents no serious difficulty for researchers; a set of appropriate situations could easily be conceived for the general population, or for almost any special subgroup. Shorter forms with fewer situations and fewer responses are also perfectly feasible and could probably be devised without loss of measurement efficiency.

The Fear Survey Schedule. An instrument developed by Geer (1965) is allied in principle to the S-R Inventory. It consists of 51 specific fears such as "looking foolish," "being alone," "blood," "driving a car," and "snakes." The subject indicates the extent to which he fears the stimulus or situation on a 7-point scale ranging from "none" and "very little" at the lower end to "very much" and "terror" at the upper end. Numerical values from 1 to 7 are assigned in order of magnitude to the possible responses.

Average scores of 76 for men and 100 for women were obtained in college samples. Correlations with the MAS of .39 for men students and .55 for women were reported; and of .42 and .57 with Welsh's A factor.

The FSS is a measure of trait anxiety which appears to be similar to the S-R Inventory in content but which has a greatly simplified system for responding by the subject. It is quicker and easier to administer than the S-R. Possible loss of predictive accuracy because of the simplified scoring can be assessed only by further research.

The Assimilation Scales. McReynolds and Acker (unpublished) have developed a series of inventories for different subject populations based on the former's "assimilation" theory of anxiety (McReynolds, 1956). The theory (which in itself is irrelevant

Table IV

Sample Items from the Assimilation Scale, Adult Male Form

0 = no unsettledness at all	1 = a little unsettledness	2 = moderate unsettledness	3 = a lot of unsettledness	
0	1	2	3	Educational plans.
0	1	2	3	Something that happened a long time ago.
0	1	2	3	My physical strength.
0	1	2	3	A woman bossing me and telling me what to do.

to the present discussion) states in essence that anxiety is a consequence of incongruent or dissonant apperceptions. Each inventory lists "a number of topics that a person may at times feel *unsettled* about," and the subject is instructed to estimate his degree of "unsettledness" about each item, on a 4-point scale. "Unsettled" is further explained in the instructions as "uncertain or undecided about it, or bothered or disturbed by it." The structure of the inventories and several of the 50 items in the form for adult males are shown in Table IV. The subject's score is obtained by simple addition.

As yet no experimental work has been published using any of the Assimilation Scales except the form intended for use with hospitalized psychiatric patients. Correlations of .32 with clinical ratings of anxiety and .52 with the MAS have been reported (McReynolds and Acker, 1966).

Affect Adjective Check List. An anxiety inventory could be composed simply of a series of items like "I am frightened," "I am upset"—that is, a number of similar, self-evaluative statements in which only the predicate adjective is changed. Since the "I am" of each item is a constant, the inventory could be simplified by omitting it and directing the subject to "Check those words that describe how you feel." The inventory then becomes an *adjective check list* in which a check mark or its absence replaces the conventional true or false responses. The measurement principle remains the same. The check list could also include antithetical adjectives like "calm" and "agreeable." Failure to check these words would contribute to the subject's anxiety score.

The approach was employed by Zuckerman (1960) in developing an Affect Adjective Check List for measuring anxiety.[3] The AACL has 11 anxiety-positive adjectives—that is, those that directly describe anxiousness—and 10 anxiety-negative items—the antithetical ones—as shown in Table V. Thus the maximum possible score is 21. Normal subject groups score about 4 to 6, whereas individuals under stress average about 15.

[3] The AACL is published by the Educational and Industrial Testing Service of San Diego in a form that combines with it check lists for the simultaneous measurement of depression and hostility.

Table V

The Affect Adjective Check List

Anxiety-plus	*Anxiety-minus*
Afraid	Calm
Desperate	Cheerful
Fearful	Contented
Frightened	Happy
Nervous	Joyful
Panicky	Loving
Shaky	Pleasant
Tense	Secure
Terrified	Steady
Upset	Thoughtful
Worrying	

The AACL has some advantageous features. It can, with a simple adjustment of the wording of instructions, be used to measure either proneness ("Describe how you generally feel") or state ("Describe how you feel now"). In the latter, or "Today," form, the AACL is one of the few instruments that taps state anxiety instead of predisposition. It is therefore particularly useful for experiments in which anxiety is induced, or in any situation in which it is assumed that the subject will become acutely anxious.

The AACL is also administratively simpler than other verbal devices and lends itself to the construction of parallel forms for repeated testing.

The major disadvantage of the check list approach is that responding involves vocabulary level and verbal fluency. A person who possesses and uses a larger vocabulary is likely to check more adjectives because of linguistic sophistication rather than emotional level. This makes little difference when an intellectually homogeneous sample, such as a group of college students, is used, but it could be a serious deficiency in an unselected sample. Valid responding also requires that the subject have a sharp awareness of his feelings. An individual who defends himself against anxiety by denial and repression of his feelings may score low on a check list even though he is very anxious.

The Subjective Stress Scale. The SSS is a 14-item, check-list type of device which is properly called a "scale." That is, weights have been empirically assigned to each of the 14 words or expressions in the scale (shown in Table VI).

Table VI

The Subjective Stress Scale

Item	*Scale value or score*
Wonderful	00
Fine	09
Comfortable	17
Steady	27
Didn't bother me	40
Indifferent	48
Timid	57
Unsteady	64
Nervous	69
Worried	74
Unsafe	76
Frightened	83
Panicky	88
Scared stiff	94

The SSS was developed for the purpose of evaluating anxiety in soldiers in simulated combat conditions (Kerle and Bialek, 1958). The subject is instructed to check the one word or expression in the scale which most adequately describes his strongest feeling. Soldiers describing their reactions to simulated combat obtain average scale scores ranging from 60 to 75, compared to about 30 in the unstressed state (Berkun, *et al.*, 1962).

The SSS is intended to measure situational anxiety only. On the face of it, the scale appears suitable for any literate population. But the scale values, strictly speaking, are not ubiquitously appropriate. They were derived from soldier samples in simulated combat; they might be considerably different for other groups in different stressful circumstances. The experimenter who uses the scale values in Table VI should understand that his subjects are being compared to soldiers experiencing simulated warfare.

Freeman Manifest Anxiety Test. The items of the conventional anxiety inventory are based on the subject's perception of himself—his feelings, mental state, and physiological reactions. Freeman's MA Test (Freeman, 1953) employs a different approach. It is structured like an attitude inventory or opinion questionnaire. It asks the respondent to agree or disagree with statements about people in general. For example, in place of a conventional item like "Looking down from a high building makes me frightened," the item reads, "Looking down from a high building is usually frightening." Instead of "I suffer from extreme fatigue," the statement is "Many people suffer from extreme fatigue."

Some of the items are true-false, some are multiple-choice, and some are in the form of a forced-choice pairing. There is a total of 56 items yielding a maximum score of 56. Normal persons average about 25 and hospitalized psychiatric patients about 30. Some typical items are shown in Table VII.

The assumption underlying the formulation of items in the

Table VII

Sample Items from Freeman Manifest Anxiety Test

If someone is easily irritated, the reason is he cannot help himself.	YES	NO
The successful person:		
(1) Takes things as they come.		
(2) Worries before each task.		
The average person:		
(1) Fears another war taking place.		
(2) Fears doing the wrong thing.		

Freeman MA Test, that the test will "bring about projection through the respondent's use of the mechanism of identification," is questionable. Although the items themselves were selected from a larger pool on the basis of their ability to distinguish between normal people and psychiatric patients, total test scores discriminate relatively poorly. In addition, the use of several different forms of test items makes for administrative inexpediency.

As in the case of the S-R Inventory, the value of the MA Test lies in the use of impersonal, rather than subjective, evaluation as a measurement approach. This may increase the effect of response set on the true-false items, but it also minimizes denial of feelings and the effect of the social desirability factor.

State-Trait Anxiety Inventory. With the exception of the Subjective Stress Scale and the Today form of the Affect Adjective Check List, all the inventories that have been presented so far are intended to measure anxiety-proneness. Because trait anxiety is theoretically a constant condition of the individual, it should not fluctuate in response to circumstances. Instruments like the MAS and the S-R Inventory ought not to be sensitive to stress reactions. Only the SSS and the AACL, Today form, are appropriate if a measure of response to emotional stimulation is required. It is advantageous to be able to measure either situational anxiety or anxiety-proneness with the same instrument. This capacity of the AACL is also found in the State-Trait Anxiety Inventory (Spielberger and Gorsuch, 1966).

The STAI is available in several parallel forms; the test's constructors recommend Form B for use. It consists of 20 self-descriptive statements to which the subject responds on a 5-point scale of intensity of the feeling, condition, or experience. The subject can be instructed to respond so as to indicate how he feels "right now," or how he "generally" feels, or both. The items are identical for determining either trait or state anxiety; like the AACL, only the instructions vary. Some items of the STAI appear in Table VIII.

The STAI is the most carefully developed instrument, from both theoretical and methodological standpoints, of those presented in this chapter. The test construction procedures de-

Table VIII

Sample Items from the State-Trait Anxiety Inventory

I am calm.	1	2	3	4	5
I feel regretful.	1	2	3	4	5
I am a steady person.	1	2	3	4	5
I am overexcited and "rattled."	1	2	3	4	5

scribed by Spielberger and Gorsuch (1966) are highly sophisticated and rigorous. The theoretical basis underlying the construction of the STAI, as outlined by Spielberger (1966), is as follows. A measure of trait anxiety should be stable and consistent. A measure of state anxiety should be sensitive to stress situations. Trait scores ought to be correlated with increase in state scores under stress for a given group of respondents.

The validating data on the STAI presented by Spielberger and Gorsuch (1966) are clearly in accord with this theoretical conception. The sole shortcoming of their work is, perhaps, that it has been carried out entirely with college student groups. Of course, this is true for most of the instruments presented in this chapter; it is noted only because it is the sole blemish on an otherwise impressive test construction process.

Test Anxiety Questionnaire. The instruments which have so far been presented have been designed to measure anxiety as a general trait or a temporary state of the respondent. In Chapter Seven we will encounter a group of psychologists who believe that the field is not yet prepared to investigate anxiety as a unitary, general phenomenon. They argue that the scientific study of anxiety should begin with in-depth investigation of specific, situational anxieties. Consequently, in studying anxiety they have chosen to focus on the academic test situation. The reaction which they seek to measure is called *test anxiety*.

The Test Anxiety Questionnaire, first of several inventory devices for the measurement of test anxiety, was developed by Mandler and Sarason (1952). The TAQ consists of 35 items deal-

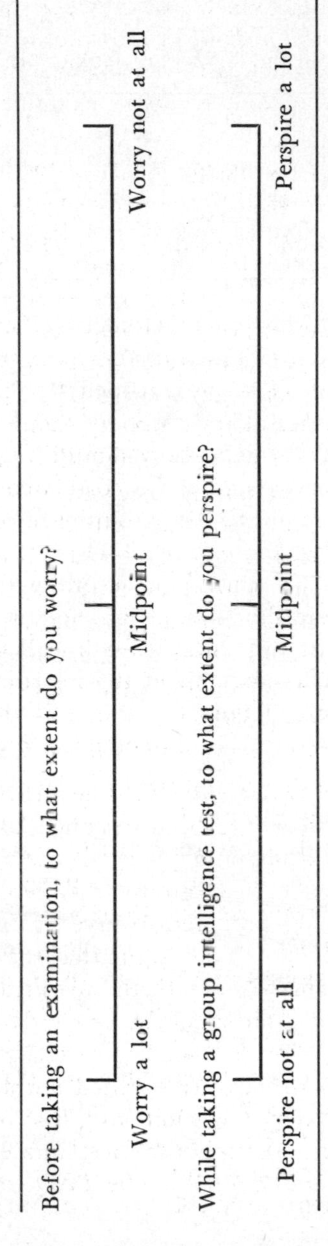

Table IX

Sample Items from the Test Anxiety Questionnaire

Before taking an examination, to what extent do you worry?

Worry a lot	Midpoint	Worry not at all

While taking a group intelligence test, to what extent do you perspire?

Perspire not at all	Midpoint	Perspire a lot

ing with reactions to facing or taking a course examination or an intelligence test. The subject indicates his reaction by marking a point on a line which is 15 centimeters long and anchored at the ends and in the middle. Some example items and scales are shown in Table IX.

The original scoring method was to divide the scale into 10 equal units and to assign values of 1 to 10 on each scale. A median value (middle score of the distribution of scores) would then be established for each item for the particular group of subjects. Subjects would then be assigned a score of 1 if their marking was above the group median, and a score of 0 if it was below it. The possible range of scores is thus 0 to 35. Scored this way, the TAQ yields an average of from 14 to 18 for college student groups.

This method of scoring is time-consuming and somewhat tedious. Instead of computing medians for one's own sample, the experimenter could use norms, provided by Sarason and Gordon (1953), based on the administration of the TAQ to more than 700 Yale students. This procedure assumes that students anywhere react much the same as those at Yale. The assumption may be a trifle shaky; students at the University of Illinois obtained a mean of about 14 on the TAQ (Endler, *et al.*, 1962) compared to about 18 for those at Yale.

The original scoring method can be simplified in at least two ways. One is simply to sum the raw scores for each subject, rather than obtaining group medians. This provides a score range of 35 to 350, and yields an average score for college students of about 170. It is also highly correlated (above .90) with the original scoring method (Mandler and Cowan, 1958).

An even simpler method is to measure the point of the subject's response along the scale and assign it a value to the nearest centimeter. Thus, the score on any item could range from 0 to 15, with a range of total TAQ scores from 0 to 525. A mean of about 250 has been reported with this method (Endler, *et al.*, 1962).

Also available is a 17-item true-false version of the TAQ called the Test Anxiety Scale (Sarason, 1958). An average of about 6 was reported for college students.

General evidence from the test construction field strongly suggests that scores furnished by mathematically derived or complex scoring methods are highly related to those obtained by simpler, logical techniques. This is very probably applicable to the TAQ, as the study by Mandler and Cowan (1958) suggests.

The Yale group has also developed a 30-item Test Anxiety Scale for children, and a 34-item General Anxiety Scale for Children (Sarason, *et al.,* 1960).

Achievement Anxiety Test. The approach to test anxiety measurement of Alpert and Haber (1960) represents a variation of the Yale procedure. Alpert and Haber reasoned that an instrument like the TAQ shows, in its extreme scores, the individual who is "debilitatingly" affected by anxiety, and the one who is unaffected. According to the Mandler-Sarason theory, there should be some individuals whose performance is *facilitated* by test-taking stress. Such people cannot be identified by the TAQ.

The Achievement Anxiety Test is composed of two independent inventories, each with 5-point response scales for its items. Nine items constitute "the facilitating anxiety scale," on which high scores presumably identify the individual whose test performance is facilitated by stress. Ten items make up the "debilitating anxiety scale," which is similar to the TAQ. Examples are given in Table X.

Although Alpert and Haber (1960) kept the two inventories separate in their original study, they can be amalgamated into a single inventory. Items contributed by the two inventories would then be keyed differently so that a high score would indicate debilitating effect, a low score, facilitating effect, and scores in the middle of the range, little or no effect. Another approach, suggested by Singer and Rowe (1962), is to compute the ratio of scores obtained on the two scales.

Another distinctive feature of the AAT is that its items were chosen from a larger pool specifically on the basis of ability to predict grade-point averages in college students. Thus it may be stated, on empirical grounds, that the characteristic defined by the AAT is related to academic performance.

This is both an advantage and a disadvantage. When the researcher's intent is to identify individuals on the basis of the way

Table X

Sample Items from the Achievement Anxiety Test

Facilitating Anxiety Items

I work most effectively under pressure, as when the task is very important.

	1	2	3	4	5
	Always				Never

Nervousness while taking a test helps me to do better.

	1	2	3	4	5
	It always helps				It never helps

Debilitating Anxiety Items

Nervousness while taking an exam or test hinders me from doing well.

	1	2	3	4	5
	Never				Always

I find myself reading exam questions without understanding them, and I must go back over them so that they will make sense.

	1	2	3	4	5
	Never				Almost always

in which anxiety affects their academic achievement, the AAT is likely to be chosen for use. Findings with the AAT cannot, however, be used to investigate the *hypothesis* that anxiety affects academic performance because a positive result is "built into" the inventory.

An Overview of Anxiety Inventories

All the inventory or check-list methods of measuring anxiety appear to be related to some extent. Similarity of results is partly a function of the respondent group. In normal samples correlations among different general or trait anxiety measures range from .20 to .45, with an average correlation of about .35. Approximately the same figures apply to relationships among general measures and test anxiety inventories. The correlations are apt to be somewhat higher for psychiatric patient groups, possibly as a function of the greater willingness of patients to admit to undesirable feelings and behaviors. There is a general impression among psychologists that correlations among anxiety measures will vary inversely with respondents' defensiveness.

Intelligence test scores and measures of academic achievement, like grade-point averages and grades in individual courses, are generally found to be unrelated to scores on general anxiety measures, and to show small to moderate negative correlations—.25 to .50—with test anxiety inventories. Much of the work in this area has, however, been done with college student populations where low IQ's are rarely or never found. It is conceivable that in random populations there is a low, negative relationship between intelligence and trait anxiety.

Scores on short forms of anxiety inventories are invariably found to be highly correlated with scores on the respective complete inventories, and variations in scoring method seem to have little or no effect on experimental results.

Sources of Anxiety in Experimental Studies

Natural and Naturalistic Conditions

The scientist whose eventual goal is the prediction and control of behavior seeks to examine this behavior in the natural settings in which it occurs. This is feasible for the zoologist and the botanist, but it is seldom practical for the study of human behavior. Phenomena like motives and emotions are extremely difficult to grapple with in the everyday milieu. Opportunities for natural observation occur infrequently, and even when they do, the researcher confronts the additional, and often impossible, task of securing the subject's cooperation. In the natural setting, methodological problems of standardization of procedures and control of extraneous factors are greatly magnified. When the purpose of the investigation is to examine a single emotion, these problems constitute an almost insurmountable obstacle to scientific study.

Despite these difficulties, anxiety has been investigated in a few circumstances in which stress occurs naturally, including learning to become a paratrooper or submariner, facing major surgery, speaking before a large audience, taking important university examinations, and being involved in combat during war. Unfortunately, such studies constitute only a tiny fraction of the total of anxiety investigations.

The effort to circumvent the problems of standardization and control without entirely sacrificing the natural setting has led to the occasional use of naturalistic conditions. In the study of anxiety, these have included artificial sleep deprivation, exposure to temperature excesses, and realistically simulated combat conditions. These conditions, though they are artificially created by the experimenter, closely resemble stressful circumstances that occur naturally. Unfortunately, the number of naturalistic studies is very small, too small to have added much to our knowledge about anxiety.

Artificial Stress Situations

Because it is so difficult to examine naturally occurring anxiety, most investigators have resorted to laboratory studies in which anxiety is induced artificially. The immediate problem in the laboratory is to find a technique that has a reasonable probability of stressing the subject appropriately. A fairly wide range of stress stimuli has been employed in laboratory studies. The two most commonly used methods involve either pain or failure, or threat of pain or failure. The pain stimulus is usually a mild electric shock. This technique has the advantage of producing a painful sensation peripherally in a limited area of the body without damaging the skin or involving more than its sensory receptors. The technique assumes, as do most theories of the development of anxiety, that pain is universally feared.

Anxiety over impending failure is considered to be a very strong, acquired drive in achievement-oriented cultures, as was indicated in the discussion of test anxiety measures. In the garden-variety laboratory situation, the subject is presented with a task involving a puzzle, a type of performance measure used in intelligence tests, or a simple motor task. Failure or threat of failure is brought about in one of four ways:

1. By harassing the subject or interrupting him so that he cannot complete the task in the required time;
2. By exposing the subject preliminarily to a set of false norms so that he appears to be doing poorly even though he is succeeding;
3. By informing the subject that he has failed or done poorly, no matter what his performance has actually been;
4. By employing a task that cannot actually be completed successfully, such as a puzzle with no solution.

Psychologists accept as a regrettable fact that artificial methods of inducing anxiety fail to produce reactions of the scope and intensity found in naturally occurring situations. The laboratory experimenter is aware that his technique is not a powerful one, but this realization need not be discouraging. An effect equal to natural stress is not required. The experimenter has only to provoke anxiety sufficient to measurably affect his criterion measure. If an artificial technique accomplishes this much, it should be regarded as successful. For research purposes, it is a valid facsimile of a natural situation.

Validity of Artificially Induced Anxiety

We may now consider a very important, and often neglected, question: How valid are laboratory stress techniques?

Procedures intended to induce anxiety in the laboratory subject are generally *assumed* to be successful. Few researchers bother to conduct an independent check on efficacy. Many negative or confusing experimental results could reasonably be attributed to failure to stress subjects adequately, but for some reason this explanation is not commonly advanced by laboratory investigators.

There are at least two good reasons why an artificial stress technique may fail in its purpose:

1. *The subject may not perceive that the technique is intended to induce anxiety.* He may simply refuse to believe that the professor or doctor will permit anything untoward to happen to him. He may even perceive the stress stimulus as benign. For example, Grinker and his associates (1957) attempted to evoke anxiety in hospitalized patients by means of a stressful interview specially structured for each patient. They found, to their chagrin, that "often the subject tended to view the experiment in a helpful context no matter how threatening the interpretation made to him. Paradoxical reassurance from the stimulus interviews was a surprisingly common occurrence."

2. *The technique simply may not be stressful to many of the subjects even though they perceive that the experimenter's intent is to stress them.* This contingency, and its impact on experimental results, is illustrated in a study by Walker and Spence (1964), one of the few in which the investigators independently checked the effectiveness of the stress technique. Walker and Spence attempted to induce anxiety by telling student subjects that their performances on two anxiety scales were "questionable," and that a faculty adviser had suggested that they be given an intelligence test. The test was the Digit Span Subtest (immediate rote memory for numbers) of the Wechsler Adult Intelligence Scale.

At the conclusion of the experiment, each subject was asked how he felt when told about his performance on the anxiety scales. Of the 52 experimental subjects, 32 indicated that they had felt bothered or upset, but 20 reported no disturbance. Table XI shows the average Digit Span scores obtained by the total experimental group, by the subgroups who reported being disturbed and not disturbed, and by an unstressed control group. The average score of the total experimental group did not differ significantly from that of the control group, but the breakdown shows clearly that this is a function of the 20 individuals who reported no disturbance. This subgroup's performance was un-

Table XI

WAIS Digit Span Scores as a Function of Reported Stress*

	No. of subjects	*Average score*
Control group	58	11.8
Experimental group, total	52	11.0
Disturbed subgroup	32	10.4
Undisturbed subgroup	20	12.0

* Data from Walker and Spence (1964).

affected, whereas those who reported feeling disturbed made significantly poorer scores than did the control group. This demonstrates clearly how the failure of an artificial anxiety-induction technique can obscure an experimental finding.

Logically, the effectiveness of laboratory-induced stress ought to be partly a function of the subject's predisposition to anxiety. We would expect that those with high predisposition would be more easily threatened and would thus be more likely to respond anxiously to artificial stress. A postexperimental inquiry conducted by Schwab and Iverson (1964) suggests that this is the case. They attempted to stress subjects by telling them beforehand that the experimental task was one which would reveal the subject's "innermost conflicts and some of the things in himself of which he is most frightened." Subjects were divided into high and low anxious groups on the basis of the IPAT Anxiety Scale. In the postsession inquiry, 45 per cent of the subjects admitted that they had felt threatened by the preliminary comments. Evidently, the stress technique was relatively ineffectual for the group as a whole. However, it was considerably more successful with the high anxious group, of whom 65 per cent admitted feeling threatened, than it was with the low anxious group, in which only 25 per cent felt threatened.

This distinction not only bears on the methodology of anxiety experiments; it also illustrates a fairly common finding. Stress techniques are usually (but not always) relatively more effective with subjects who have a high predisposition to anxiety.

Experimental Design in Anxiety Studies

Suppose that a group of people is exposed to stress, and their psychological or physiological reactions are measured. Do the data furnish a basis for making inferences about the reactions to stress? If they are considered in isolation, they do not. We must have reason to believe that the stressful situation *alters* the behavior of the subject before we can draw any inferences about anxiety. We need some sort of control or baseline measurements.

The scientist calls the experimental conditions the *independent variable*. The measure of the effect of these conditions is called the *dependent variable*. The making of inferences requires that the independent variable be a true variable. In other words, there must be a stressful and an unstressful condition, or their equivalents. There are three primary ways of accomplishing this requisite:

1. *Pre-experimental measurement*. Experimental measurements are obtained from the same subjects both before the stressful condition and during or immediately after it. A change in level may then be reasonably attributed to the stress condition. This is customarily called an "own-control" design.

2. *Levels of stress*. Several independent groups of subjects are exposed to different intensities of stress. The degree of reaction as measured by the dependent variable should then correspond to the varying levels of induced stress. If it does, we may assume that anxiety was actually evoked.

3. *Subject selection*. Instead of applying different levels of stress to independent groups, the experimenter may divide his original sample into subsamples according to their scores on an anxiety inventory administered before the experiment. The "high anxious" subgroup would consist of those subjects who have scored, for example, above 25 on the MAS, or who represent the top 20 per cent of the distribution. The "low anxious" sub-

group would be those who scored below 7, or in the lowest 20 per cent of the distribution. The use of two extreme groups is most common, but occasionally an investigator will include a "moderately anxious" group taken from the middle of the distribution.

Another method of obtaining groups with contrasting anxiety levels is to use psychiatric patients, individuals who have diagnosed emotional or mental illnesses, and to compare them with normal subjects. The assumption is that the average anxiety level in the patient group will be higher than that of nonpatients. This is especially probable if the patients have been selected so as to include only those who have been diagnosed as having anxiety as a primary symptom.

In experiments in which anxiety is artificially induced or in which psychiatric patients are used as subjects, the independent variable is state or transient anxiety. In experiments using a subgroup identified by a pre-experimentally administered anxiety inventory, the independent variable is predisposition or proneness level.[4]

It is simple enough to see that the two types of independent variables could be used conjunctively in a single study. The investigator would then have a measure of the effect of proneness level on the transient state. Such a design could, in theory, furnish more revealing data than one in which only one independent anxiety variable was employed. Nevertheless, the bulk of anxiety experiments—about 70 per cent, judging by Sarason's review (1960)—are not of the multifactor type. The reason is, most likely, largely administrative.

Suppose, for example, that a sample of 90 subjects is subdivided into three groups of 30 each, representing varying proneness levels as defined by an inventory measure. Now suppose that the experimenter wished also to examine three levels of induced stress intensity. Each of the original three groups must then be trichotomized, resulting in nine groups with only 10 subjects in each. This number is regarded as too small to permit reliable measurement. In order to maintain 30 subjects in each sub-

[4] When the fractionation is based on scores obtained from trait anxiety measures like the MAS or the IPAT scale, "high anxious" or "high anxiety" actually means "anxiety-prone" or "having a high predisposition to anxiety."

sample, an original sample of 270 subjects would be needed. If four degrees of stress intensity were used, an original sample of 360 would be required.

Unfortunately, samples of this magnitude are rarely available to investigators in the behavioral sciences. About four out of five experiments necessarily employ sample groups of fewer than 100 subjects.

An experimenter could decide to set up the more complex design and collect some of his data now, some next year, and some the year after. But it is methodologically unsound to permit long periods of time to intervene between collections of data for any one experiment. Time itself then becomes an uncontrolled factor whose effect on experimental results is unpredictable—as, for instance, in the Mednick (1957) experiment described in the next section (the time interval was only three weeks).

Sampling Variations

Some years ago a psychologist remarked, with rather bitter sarcasm, that a large majority of experiments in psychology used as subjects the Norway rat and the college sophomore. This imbalance is expedient; both species are hardy, easily available, and seldom in a position to object to participating. The degree to which the overuse of these particular groups limits our knowledge of human behavior is a moot question. We are constantly faced by the possibility that an experimental finding based on the behavior of the college student does not advance our knowledge about his parents, his younger siblings, or his age peers who did not complete high school.

The bulk of scientific studies of anxiety have employed as subject either the student or the rat. Researchers and theorists may have been led down many a blind alley or cold trail by incautiously overgeneralizing from the behaviors of these species. The possibility is strongly suggested by a comparison of the findings of two investigations (Wenar, 1954; Kamin and Clark, 1957) dealing with the effect of anxiety on simple reaction time. In these studies, the subject was instructed to press a key whenever he heard a buzzer. An electrode was attached to his finger, and if his response was too slow, he received an electric shock.

Wenar used the conventional college student group. He found that subjects with high MAS scores tended to react more quickly. Kamin and Clark tested adult males who were in basic training with the Canadian Air Force; none of these subjects had gone to college, and they were, on the average, several years older than Wenar's students. They found that the high MAS scorers tended to react *more slowly*.

Now, it is conceivable that this sharp conflict in findings is a function of unobserved differences in the experimental situation. It is also perfectly likely that the sample difference is at the root of the matter. One might speculate as follows. Ordinarily, an individual with high predisposition to anxiety would be more fearful of pain. The experimental situation might well be considered to involve a one-response task, with no competing response tendencies. The anxious student therefore responds more quickly.

On the other hand, the anxiety-prone soldier, who wishes to perceive himself as a tough, rugged, unafraid person, denies his anxiety by reacting relatively slowly. Possibly this illustrates a counterphobic reaction. The less anxious soldier, who is more certain of his self-image, does not need to deny his anxiety, and hence is energized.

Extraneous Personal Factors Affecting Anxiety Experiments

Experiment Anxiety and Experiment Sophistication

One of the situations in the S-R Inventory reads, "You are going into a psychological experiment." It is included as a stressful situation because psychologists have frequently observed that many people seem to experience some anxiety merely because they are participating in an experiment, regardless of its nature. The anxious reaction appears to be a function of the novelty of the situation, the subject's lack of knowledge about what is going to happen to him. It occurs most often when the study involves drugs, hypnosis, or an injection, or when the subject must handle, or is fastened to, an apparatus, but none of these is a requisite.

"Experiment anxiety" can have some serious consequences for the investigator, especially if he is unaware that it exists. It can be a nasty complication which distorts experimental findings.

When anxiety is a primary variable, the effect of experiment anxiety will depend on the experimental design, but in most instances it will be advantageous. In fact, it is quite conceivable that even if the artificial technique deliberately employed to stress subjects fails, the experiment will proceed to a meaningful conclusion because of experiment anxiety.

The main source of difficulty is that experiment anxiety is a variable among subjects, most probably as a function of previous experience. College students have widely varying experience. One investigator may obtain positive results because he used mainly naïve subjects who were greatly inclined to experiment anxiety. An identical study may yield negative results because the subjects tested were sophisticated about participating in experiments. In the own-control type of study, experiment anxiety is likely to be greater in the pre-experimental phase, which is being used to establish an unstressed baseline. It will be lowered during the stress period of the experiment because of the increment in experience. The net result may be a neutralizing or attenuation of unstressed-stressed differences on the dependent variables.

The experimenter who fractionates his sample in order to obtain groups of differing anxiety-proneness may fall victim to a sampling bias brought about by the experience factor. The effect of such a bias is pointedly illustrated in a study by Mednick (1957) which also exemplifies the general effect of experiment anxiety on experimental results.

Mednick was actually concerned with the effect of anxiety-proneness on stimulus generalization. His subjects, divided into low, medium, and high anxiety groups as measured by Heineman's scale, were faced with a board containing eleven lamps and were instructed to respond by releasing a key as quickly as possible only when the middle lamp was lit. Without warning,

Mednick varied the procedure on some trials by lighting one of the peripheral lamps. He hypothesized that the number of key-releasing responses to incorrect lamps would increase with anxiety-proneness. This would demonstrate the influence of anxiety on stimulus generalization.

Table XII

Original Tabulation of Results in the Mednick Experiment: Average Number of Incorrect Responses by Anxiety Level Subgroups

Low	*Medium*	*High*	*All subjects*
5.0	8.5	5.5	6.0

Table XII shows Mednick's results as originally tabulated. The high and low anxiety groups hardly differ, but, surprisingly, the medium group very clearly manifested the most generalization.

These findings were so completely unexpected, especially since they run exactly opposite to the Yerkes-Dodson principle which is described in Chapter Seven, that Mednick apparently began to root around for some possible explanation. Investigation of the immediate backgrounds of his subjects disclosed that those in the high and low groups had already participated in at least five psychology experiments, but about half of those in the medium group had had no previous experimental experience.[5] Furthermore, each of the three groups consisted of two subgroups which participated three weeks apart. In the interim, all subjects had participated in two or three other experiments. The late participators were relatively sophisticated compared to the early ones.

Then Mednick analyzed his results according to time of participation as well as anxiety-proneness level. The results are shown in Table XIII. Obviously, all three late-participator groups man-

[5] This disparity was very probably a function of the frequent use of high and low anxious groups in anxiety experiments. A middle group is seldom included.

Table XIII

Breakdown of the Data in Table XII
According to Time of Participation

	Low	*Medium*	*High*	*All subjects*
Participated early	5.5	9.0	6.5	6.5
Participated late*	4.5	6.5	4.5	5.5

* A three-week interval.

ifested less generalization, the decrement being most marked for the medium group.

The effects of experiment anxiety and experiment sophistication constitute the most plausible explanation of Mednick's curious results. Their effect appears both in a sampling bias that channeled the unsophisticated subjects into the medium anxiety group, and in the systematically different performances of the subjects who participated early and late in the experiment.

Evaluation Apprehension

For the experimental subject, another source of naturally occurring anxiety is fear of being exposed to an evaluation of one's emotional stability, mental health, or personal adequacy. This *evaluation apprehension,* as Rosenberg (1965) terms it, is probably indigenous to the investigation in which the experimenter is, or is perceived as, a mental health professional. Evaluation apprehension is also likely to be partly a function of the nature of the experiment, at least as it is interpreted by the subject.

Frequent expression of such a fear by experimental subjects has led to its deliberate exploitation as an artificial stress technique, as, for instance, in the studies of Schwab and Iverson (1964) and Walker and Spence (1964).

Evaluation apprehension is similar to experiment anxiety in its potential effects on experimental results. These may be either facilitative or confounding, depending upon the design. Furthermore, the two fears may cumulate or interact in some subtle fashion, yielding, in effect, a third influence.

Anxiety in the Experimenter

The pioneer work of Rosenthal (1966) suggests that the *experimenter's* anxiety level may also affect experimental findings. In a series of ingenious studies Rosenthal has shown that personal characteristics of the researcher, including his particular hypothesis, can bias results. A classic study (Rosenthal, *et al.*, 1963) indicates that experimenter bias—the unwitting influencing of subjects so as to obtain data in accordance with a hypothesis—is more pronounced among experimenters who score high on the Manifest Anxiety Scale. Supporting evidence has been furnished by Winkel and Sarason (1964), who have shown that the experimenter's anxiety level can influence verbal learning in experimental subjects. One could speculate that the more anxiety-prone investigators also evoke more incidental anxiety from their subjects, or that other characteristics of a researcher incidentally affect anxiety level in subjects, and thereby influence results.

Summary

Physiological systems have not proven useful in the experimental measurement of anxiety. This appears to be primarily a result of broad individual differences in autonomic nervous system reactivity to emotion, and the lability of physiological indexes.

Among psychological measures, projective techniques offer some advantages, but these are outweighed by disadvantages. The inventory is by far the most popular instrument for the experimental measurement of anxiety. An inventory is made up of statements or words which describe the respondent's feelings or attitudes about himself or his environment. Inventories are subject to certain response biases, primarily those which result from the tendency of most people to present themselves in a desirable light. However, these shortcomings appear of less moment than the ease of administration and scoring of the inventory.

Most inventories deal with anxiety-proneness or predisposition as a general characteristic of the respondent. Test anxiety and achievement anxiety inventories illustrate the attempt to measure an important, specific, situational fear rather than the general trait.

Correlations among scores on anxiety inventories average about .35. General anxiety inventories are usually found to be unrelated to measures of intelligence or of intellectual performance, while test anxiety measures show moderate negative correlations with measures of academic achievement and intelligence. The use of short-forms or variations in scoring systems appears to have little or no effect on experimental results.

Among the possible shortcomings of research on anxiety are the widespread use of artificial data-collection situations and artificial stressing techniques, limited research populations, experiment anxiety, experiment sophistication and evaluation apprehension among subjects, and anxiety in the experimenter. The extent to which these factors have affected studies of anxiety is unknown.

6

THE PHYSIOLOGY OF ANXIETY

Few people need experimental investigation or a learned text to be aware that the experience of a strong emotion like anxiety, anger, or sexual excitement has marked physiological accompaniments. The pounding heart, peculiar feelings in the pit of the stomach, sweating, and dry mouth are as well known to writers of fiction as they are to physiologists. While the simple fact of the cofluctuation of the psychological-behavioral and the physiological is unquestioned, the relationship itself has given rise to several significant problems with which the scientist concerns himself. These may be presented in terms of three primary questions:

1. Why do emotional states have physiological concomitants, and how are these concomitants mediated?
2. Does the pattern of physiological reaction differ among emotional states; can these patterns be used to differentiate among the emotions?
3. Do mental and emotional illnesses have physiological causes, or at least identifiable physiological correlates?

Physiological Reactions to Emotional Stimulation

The physiological responses to emotional stimulation are *autonomic*. The function of an autonomic response is to make an automatic, internal adjustment in the body without a conscious or voluntary effort by the individual. There are two kinds of autonomic responses: the *sympathetic,* the function of which is to

Table XIV

Examples of Actions of the Autonomic Nervous System

Organ or function	*Sympathetic effect*	*Parasympathetic effect*
Heart-beat rate	Increased	Slowed
Blood vessels	Constricted	Dilated
Body temperature	Raised	Lowered
Blood sugar	Increased	Decreased
Gastrointestinal	Action inhibited	Action enhanced
Sweat glands	Increased secretion	None

activate body processes, and the *parasympathetic,* which acts to conserve bodily resources. Examples of actions of the autonomic nervous system are presented in Table XIV. Comparison of the two kinds of responses indicates that the concomitants of emotion are largely sympathetic, with a few parasympathetic, such as increased gastrointestinal activity. Experimental studies of emotion, especially of anxiety, generally support the predominance of the sympathetic reaction. However, a wide range of responses, both sympathetic and parasympathetic, has been reported. Individual variation is extensive, and in a few people parasympathetic reactions predominate.

These immediate, physical correlates of emotion are manifest and can be measured with relative facility. The question as to how they come about, how they are mediated within the individual, has not yet been answered completely.

Theories of the Neurophysiology of Emotion

James and Lange

The earliest scientific attempt to explain the relationship between the subjective experience of emotion and its physiological accompaniments was advanced in 1884 by the psychologist William James, and independently a year later by the Danish physiologist Carl Lange. Briefly, the James-Lange theory proposed that the individual first senses or perceives the exciting stimulus and that this perception directly provokes autonomic reactions. The person's awareness of the physical changes in himself, rather than perception of the stimulus itself, leads to the subjective experience of emotion. The neural pathway must go from receptor to the cerebral cortex of the brain to the internal organs and back to the cortex. Neural impulses travel so rapidly that a person is unaware of the sequence. Everything appears to be happening simultaneously.

Cannon and Bard

Not a great deal was known about the functioning of the brain at the time that the James-Lange theory was proposed, and it seemed reasonable enough. It endured for more than forty years before it was finally overturned by the discovery of facts that it could not explain. In the 1920's, the physiologists Walter Cannon and Philip Bard demonstrated clearly that manifest behavioral responses to emotional stimulation occur in animals which have been deprived neurosurgically of all autonomic reactivity. According to the James-Lange theory, this occurrence would be impossible.

Cannon and Bard suggested that physiological reactions and emotional experience arise simultaneously, mediated by two lower brain centers called the *thalamus* and the *hypothalamus*. Recent advances in neurophysiology have shown that the Cannon-Bard theory was too simple, though it pointed in the right direction.

Papez and McLean

Current theory, identified by the names of J. W. Papez, a neuro-anatomist, and Paul D. McLean, a neurophysiologist, began with Papez' speculation that the seat of emotional control in the brain is an area called the *limbic system*. The limbic system is located on the medial underside of the brain and is composed primarily of *paleocortex*, phylogenetically the most primitive part of man's enormous cerebral cortex, together with parts of the hypothalamus. Neurosurgical investigation has shown beyond any question that the limbic system is involved in emotional expression. The techniques include surgical removal of all or part of the brain; direct stimulation of brain tissue either chemically or electrically; and creation of a lesion or removal of a specific area of brain tissue. Marked emotional responses, or alterations of expected emotional responses, have been shown to occur when these procedures are applied to the limbic system.

The "Anti-Anxiety" Area

Incontrovertible support for the involvement of the limbic system in emotional response is based on a relatively recent method of studying brain function. It employs permanent (or "chronic") implantation of a tiny electrode directly in the brain of an experimental animal. Relatively little destruction of brain tissue occurs. A minute area of the brain can be stimulated, without otherwise disturbing the animal, by means of a flexible cable attached to the electrode.

The method was adapted by Olds and Milner (1954) to permit a rat to electrically stimulate *its own brain* by pressing a bar. In this way, it has been established that the rat will work very hard to stimulate certain areas of the limbic system, especially the septal area. The animal will press the lever at a furious rate—as many as 5,000 times per hour—if this behavior leads to an electrical impulse to the brain every eight or ten bar presses. It is inferred, of course, that the animal maintains intracranial self-stimulation because it is "pleasurable." There is some evidence that a rat will elect to stimulate certain limbic system areas rather than to sleep, eat, drink, or mate.

The discovery of these "pleasure sites" is dramatically indicative in itself, but the consequent work of Brady and his associates at Walter Reed Institute of Research is even more relevant. In order to understand the significance of this unusual research, a brief discussion of the induction of anxiety in laboratory animals is necessary.

It is simple to produce a fear response in an experimental animal. If the sound of a clicker and a painful shock to a rat's feet occur simultaneously or close together a number of times, the animal will shortly respond to the sound of the clicker alone with such obvious signs of fear as cowering, urinating, and defecating. Brady and his coworkers (1958) found that the clicker failed completely to elicit these conditioned fear reactions in rats which were allowed simultaneously to engage in self-stimulation of the limbic system pleasure sites. Nor did the lever-pressing behavior leading to the self-stimulation cease. In fact, even the electric shock applied to the feet now failed to produce fear reactions! (No lasting immunity to fear occurred, however. The animals could easily be reconditioned to fear the clicker when brain self-stimulation was discontinued for a time).

The original Olds-Milner findings have since been reproduced in many experiments in different laboratories and extended to a number of species of organisms ranging from fish to human beings. The studies of humans have come largely from Heath's laboratory at the Tulane University School of Medicine (Heath, 1964a), where electrodes have been chronically implanted in the brains of more than four dozen people. None of Heath's subjects could be classified as normal; they were either severely psychotic, epileptic, or suffering from the intractable pain of terminal cancer. The evidence suggests that the distribution of pleasure sites in the human brain is similar to that which had been previously mapped for lower animals. Verbal reports and clinical observation indicate that Heath's patients experienced considerable symptom relief through intracranial self-stimulation of limbic system areas. Among the reported and observed consequences were increased alertness and more attention to the environment, dramatic shifts of mood, especially elimination of depression and anxiety, enhanced memory recall and psychomotor activity, "striking and immediate" relief of pain, and reports of "feeling wonderful," "happy," and "drunk." Stimulation of some areas produced autonomic reactions suggestive of sympathetic arousal, anger or fear or both, and drowsiness and sleep. Furthermore, some evidence (Bishop, *et al.,* 1964) suggests that there is an optimal intensity of electrical current to the pleasure sites. Intensities below the optimum produced little reaction, whereas intensities above it were reported as unpleasant.

The Reticular Activating System (RAS)

Another region of the central nervous system whose potential importance for a theory of emotion was first pointed out by Lindsley (1951) is the *reticular formation.* This rather diffuse and not clearly defined area is centered in the brain stem, the brain's connection to the spinal cord. The anatomy of the reticular formation suggests that it exercises a broad influence on central nervous system functions. It receives a collateral branch from every channel of nerve connection between a sense organ and the cerebral cortex, and it interconnects extensively with systems of motor nerves.

The reticular system is known to be intimately concerned with the sleep-waking continuum. Direct electrical stimulation of certain reticular areas will cause an organism to immediately fall asleep or to immediately awaken. For this reason, it is often called the reticular *activating* system (RAS). It is also plausible, though not as clearly demonstrated, that the reticular system is involved in regulating levels of wakefulness, of which the extreme upper level would logically be emotional arousal.

Malmo (1957) hypothesizes that the cerebral cortex and the reticular system are involved in a feedback-control operation whose purpose is to maintain an optimal stimulation level. Sensations reaching the cortex are constantly fed back to the reticular system. When the frequency of impulses becomes too great, an inhibitory area of the RAS discharges, sending inhibitory impulses back to the cortex, damping its activity. When environmental stimulation is low and the sensations reaching the RAS through the cortex are insufficient, the former "must fire diffusely," sending activity-provoking impulses to the cortex. In other words, the activity of the RAS is directly reciprocal to cortical activity.

Malmo suggests that the experience of anxiety is a result of a weakening of the inhibitory aspect of the RAS. This weakening permits too many facilitative impulses to be discharged to the cortex, leading to an arousal level beyond the optimal. He also suggests that the total function of the RAS may be altered if the arousal level is kept constantly high over a long period of time.

Endocrinology of Anxiety

Since Cannon's time it has been known that a pair of little organs located near the kidneys, the *adrenal glands,* are critically involved in emotional arousal. It is also known that the adrenals will secrete their hormones into the blood stream when stimulated by secretions of the pituitary, the so-called master gland. No one questions that these glands are involved in emotion, or that endocrine and brain systems are involved together in the process of emotional arousal.

A critical question, as yet unresolved, concerns the exact nature of the endocrinological response in emotional stimulation. There are, in essence, two opposing points of view, each of which we shall take up in turn.

Anxiety, Anger, and Adrenaline

The adrenal gland consists of two parts, the *cortex* and the *medulla.* The latter is of primary concern here, because it is the source of adrenaline, a hormone which mobilizes activity of the sympathetic nervous system. The function of adrenal arousal of the body appears to be to prepare the individual for violent activity. Cannon, who applied the now famous expression, "fight or flight," to this gross reaction, regarded it as nonspecific to emotional arousal. It was, he believed, indistinguishably associated with any strong emotional state that is characterized by excitement or arousal.

Cannon was aware that the adrenal medulla secreted two hormones, but he was unable to identify them functionally. We have now clearly distinguished these two substances, which are called *adrenaline* (or epinephrine) and *noradrenaline* (norepinephrine). Both bring about primarily sympathetic responses, but their actions are somewhat different.[1] Adrenaline has more

[1] Determining glandular action by direct assay of a hormone level in the blood stream is a difficult matter. The volume is not constant for any length of time, for hormones are continually being metabolized, altered, and excreted. One would be hard pressed to know at exactly what point in time a

pronounced central effects, including the raising of systolic (central) blood pressure by increasing heart action, decreasing blood volume at the skin level but increasing it in the muscles and brain, increasing blood-sugar level, and so forth. The primary subjective effects noted by the individual are tremor of the muscles, heart palpitation, rapid breathing, and sometimes a feeling of flushing in the face.

Noradrenaline has a more limited action, most of which is peripheral. For example, it increases blood pressure, but it does so by constricting the peripheral blood vessels rather than by increasing heart action.

During the past fifteen years, the results of several studies have suggested that the pattern of physiological responses to anxiety is produced by adrenaline, whereas the pattern for anger is largely determined by noradrenaline. Martin (1961) and Breggin (1964) have reviewed the evidence. The data in Table XV are adapted from three of the main studies reviewed by Martin. According to the adrenaline-noradrenaline hypothesis, it would be expected that systolic blood pressure and heart rate increases would be greater in the experience of anxiety, and that diastolic blood pressure would be greater in anger. Commenting on the data, Martin notes that "in spite of some inconsistencies among the studies, there does appear to be evidence for distinguishable response patterns that can be tentatively associated with the constructs of fear (anxiety) and anger." Martin believes that anxiety may be associated with a purer adrenaline reaction, and anger with a mixed adrenaline-noradrenaline reaction, but he cautions against "any too ready acceptance of some particular pattern as being *the* anxiety or *the* anger pattern."

Breggin, though he seems more convinced of the adrenaline-anxiety and noradrenaline-anger isomorphisms, displays some ambivalence. At one point he states, as a *hypothesis,* that "the proportion of epinephrine secreted by the adrenal medulla dur-

blood sample should be drawn. A veritable host of factors too slippery to control are involved. It is a simple matter, however, to inject a known amount of the hormone into a person and to make physiological measurements after a standard time interval. When the physiologist says that an injection of adrenaline is "sympathomimetic," he means its effect is like that of the natural release of the hormone into the blood stream.

Table XV

Increases in Physiological Measures as a Function of Induced Anxiety and Anger: Data from Three Experiments*

Study	*Anxiety*	*Anger*
	Systolic blood pressure	
1	20	19
2	23	21
3 †	20%	13%
	Diastolic blood pressure	
1	14	18
2	14	15
3 †	10%	23%
	Heart rate	
1	30	26
2	10	11
3 †	33%	7%

* Data adapted from Table 1 in Martin (1961).

† Increases are expressed in percentage of the resting, baseline measure in Study 3, and in absolute units in the other two.

ing anxiety is greater than during other responses, such as anger." Two pages later, he advances the same statement as a fact, though he presents little of his evidence in the intervening paragraphs.

The data are suggestive but, as Martin points out, certainly not conclusive, especially in view of Buss's (1961) critique of the methodologies of some of the chief studies cited by Martin and Breggin.

One may argue that though we have not yet clearly distinguished among states of arousal, enough progress has been made to suggest that we shall eventually be able to do so. The adrenal medulla does not present the only possibility for study. One of the many hormones of the adrenal cortex, *plasma hydrocortisone,* is also associated with emotional arousal (Persky, 1962). Hydrocortisone is known to assist in the repair of damaged tissue, but its specific role in emotional arousal is still unclear. Studies at the Indiana University Medical Center's Institute of Psychiatric Research suggest that hydrocortisone may be involved in preparing the individual to experience anxiety (Weiner, *et al.,* 1963), and in prolonging the anxiety experience (Levitt, Persky, Brady, and Fitzgerald, 1963). Whether or not it may also mediate other aroused states is unknown.

The Theory of General Arousal

One may reasonably elect to agree with the cautious optimism of Martin and Breggin and assume that the discovery of specific endocrinological patterns of emotional reaction awaits refinement of measuring instruments and additional accumulation of basic data in the areas of neurophysiology and neurochemistry. An alternative position argues that the search for specific patterns is a blind alley, that emotional arousal is physiologically nonspecific. In any aroused emotional state, the physiological reaction is simply general arousal or activation. The subjective experience of a specific emotion exists solely on the cognitive or psychological level.

In a sense, this view is a re-establishment of the earlier position of Cannon, though it may be found as early as William James, who pointed out that fear and anger are very often aroused by the same stimulus, and that the experienced emotion is determined by intellectual awareness of circumstances. General arousal theory is in accord with Selye's concept of the *general adaptation syndrome* (Selye, 1956), which will be discussed more fully on pages 104–105 of this chapter.

The general arousal or activation theory has been the brainchild primarily of behavioral scientists, notably Duffy (1941) and, more recently, Malmo (1957, 1959). According to Duffy (1962) two factors are involved in an emotional state: a degree of activation, either high or low, of the organism; and a direction. The activation or arousal aspect takes place on the physiological level and is nonspecific, though it varies among individuals. Thus, various measures of arousal, such as blood pressure, heart rate, and so forth, will be found to be consistently interrelated in the individual, though not necessarily among individuals. The direction aspect exists on the psychological-behavioral level. When a person says, "I am afraid," or, "I am angry," his level of physiological arousal may be the same, but the direction of his behavior is likely to be very different. The individual who experiences a feeling of fear is likely to move away from the stressful stimulus. The angry person is likely to move toward the stressful stimulus.

On the basis of the arousal hypothesis, several predictions can be advanced. Emotions like anxiety and anger are so intertwined by means of learning experiences that individuals commonly report mixed feelings resulting from stimulation, or are unable to distinguish reliably between the two feelings.[2] The experience of joy or mirth, however, is distinctly different from that of anxiety and anger. According to arousal theory, the physiological accompaniments should be much the same.

Several studies suggest that this is, in fact, the case. Levi (1963) showed his subjects the tragic war movie, *Paths of Glory*, and the comical film, *Charlie's Aunt*. Behaviorally and in self-reports, the subjects reacted as expected, but both films brought about approximately the same increases in adrenaline and noradrenaline secretion.

In another relevant experiment (Schachter and Wheeler, 1962), one group of subjects received an injection of adrenaline; another, an inert placebo; and a third, chlorpromazine, a drug that inhibits emotional arousal. All groups were then shown a brief, funny movie. Manifest reactions of amusement were noted and cumulated into an "amusement index." The adrenaline-injected group had the highest amusement index, with the placebo group next, and the chlorpromazine group showing the least amusement. Sixteen per cent of the adrenaline-injected subjects responded at some point with a "belly laugh," whereas not a single placebo subject did.

The Levi study suggests that stimulation of the adrenal medulla accompanies aroused states that are, subjectively and

[2] The relationship has been expounded in detail in neo-Freudian theory, especially in the views of Horney.

behaviorally, distinctly different from anxiety and anger. Furthermore, it appears likely that the degree of adrenomedullary activity is much the same for the positive and the negative states. A logical inference from the Schachter-Wheeler study is that adrenaline causes a state of arousal whose direction is then determined by an external stimulus that is perceived independently by the subject.

The Schachter-Wheeler experiment is in accord with Duffy's idea that the direction of emotion is determined by the individual's perception of the situation within which he experiences general arousal. Schachter (1964) states the hypothesis:

> Given such a state of arousal, it is suggested that one labels, interprets, and identifies this state in terms of the characteristics of the precipitating situation and one's apperceptive mass. This suggests, then, that an emotional state may be considered a function of a state of physiological arousal and a cognition appropriate to this state of arousal. The cognition, in a sense, exerts a steering function. Cognitions arising from the immediate situation as interpreted by past experience provide the framework within which one understands and labels one's feelings. It is the cognition which determines whether the state of physiological arousal will be labeled "anger," "joy," or whatever.

Schachter and Singer (1962) devised an experiment to test this hypothesis directly. Three groups of subjects were injected with a small quantity of adrenaline. One group was then given accurate information about the expected physiological effects. A second group was told nothing, and a third group was deliberately misinformed about the effects.

Each group was then divided into two subgroups. An accomplice of the experimenter was then brought into a room with each of the six subgroups. In half of the subgroups, the accomplice behaved in a merry manner, clowning, joking, and so forth. In the other half, the accomplice and the subjects were required to complete a questionnaire that included offensive personal questions, such as, "With how many men (other than your father) has your mother had extramarital relationships?" The accomplice deliberately became increasingly angry and finally stomped out of the room in a rage.

All subjects were now required to complete a rating scale describing their feelings. The informed group, which was aware that the effects of the injection resembled ones they associated with fear, reported fewer feelings of euphoria and anger. The subjects who had not been informed about the true effects of adrenaline, or who had been misinformed, were more amused and more angered in the respective experimental conditions designed to provoke these effects.

We may infer with Schachter that the subject who had received no explanation for his altered physiological state tended to describe it "in terms of the cognitions available to him," that is, amusement and anger. The individual who had a completely appropriate explanation for his feelings did not need to use any "alternative cognitions available" to account for them. The findings appear to support the general arousal hypothesis advanced by Duffy and others.

Does Mental Illness Have a Physiological Cause?

The specific causes of mental and emotional illness remain a proper subject for investigation, but it has been accepted, since the peak of Freudian influence, that the causation is essentially psychosocial. This has not discouraged a small group of researchers from seeking physical bases for mental illness. Their rationale is appealing. Psychosocial development, spanning many years and influences, has a flavor of irreversibility. An architect can buttress a badly constructed building, but he cannot make it perfect without rebuilding it entirely. But if the etiology resides in a hormonal imbalance, a defect in metabolism, or a distinctly neurophysiological phenomenon, the illness might be completely cured by appropriate chemotherapy, diet, or surgical procedure.

Investigators have been encouraged by well-established demonstrations that severe mental illness may result from excessive doses of certain drugs or from extreme deprivation of such vitamins as thiamine and riboflavin. In most instances the malignant condition is reversed completely by discontinuing the toxic substance, or by supplementing the diet. Toxic and deprivation psychopathology are relatively infrequent. The potentiality of the connection between the physical and the psychological provides the encouragement.

The Concept of the General Adaptation Syndrome

The work of Selye (1956) has also stimulated the quest for physiological bases of mental illness. His concept of the general adaptation syndrome (GAS) applies primarily to physical disease, but it has been extended in theory to emotional and mental illnesses. The GAS comprises three stages:

1. The "alarm reaction," which is a generalized, nonspecific arousal of the organismic processes to rectify some bodily pathology;
2. The "stage of resistance," during which the body system best adapted to cope with the condition becomes specifically active;
3. The "stage of exhaustion," which comes about if the stage of resistance fails. It is characterized by a spreading of the reaction to more body systems.

Suppose the body suffers a wound. Pain is accompanied by an adrenal response which prepares many systems of the body to become active. If infection at the wound site threatens, white blood cells concentrate to combat it, and plasma hydrocortisone accumulates to speed the repair of the damaged tissue. If these reactions fail, the infection spreads into the blood stream, causing more systems to become involved. Body temperature rises, heart rate increases, and so forth. If these "auxiliary channels" are ineffective, the organism eventually dies.

According to Selye, many diseases result from the GAS, including nervous and mental illnesses. But Selye refers to the rare instances in which temporary mental aberration, or a brain lesion, results from hormonal imbalance. He has never contended that the so-called functional emotional illnesses like schizophrenia or anxiety neurosis—those without known organic etiology—are also consequences of the GAS.

The general adaptation syndrome can, in theory, be extended to involve anxiety and emotional illness, as has been suggested, for example, by Fox and his associates (1957). The alarm reaction is the experience of anxiety itself, the "signal of danger," as Freud put it. The stage of resistance corresponds to the mobilization and functioning of defense mechanisms. The stage of exhaustion is analogous to the collapse of the defenses and the overwhelming of the individual by anxiety, with its attendant psychopathological symptomatology.

The physiological concept and the psychological concept of the GAS actually need have no relationship whatsoever. The striking parallel, more than anything else, has encouraged investigators who are searching for physiological etiologies of emotional illnesses.

Physiological Research on Anxiety

The conventional methodology of the study of physiological correlates of mental illnesses is to contrast psychiatric patients and normal control subjects. Because he is behaviorally the most divergent from normality, the psychotic individual has been the focus of research attention. A number of studies of schizophrenia, the most common psychosis, have been reported. The body systems that researchers have most often studied have been brain function as represented by the electroencephalogram (brain-wave measurement) and components of the blood stream. The results, viewed as a whole, are disappointing. Electrical action of the brain would seem to be a logical phenomenon to investigate. But for every positive study, there is at least one counterbalancing negative study, to say nothing of the likelihood of others that have not been published. The absence of definitive findings constitutes a serious setback to exponents of the physiological basis.

A large number of substances are found in human blood, and more are being isolated each year as methods of biochemical assay become more sophisticated. Periodically, a dramatic report will appear alleging that some newly isolated chemical or hormone has been found in excessive quantities in the blood of schizophrenic patients. Invariably, other investigators fail to replicate this finding, and it is eventually chronicled as another of the peculiar accidents with which chance continually bedevils the scientist.

Recent experimentation on the physiological correlates of mental illness has been reviewed by Stern and McDonald (1965), who were originally asked to write on the "physiological bases of mental disease." They began by pointing out that a change of title was necessary because "to the best of our knowledge, no physiological bases for any of the major mental diseases have been found. . . . A chapter reviewing the evidence for causes would have been short and unequivocal."

Kety (1965) and Feldstein (1965) have arrived at similar conclusions based on reviews of the available experimental literature. Feldstein notes, in summary:

> Not only has the "schizochemist" failed to establish a causal relationship between any given metabolic abnormality and schizophrenia, but he has failed to establish convincingly that abnormalities exist, causally related or not causally related.

The significance of these conclusions is enhanced by the fact that both Kety and Feldstein are exponents of the idea that emotional illness is primarily a result of metabolic disorder.

Problems of Physiological Research

In ending this brief section on such a gloomy note, it is only fair to point out that research in this area is fraught with problems. Possibly they are no more numerous or slippery than those which face investigators in other areas of behavioral science, but some are unique. The problem of defining a diagnostic group or groups is common to all researchers who use the mental patient as a subject. The terms "schizophrenic" and "sociopath" slide easily from the tongue of the clinician. Often it hardly matters, as far as treatment is concerned, whether the label is accurate or not. The researcher, unfortunately, cannot afford such comfortable looseness. Findings are likely to be obfuscated if the experimental sample is not reasonably homogeneous. Schizophrenia is a notorious catch-all label; it is usually applied to any psychotic who does not evidently warrant another diagnosis.

A substantial number of factors affect physiological measurement at any moment. These include diurnal fluctuations of bodily processes, diet, medication, exercise, and use of common stimulants like coffee and tobacco. A previous pathological condition may have left permanent physiological alterations whose effects on current response may be difficult to assess.

It is not remarkable that examiners of the physiological have as yet established nothing conclusive. Whether or not they will ever succeed in doing so is a question that can be answered only by continued experimentation.

Summary

Contemporary theory of the physiology of emotional states places the mediating brain centers in the limbic system and the reticular formation. Evidence suggests that the paleocortex contains areas whose stimulation can neutralize anxiety and pain. The RAS is thought to be involved with the cortex in the process of maintaining an optimal level of sensory stimulation in the individual.

There is tentative evidence that the hormonal reaction patterns in aroused states like anxiety and anger may be different with adrenaline predominating in anxiety and noradrenaline in anger. In contrast, the theory of general arousal as advanced by Duffy and Malmo postulates that an aroused emotional state is, at the psychological level, a condition of nonspecific activation. The specific experience of emotion depends upon perception of the environment. A series of pertinent experiments appears to support this point of view.

Research attempts to discover endocrinological or metabolic causes for mental illness continue, but nothing conclusive has as yet been discovered. The absence of findings might conceivably be attributed to methodological difficulties in experimentation

7

ANXIETY AND LEARNING

The ebb and flow of anxiety is found in every facet of human existence. Behavior at a moment in time and over the entire course of a human life may reflect its impact. Long-range effects are ferreted out by the clinical practitioner; they are slippery, devious, and subject to the distortions of recollection and the imprecisions of verbal communication. The experimentalist, because of the requirements of scientific methodology, usually restricts his study of anxiety to the immediate present. He examines a bit of behavior, a standard performance required by the design of his experiment. Occasionally, his investigation has an immediate applied value, but most often he is interested in a particular construct and he views the performance as an operational definition. One such construct, which is of great significance in human life, is *learning*.

A Definition of Learning

"Learning" is a very common word, one that is not usually regarded as needing definition. Yet psychology, the science that has been most concerned with learning, has been unable to formulate a completely acceptable, vernacular definition of learning. Some definitions are so broad that they encompass almost any human behavior under any circumstances. Others are too narrow to cover behaviors which many theorists regard as instances of learning.

Most theorists agree that an opportunity to practice behavior must be provided before we can properly speak of learning, or at least that a time element must be involved. But even this consensus is not unqualified. Practice may have preceded the learning situation, or it may be built into it. In the experimental situation the individual brings his past experience with him; such experience is quite likely to include practice of many forms of behavior required by a laboratory learning experiment. Sometimes the experimenter pointedly incorporates the practice factor. Performance is divided into *trials*. A trial is a single presentation of the substance that is to be learned, and a subsequent performance by the subject. Or the time factor may be implicit, as when the performance itself is repetitive and requires a considerable time to complete.

The distinction between learning and *performance* is equivocal. Learning must be operationally defined by performance, but it is not always certain when performance is a paradigm of learning. The most influential theories of the effect of anxiety on learning do not make the distinction sharply.

The distinction between learning and *memory* is similarly unclear. The effect of practice implies memory in some form; it is literally impossible to conceive of learning completely apart from mnemonic process. The two constructs are so closely related that it appears that they could be employed interchangeably. The choice of a construct label seems to be more a matter of vogue than anything else. In the early years of psychology, memory was an important construct. Many of the experiments that are currently called "learning studies" would have been subsumed under "memory" in the past. Today, memory as a construct has practically disappeared from the experimental literature. Studies once thought to deal with memory are now placed under the heading of learning.

We need not be overly concerned with defining learning, for a chapter title is merely a conventional structure that houses a related group of findings and discussions; if they are loosely linked, or even if some do not actually belong in the structure, no great harm is done. Nevertheless, I feel obliged to attempt a vernacular definition of learning.

Learning is defined as a *relatively permanent change in be-*

havior which comes about as the result of past experience. For experimental purposes, all or most of the past experience takes place within the experimental setting. Learning is usually, but not invariably, measured by an increment or improvement in performance over a period of time.

This definition is expedient, and doubtlessly would not stand the test of critical analysis. It has the virtue, however, of encompassing with reasonable adequacy most of the experiments that will be described in this chapter.

Measuring Learning in the Laboratory

Learning has probably been investigated more often than any other phenomenon, if we include experiments with animals as well as those with humans. A broad range of behaviors has been studied, and many methods and procedures have been employed. A comprehensive discussion is beyond the limits of this chapter, but it will be helpful, before going on, to note some typical methodologies in the experimental investigation of the influence of anxiety on learning.

A common type of experiment deals with *verbal learning.* The task is to learn lists of words or syllables. Sometimes the experimenter will use *nonsense syllables,* combinations of letters, like VIJ or CEQ, which do not actually make a word. An advantage of nonsense syllables is that subjects are unlikely to have had prior association with them.

Another task is called *paired associates.* The subject must learn a list consisting of pairs of words, like *high-low* and *light-dark* (these are easy associations to learn) or *crush-pin* and *orange-desk* (these are difficult ones). The subject is then given the first word of the pair and must respond with the mate.

The lists of verbal material are presented in a fixed order, usually by means of a memory drum, a cylindrical apparatus which presents one stimulus at a time. Performance frequently is based on the *anticipation method,* in which the subject is required, upon presentation of a stimulus, to respond with the stimulus that will next appear on the drum.

Another kind of learning experiment involves *conditioning,* which is roughly synonymous with learning by association. There are a number of forms of conditioning; the one which has been frequently used in learning experiments deals with the *corneal reflex,* customarily called by psychologists the *eyelid* or *eye-blink reflex.* As a protective device, the eyelid will blink or partly close reflexively whenever a stimulus touches the cornea, the transparent part of the outer coating of the eyeball. The blinking response can be elicited easily by blowing a puff of air at the eye. The conditioning technique consists of creating an association between the puff of air and another stimulus, usually an auditory one, like the sound of a buzzer. First the buzzer is sounded; the puff of air follows almost immediately. Conditioning is demonstrated when the eyelid reflex occurs at the sound of the buzzer, without the puff of air.

Although eye-blink conditioning has not been employed to any great extent in recent studies of the effect of anxiety on learning, it was used in a large number of investigations in the 1950's. Some of these studies have theoretical significance and for this reason the phenomenon is accorded special mention here.

Some of the subtests of the Wechsler Adult Intelligence Scale have been used as tasks in experiments dealing with intellectual factors. The most commonly used is the Digit Symbol Subtest. The subject is provided with a key which lists the numbers one through nine and a simple symbol for each number. The task is to fill in the correct symbol in blank boxes under the numbers, which are arranged in various random orders in rows. The subject may refer to the key while performing the task.

It is not certain whether the Digit Symbol task should be regarded as a measure of learning or as a measure of a perceptual-motor performance distinct from learning. Probably it depends on the individual's mode of approach. In many instances, the subject learns much of the key as the task proceeds, thereby facilitating performance, but some may continue to refer to the key throughout the task.

On most tasks, learning can be measured in a number of different ways:

1. The number of errors in a given number of trials;

2. The number of correct responses in a given number of trials;
3. The number of trials required to reach perfect performance or a given level of accuracy;
4. The time required to complete the task.

Theories of the Effect of Anxiety on Learning

In psychology it is conventional to break down the study of human behavior into areas like perception, motivation, and learning. This should not be permitted to obscure the fact that human behavior is unitary. Nevertheless, theorists place varying emphasis on different areas of investigation. Psychoanalysts, for example, are preoccupied with motivation and scarcely concerned with learning. The study of learning and the formulation of theories of learning have been largely the work of experimental psychologists. It is not surprising, therefore, that the literature does not reveal a psychoanalytic position on the effect of anxiety on learning. Nor is it surprising that the few theories which are sufficiently worked out to be considered seriously have come from experimental psychology.

Anxiety as an Energizing Drive: The Iowa Theory.

A great deal of experimental work dealing with the effect of anxiety on learning has been carried on at the University of Iowa under the direction or influence of the former chairman of its psychology department, Kenneth W. Spence. The Iowa studies, like those of Dollard and Miller, were influenced by the theorizing of Hull, but there are some important divergences and elaborations.

Spence (1960) conceives of anxiety as an acquired drive which has the capacity to generally energize the organism. Anxiety ought thereby to facilitate performance and increase the speed of learning. Clinically, one thinks of the tense, "jumpy" person who responds quickly and with relative intensity to minor stimuli.

Spence's theory is straightforward when applied to learning

situations in which only one response is possible and occurs invariably, as is the case with the conditioning of a reflex, like the eyelid reflex. The individual either responds to the conditioned stimulus with the reflex act, or he does not respond; there is no choice of responses. In this kind of situation, a high anxiety level should, by energizing the individual to behave, facilitate learning.

The one-response learning situation does not occur frequently in human life. In most learning circumstances, a variety of possible responses is available to the individual. Each of these response tendencies or "habits"[1] has a certain strength or probability of occurrence, depending upon the individual's past experience. These responses could, theoretically, be arranged in a *hierarchy* of habit strength.

Spence's theory holds that anxiety will energize or strengthen each of the habits in the hierarchy in proportion to the initial strength of the habit. The relationship is multiplicative. For example, suppose that there are two response tendencies, H_1 with an initial strength of three, and H_2 with an initial strength of four. Assume that the strength of anxiety as an energizing drive is represented by the quantity 10. In the learning or performance situation, the energized value of H_1 becomes $3 \times 10 = 30$, and H_2, $4 \times 10 = 40$. The absolute difference between the values of H_1 and H_2 has been increased from one to 10. Thus, H_2 is more likely to occur than it would be without the energizing effect of anxiety.

In some learning situations the correct response tendency will initially rank high in the hierarchy for most people. Suppose that the task is to learn to associate the word *low* with the stimulus word *high*. Most people have been exposed to other associations with the stimulus word, like *high-mountain* or *high-light*. But the association with "low" has doubtless occurred many more times in the past and thus has a greater habit strength. Anxiety will energize the correct response to a greater extent than it will the incorrect ones, and will thus increase the speed of learning.

[1] A habit, as the psychologist employs the word, is not a behavior which is carried out solely because it has been repeated many times in the past. It is usually considered to have a motivational aspect which also plays a part in maintaining the behavior.

This particular learning task is evidently a simple one. In fact, one way in which to define a "simple task" is to say that for most people the correct response initially ranks high in the habit hierarchy. Most human learning, however, is complex. A complex situation is one in which there are a number of competing response tendencies, all of which are equally weak in habit strength. The effect of anxiety as an energizer is to increase the habit strength of the many incorrect response tendencies to the disadvantage of the lone correct response. Learning will thus proceed more slowly.

If there is enough practice, sooner or later the correct response will begin to occur more frequently, and its position in the habit hierarchy will be improved. As this happens, the effect of drive will be to increase the habit strength of the response more and more, so that eventually a point is reached at which learning is facilitated.

A simple mathematical formula describes the effect of anxiety on any one response tendency: R(esponse) = D(rive) × H(abit strength). But Spence has never been able to proceed to the point of formulating an equation to predict the effect of anxiety in a learning situation involving more than one habit. The reason is that it is difficult to establish habit hierarchies for learning tasks. The habit hierarchy is likely to be a function of the individual's past experience; for each task and within each group of people the hierarchy will be a variable. An investigation of the effects of anxiety as a drive on complex learning would thus be an exceedingly complex task itself. It is more feasible to deal with the learning tasks themselves, and much of the Iowa experimentation has therefore been concerned with measuring the effect of anxiety as a function of task difficulty.

Anxiety as a Situationally Determined Reaction: The Yale Theory

In the Iowa theory anxiety is evidently used in the sense of a constant characteristic or trait of the individual. The exclusive use of the MAS as a measure of energizing drive indicates that the evoking of anxiety in the anxiety-prone individual is regarded primarily as a function of a condition of the individual, and secondarily as a function of external stimuli. An opposing view has been advanced by psychologists at Yale led by Mandler and Sarason (Mandler and Sarason, 1952; Sarason, *et al.*, 1960).

The essence of the Yale position is expressed in the following points:

1. Anxiety is a strong learned drive which is situationally evoked. A particular circumstance or class of circumstances may be stressful for a person though he is not made anxious by other situations. Individuals may react differently to the same circumstances.

2. The individual has learned or developed characteristic responses to anxiety which he brings with him to the current situation. These reactions may be *task-irrelevant*—that is, tending to disrupt performance. Examples are feelings of inadequacy, fear of failure, desire to quit the situation. Or they may be *task-relevant*—facilitative of performance, because they move the person to reduce anxiety by completing the task successfully.

3. The effect of anxiety is also a function of such aspects of the situation as the attitude of the experimenter or teacher and the meaning of the task as perceived by the individual. These factors are of greater significance than the complexity or difficulty of the task per se.

4. There may be a general trait of anxiety, but behavioral science is not yet prepared to investigate it. It is first necessary to thoroughly study important situational anxieties.

According to the Yale theory, the study of anxiety should begin with examination in depth of particular stressful situations. In theory, researchers may choose from a limitless number of such situations. There would obviously be little profit in attempting to investigate many of them; few of us have confronted a charging lion or teetered on the edge of the top of a tall building. Nor can such circumstances be arranged artificially. In selecting a stressful situation to study in depth, the Yale researchers were guided by the implicit reasoning that we live in an achievement-oriented society, in which great emphasis is placed on successful performance from an early age. Not achieving—not accomplishing, not performing up to a standard—is regarded as highly undesirable. Anxiety about failing becomes a pervasive phenomenon.[2] We might call such a fear *achievement anxiety,* as some have done.[3]

Many specific situations might evoke achievement anxiety, depending upon the individual's personal goals and values. Achievement anxiety, although narrower in scope than general anxiety, was still too broad a concept for the Yale theorists.

They selected for study a limited area of the concept, called *test anxiety.* In this context "test" refers primarily to the ordinary classroom evaluation. Almost all of us have been subjected to tests, some of us with considerable frequency and over an extended period of time. Test anxiety, the Yale group points out (Sarason, *et al.,* 1960) is a "near-universal" experience, especially in this country, which is "a test-giving and test-conscious culture." Test performance has great significance for the individual; not infrequently, it may seriously affect the course of his life.

If one accepts the assumption that the most fruitful approach to the analysis of anxiety should begin with the study of specific stressful situations, test anxiety appears to be an ideal area of investigation. Even if the assumption is rejected, the study of test anxiety is potentially profitable in its own right.

The Yerkes-Dodson Law

A scientific law or principle is a statement of a basic relationship in nature. An experimental finding must be verified beyond question before it can be called a law. Behavioral science has probably not yet produced any results that really warrant

[2] A general, if implicit, acceptance of this viewpoint explains the common use of contrived or purported failure as a method of inducing anxiety in laboratory studies. It should be noted that many experimenters who employ failure stress do not accept other aspects of the Mandler-Sarason position, especially the contention that the study of general anxiety is premature as yet.

[3] The distinction between achievement anxiety, or fear of failure, and the conventional, general concept is not of recent vintage. It was advanced by Alfred Adler, one of Freud's original circle of adherents, some forty years ago. It appeared most clearly in Murray's classic study of personality (1938). He referred to general anxiety as [a need for] "harmavoidance," in contrast to [a need for] "infavoidance," which is a fear of failure and humiliation.

this lofty designation, though the term has occasionally been applied to a relationship. Perhaps this reflects more the striving of a young science for maturity than the solidity of the finding.

One of the closest approximations to a true scientific principle is the so-called *Yerkes-Dodson Law* (Yerkes and Dodson, 1908). It is one of the earliest, experimentally-based statements of relationship between drive and learning, at least for infrahuman mammals. Essentially, the Yerkes-Dodson Law holds that the relationship between fear, conceptualized as a drive, and learning is *curvilinear.* A low level of drive facilitates learning only slightly or not at all, presumably because the motivation it provides is inadequate to affect performance. A high drive level interferes with the learning process so that performance is similar to, or worse than, that obtained with low drive level. The level of drive which stimulates optimal performance lies somewhere in the middle range of drive intensity.

The law states further that the relationship between drive and performance is a function of task complexity. The optimal drive level is higher when the task is simple than when it is complex; a drive level that facilitates performance on a simple task may disrupt it when the task is more difficult.

When performance is measured in terms of errors, time to complete the task, or number of trials to reach a criterion level, the curve describing the relationship is U-shaped. It is an inverted-U when the measure is the number of correct responses in a given time or number of trials.

Figure 3 is a graphic depiction of the original data obtained by Yerkes and Dodson. The subjects were mice which were required to learn that entering a white box permitted a return to the nest, but that entering a black box resulted in an electric shock. Curve II represents the data obtained when the brightness difference between black and white was very great and the discrimination was thus simple. Curve III represents data obtained with a minor difference between colors which made discrimination difficult. The brightness difference yielding the data for Curve I was medium, compared with other conditions, and thus the task was of medium difficulty.

Curve II indicates that drive level did not affect performance

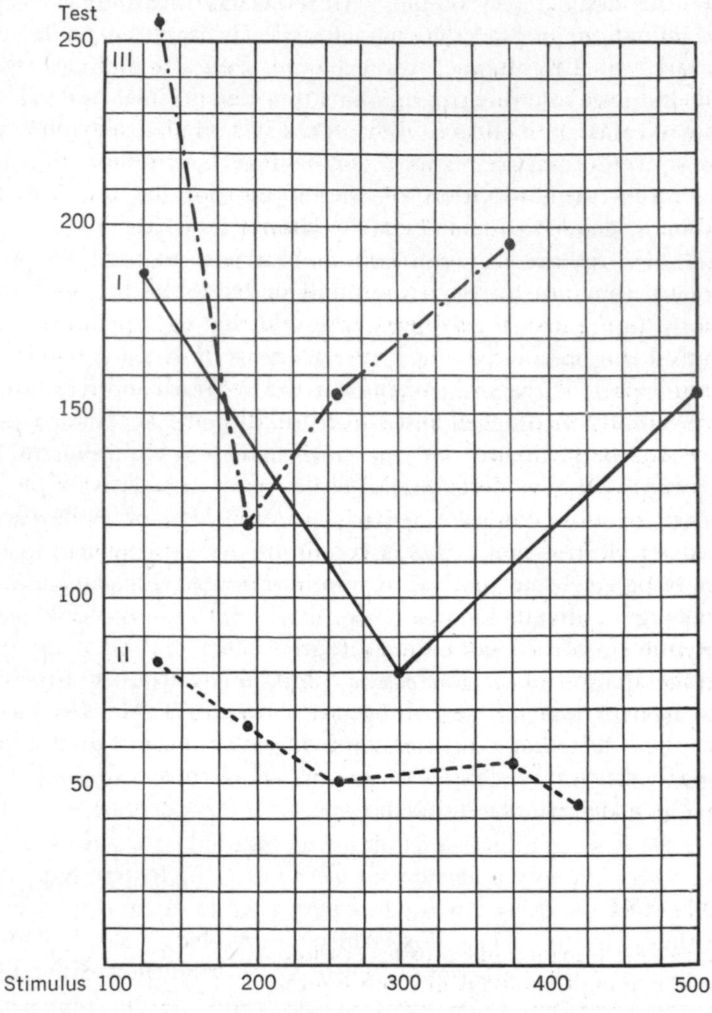

Figure 3. The original finding of the U-shaped curve relating drive level and learning (Yerkes and Dodson, 1908). Numbers along the ordinate represent trials required to learn to a criterion of perfect performance. The abscissa shows drive level in units of intensity of an electric shock. Curve II represents the findings when the task was easy, Curve III when it was very difficult, and Curve I when it was of medium difficulty. *Reproduced from Yerkes and Dodson (1908) by permission of the Wistar Institute of Anatomy and Biology.*

when the task was very simple. Performance on the more difficult discriminations yielded the characteristic U-shaped curve. When the task was difficult, the optimal drive level was 100 electrical units less (or about one-half as great) than the optimal level when the task was of moderate difficulty. (The reader may find it instructive to compare Figure 3 with Figures 4, 5, and 6).

A recent demonstration of the application of the Yerkes-Dodson principle to human behavior has been reported by Stennett (1957). He required a small group of subjects to perform on a tracking apparatus directed by sound under three different conditions. In the first, the subjects were told that the apparatus was simply being calibrated; they were unaware that this phase was actually part of the experiment. In the second condition, they were verbally encouraged and offered small monetary rewards for successful performance. In the third condition, by performing successfully the subjects could either earn a relatively large amount of money or earn a fairly large amount of money and avoid an electric shock. These conditions were presumed to reflect respectively no motivation, optimal motivation, and excessively high motivation.

Stennett recorded both the average number of errors and the average amount of tension in the subject's left arm, the one not used in performing. The findings are shown in Table XVI. The data show first that the amount of muscular tension in the left arm was directly related to motivating conditions, a finding that suggests a degree of validity for the assumed differences among

Table XVI

Average Performance and Muscle Tension
Under Varying Conditions of Motivation *

	CONDITION		
	Calibration	*Optimal*	*High incentive*
Muscle tension	129	145	210
Errors	10	6	8

* Data from Stennett (1957).

the conditions. The differences among the average number of errors under the three conditions of motivation are small, but they are clearly in line with the Yerkes-Dodson Law. The calibration (no motivation) condition and the high motivation condition both yielded a greater average number of errors than did the optimal motivation condition.

The Yerkes-Dodson Law calls for transient or situational anxiety as the drive, as in the Stennett experiment. It is not clear whether the principle ought to hold, in theory, for anxiety-proneness as well. A study by Matarazzo and his associates (1955) suggests that it might.

These experimenters divided 101 male subjects into seven groups according to their scores on the Manifest Anxiety Scale. Subjects with scores from 1 to 5 constituted Group 1, and those with scores from 31 to 35 made up Group 7, with the others grouped in similar fashion in between. Subjects were then required to learn a stylus maze to a criterion of three consecutive correct performances. The relationship between time required to reach the criterion and MAS scores is shown graphically in Figure 4. The inverted-U pattern is evident; maximum speed of performance was attained by those with MAS scores in the middle range. The high and low scorers learned relatively more slowly.

Application of the Yerkes-Dodson Law to human learning and performance seems eminently sensible. A small amount of anxiety is insufficient to improve performance. A moderate amount energizes the individual and thereby improves performance. Further increments are likely to be disruptive. We seem to see this relationship in many areas of human endeavor, and we will encounter it several times in subsequent chapters.

Some Factors Affecting the Relationship Between Anxiety and Learning

Task Complexity

Many experiments have been concerned with the effect of anxiety on learning as a function of relative difficulty of the learning

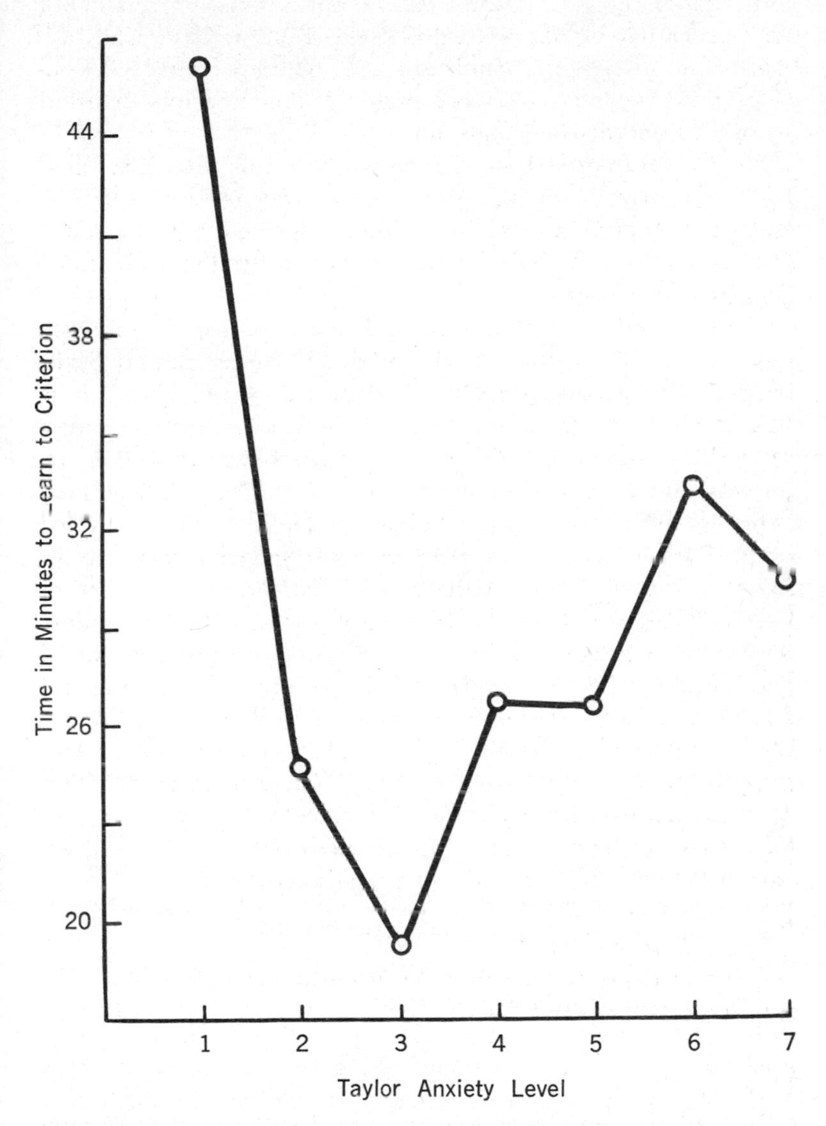

Figure 4. Anxiety proneness and learning. *Reproduced from Matarazzo, et al. (1955), by permission of the Journal Press.*

task. According to the Iowa theory, anxiety should facilitate performance on simple tasks through its energizing effect; it should disrupt learning of complex tasks because of competing response tendencies. The Yale theorists have not adopted a clear-cut point of view, for they do not regard task difficulty as an influential variable affecting learning. It might be inferred from their position that fear of failure is itself a function of relative difficulty of the task; anticipation of failure is likely to be greater when the task is complex than when it is simple. Hence, when the task is difficult, task-irrelevant responses are more likely to occur and thus to interfere with performance. Performance on simple tasks should be unaffected.

Approaching the experimental literature dealing with the effect of task difficulty, we immediately encounter a problem. The assignment of the descriptive adjective "simple" to a task is paradoxically complex, for this word may be defined in more than one way. One-response learning, as represented by the reflex, is evidently simple. A task having a very large number of possible correct responses can also be thought of as simple. In line with Spence's view, a task is simple if the correct response initially ranks high in the habit hierarchy. The correct response to the addition problem, $2 + 2 = ?$, unquestionably has a far greater habit strength for almost all people than any of the infinity of other possible responses. Obviously, a problem like this cannot be used to measure learning; everyone will perform without error on every trial, including the first one. With the exception of such unusable tasks, it is a sticky business to determine the position of the correct response in the habit hierarchy before the experiment is carried out.

One way of attempting to circumvent the absence of knowledge about particular habit hierarchies is to define "simple" in relation to "complex." Differential equations are obviously more difficult to solve than long division problems. It is easier to learn to spell "cat" than "serendipity."

Let us see what the experimental reports can tell us about the effect of anxiety on simple learning as defined in these various ways.

One-Response Learning

Taylor (1951) and since then a number of other investigators (see Spence, 1964) have shown that subjects who score high on the Manifest Anxiety Scale will condition the eyelid reflex more rapidly than low scorers. Spence's review indicates that this finding has been reported in 21 of 25 investigations, a circumstance which he regards as "substantial confirmation" of his theory that anxiety is an energizing drive.

Now, the eyelid reflex is a defensive, avoidance phenomenon, nature's way of protecting the eye from potential harm. Hilgard and his associates (1951) have suggested that anxiety-prone individuals demonstrate more rapid eyelid conditioning *specifically* because of stronger fear of bodily harm rather than because of the energizing effects of anxiety. Thus, a stringent test of Spence's position requires an investigation of the effect of anxiety on one-response learning when the reflex is nondefensive. Although there are, of course, many such reflexes, unfortunately none of them is as suitable as the eyelid reflex for laboratory conditioning experiments with human beings.

An investigation of conditioning of a nondefensive reflex was undertaken by Bindra and others (1955). They attempted to condition the salivary reflex of the mouth to the sound of a doorbell. Subjects were induced to salivate by the sight of a lollipop, and the amount of salivation was measured by absorption in a cotton roll placed in the mouth. High and low anxiety-prone subjects, as defined by the MAS, showed no difference in the amount of salivation during the critical test trials. This finding, although hardly conclusive, at least suggests some validity for the contention of Hilgard and his associates that the effect of anxiety on speed of conditioning of the eyelid reflex is specific rather than general. It also casts a shadow of doubt on Spence's concept of anxiety as an energizing drive.

Multi-Correct Response Learning

The effect of anxiety on simple learning conceptualized as a task for which many correct responses are available is illustrated by a study by Davids and Eriksen (1955). The task was to "chain associate" to each of one hundred common nouns. Chain associating means to write down as many different words as come to one's mind when a stimulus noun is presented. *Any* word is a correct response; performance is measured merely by the number of responses. Davids and Eriksen found a significant positive correlation between the number of associations to all nouns and scores on the MAS. Thus we may say that anxiety-proneness facilitated performance of this kind of simple task. We might add that, because there was only one trial, Davids and Eriksen were dealing with performance rather than with learning. It is not certain that generalization to the customary, multi-trial learning situation is warranted, but a least this experiment is a first demonstration suggesting that anxiety-proneness does have a facilitating effect.

Relative Definition of Simple Learning: Simple Versus Complex Tasks

A number of experiments have been reported in which the influence of anxiety on a relatively simple and a relatively complex task was examined. There are two kinds of findings. The first is illustrated by an experiment in serial learning of nonsense syllables (Montague, 1953). Montague divided his subjects into high and low anxious groups on the basis of MAS scores and required both groups to learn two lists of twelve nonsense syllables each. It had been determined, on the basis of independent empirical study, that the difficult (or complex) list was more than three times as hard to learn as the easy (or simple) one.

The average number of syllables learned over the trials is shown in Table XVII, which is a simplified version of the corresponding table in Montague's report. The interaction of anxiety-proneness and task difficulty is evident. On the easy list the high anxious subjects were able to give an average of a little better than one syllable more than the low anxious subjects. On the difficult list the results are almost precisely reversed.

Findings like those of Montague are more or less in accord with Spence's theory. The second kind of result supports the

Table XVII

Average Number of Nonsense Syllables Learned as a Function of Anxiety and Task Difficulty *

	GROUP	
Syllable list	*High anxious*	*Low anxious*
Hard	4.5	5.8
Easy	9.9	8.7

* Data from Montague (1953).

Mandler-Sarason position. It is exemplified by an investigation by Korchin and Levine (1957) in which the simple and complex tasks were different in substance. The simple task was a word association test in which the subject was presented with a familiar word, like "man," and was required to learn that the associated response was "boy." The complex task consisted of learning a series of incorrect multiplications, like $3 \times 5 = 6$. Three different groups were tested. Two consisted of college students scoring respectively high and low on the MAS. The third group was composed of psychiatric patients who had anxiety as a primary symptom.

Korchin and Levine found that all three groups learned the simple task more quickly than the difficult one, but that there were no differences among groups on the simple task. Differences on the complex task were manifest, with the low anxious group demonstrating the fastest learning.

Differences between the Montague and the Korchin-Levine studies are evident, even if we agree that one task was relatively simpler than the other in both experiments. The conflict in findings may be owing to these differences. It may also be caused by the degree of simplicity of the simple task relative to the difficult task. To illustrate the point, assume a hypothetical 10-point scale of task difficulty. Assume further that the interaction effect obtained by Montague occurs when the simple task has a difficulty value of 1, and the complex task, a value of 9. How are the findings affected by using a simple task with a value of 5? Quite possibly, the performances of the high anxious subjects on the simple task would begin to be impaired, and the difference between groups that existed when the simple task had a value of 1 would become attenuated or disappear entirely. The results would then approach or duplicate those of Korchin and Levine.

Nature of the Task

Mandler and Sarason maintain that reactions to anxiety are task-relevant or task-irrelevant depending in good part on the specific nature of the task itself. This hypothesis is not as easy to test as it might seem at first glance. Every task is somewhat different from every other one, unless we are talking about literally identical tasks. The incautious reviewer of the literature could easily be led into a tautological blunder. If anxiety is found to have a disruptive effect, this finding could be attributed to the nature of the task. If it is found to be facilitative, or if there is no effect, this too could be claimed to be a function of the task itself.

Observation of the everyday world suggests that people with high predispositions to anxiety do not invariably fail. In fact, many are quite successful by community standards. But this is not a true empirical demonstration.

One way in which to test the hypothesis concerning the nature of the task is to deliberately structure a learning situation in which, theoretically, the anxiety-prone individual should perform more effectively than his less anxious peer even though the task can hardly be considered a simple one. This was essentially the approach taken by Ruebush (1960). The task he presented to a group of sixth-grade pupils was to locate a figure imbedded in a matrix of lines. The problem is familiar to many children; one can find such puzzles on the pages of the Sunday comic section.

In this particular task, the subject did not know whether he had performed satisfactorily or not, and he was free to work as slowly or rapidly as he pleased, but the most efficient performance was obtained by working slowly. Now, it has been shown frequently that individuals with high predisposition to anxiety consistently require more time to complete complex tasks of various kinds. It would be expected that the anxiety-prone children in Ruebush's sample would be slower and more cautious in their approach to the task. This is exactly what Ruebush found to be the case. Correspondingly, he found that these children successfully solved more of the figure problems in any given period of time, undoubtedly as a function of greater circumspection.

Thus it appears that on at least one kind of complex task performance is facilitated by anxiety. A likely inference is that when the nature of the task requires deliberate, careful performance which is best achieved by slowness and compulsive attention to detail, anxiety will facilitate performance. This does not, however, in itself constitute a rigorous test of the Yale contention. It is also possible that this is the only sort of task on which anxiety and performance are positively related. Even this relationship cannot be said to be conclusively demonstrated by any one investigation.

Intelligence

Most learning which takes place outside the psychologist's laboratory and which has any significance in human life is affected by a variety of factors other than anxiety. One of the most important of these—indeed, probably the most important—is general intelligence.

No one can be expected to learn something which is beyond his basic comprehension, regardless of drive or anxiety level. We may say that *on the average* there is a relationship between task complexity and the effect of anxiety on learning. In the *individual case,* "complexity" itself depends upon the person's intelligence. A task that is difficult for an individual whose IQ is 80 would be simple for one whose IQ is 125. A task that is complex for the latter would be completely beyond the capacity of the low-IQ individual.

It is not surprising, therefore, to find that the results obtained by Ruebush (1960) held for the low and middle range of intelligence only. Anxiety-prone children solved more problems as long as the task presented a challenge. When the subjects were of high intelligence, the intellectual factor was so prepotent that it canceled out the effect of anxiety on learning.

The effect of intelligence was even more clearly demonstrated by Spielberger and Katzenmeyer (1959), who examined the relationship between anxiety and general scholastic achievement at the college level. They divided a large group of students into three subgroups on the basis of intelligence test scores: the lowest 20 per cent, the middle 60 per cent, and the highest 20 per cent. Then they computed the correlation between grade-point averages as a measure of college achievement and scores on the Manifest Anxiety Scale. They found no relationship between the GPA and anxiety for the highest and lowest intelligence groups, and a small, negative relationship in the middle IQ group.

Thus the student of low intelligence simply cannot do any better because of his intellectual limitations, regardless of his drive level. Academic achievement comes so easily to the student of high intelligence that anxiety cannot affect his performance. Only in the middle range of intelligence, where capacity is neither limited nor extensive, has drive any effect on scholastic achievement.

The point is further illustrated in another study by Spielberger (1962), in which he followed up anxiety-prone college students after three years. He found that more than 20 per cent had dropped out of school. But of those in the highest IQ bracket, only 9 per cent had dropped out.

Naturally Occurring Stress

Some of the methodological problems involved in studies of anxiety were discussed in the previous chapter. One of the most serious is the validity of artificial anxiety-inducing techniques. All these techniques seem relatively mild compared to naturally occurring stress situations.

Investigations of learning in natural stress situations are usually difficult to carry out. Those few that have been accomplished are, perhaps, more revealing because there is less doubt about the intensity of the emotion. Among such rare studies are two dealing with paratrooper training. One (Basowitz, *et al.,* 1955) reported that soldiers involved in the fearsome procedures of learning to jump out of an airplane performed somewhat more poorly on a number of simple tasks than did a control group. A study by Walk (1956) dealt directly with a single stressful aspect of paratrooper training: learning to jump from a 34-foot tower. The trainee falls nearly eight feet before his descent is halted by straps fastened to his parachute harness. The purpose of this training is to teach the proper form in jumping from an airplane in flight. Apart from the context, the task is a very simple kind of motor behavior, clearly within the capacity of anyone physically sound enough to qualify for the paratrooper training course. Failing to learn the proper form or refusing to jump are grounds for elimination from the course.

Walk asked a group of paratrooper trainees to rate, on a 10-point scale, the amount of fear they experienced just before jumping from the tower. On the average, the group's self-rating was about 6 before the first jump and then gradually declined over the next six jumps, reaching an average of about 3 by the seventh jump.

Thirty-one of the trainees failed to complete the course. This group consistently acknowledged more anxiety before all jumps than the group which passed. The correlations between self-ratings of fear and number of errors in jumping as rated by instructors ranged between .40 and .50 from the third jump on.

The Basowitz and Walk studies are unusual, not only because the stress situations were natural, but also because the anxiety stimulus and the learning task were the same. In most laboratory studies, the stimulus and the task are independent, as, for example, electric shock and nonsense syllables. An investigation by Beam (1955) combines features of the paratrooper and laboratory studies. The stress was natural, but the learning tasks were independent of it.

Beam tested groups of college students and staff members just before they experienced one of three stress situations:

1. Presenting an oral report as a college course requirement;
2. Taking a preliminary examination for a graduate degree;
3. Appearing in a play before a large audience.

All subjects were also tested under neutral conditions. The learning task was a standard list of nonsense syllables which had to be learned to a criterion of two consecutive errorless trials.

Under stress, subjects required 50 per cent more trials to reach the criterion and made 50 per cent more errors, on the average. Only four of 50 subjects failed to manifest the need for more trials; among those who were adversely affected, some took six times as long to reach the criterion under stress. The average number of errors made under stress was 195, while in the neutral condition this figure was only 127. Only five subjects did not conform to this trend.

These studies suggest that naturally occurring anxiety impairs learning both when the learning task is itself anxiety-evoking and when it is independent of the stress situation. When the task is inherently stressful, learning may be inhibited even though the task is relatively simple.

Experimental Relief from Anxiety

Let us assume, with Mandler and Sarason, that the interfering effect of anxiety on learning is a consequence of the learner's fear of failure. If this is so, the experimenter might be able to improve learning by reducing this anxiety. A manipulation of this kind was undertaken by Sarason (1958).

Subjects were divided into high and low anxious groups on the basis of Test Anxiety Scale scores. Each group was then further divided into two subgroups.[4] Subjects were required to learn a list either of 17 two-syllable words or of 17 two-syllable nonsense words.

One of the subgroups in each of the high and low groups was given standard instructions. Both the other subgroups were first offered the following reassuring "therapy" for possible anxiety feelings:

> Before we start, perhaps I could mention a few things that will be helpful to you in learning the list I am going to show you on this memory drum. Many people get unduly upset and tense because they

[4] The experimental design was actually more complex. It is presented here in simplified form so that the major finding can be emphasized.

do not learn the list in just a few trials. If you don't worry about how you are doing, but rather just concentrate on the list, you will find you learn much more easily. These kinds of lists are hard, and so it's no surprise or matter of concern if you progress slowly at first and make mistakes.

Table XVIII shows the average improvement per subject from the first block of five trials to the last block. Looking along the standard condition row, we see the expected, disruptive effect of

Table XVIII

Effect of Reassurance on the Relationship Between Anxiety and Verbal Learning *

	GROUP	
Condition	*High anxious*	*Low anxious*
Standard	9.1	11.6
Reassurance	11.0	9.5

Data are in terms of increment in average number of words learned over trials.

* Data from Sarason (1958).

high test anxiety under ordinary test circumstances. On the average, the low anxious subjects improved their performances by 11.6 words from trial block 1 to trial block 5, as compared with an improvement of only 9.1 words for the high anxious group.

The column for the high anxious group reveals that the experimenter's reassurance had a facilitative effect. Under the reassurance condition, the improvement over trials for the high anxious group jumped to 11.0, an increment of more than 20 per cent over the standard condition. The low anxious subjects, however, did not do as well under the reassurance condition as they had done in the standard condition, a finding which suggests that Sarason's brief "therapy" actually *interfered* with their learning.

Sarason's reassurance was calculated to reduce fear of failure in the high anxious group by suggesting that the experimenter was a benign fellow who did not want to pressure his subjects unduly and who would not mind if they performed poorly. The consequent decrement in anxiety lowered the drive level in the high anxious group so that it became energizing instead of disruptive. The anxiety reduction in the low anxious group apparently depressed the drive level to a point where it no longer energized performance. This explanation not only supports the Yale position but also is in accord with the Yerkes-Dodson Law.

A supporting result was obtained by Paul and Eriksen (1964) in an ingenious little study. An equivalent form of a regular class examination was administered to a group of students who had recently taken the real test in an introductory psychology class. The examiners carefully explained that their purpose in administering the equivalent form was experimental and would have nothing at all to do with the student's course grades. Average class scores for the two examinations were almost precisely alike, but scores on the real exam showed a low, negative relationship with scores on the TAQ, whereas scores on the equivalent form, administered under unthreatening conditions, were unrelated to TAQ scores. The absence of correlation, together with the fact that the average scores for the two examinations were the same, suggests that some of the students with high test anxiety improved in performance on the experimenter's form of the examination, whereas some with low test anxiety performed more poorly, an outcome which is much the same as that of Sarason's experiment (1958).

Learning and Muscle Tension

Tension in the striated or voluntary muscles of the body is one of the most common concomitants of anxiety. It is a correlate which anxiety shares with activity in general, either motoric or intellectual.[5] This relationship could conceivably explain how anxiety facilitates various kinds of performance, as Spence's theory suggests. Spence has never been particularly concerned

[5] Which explains why purely intellectual work can sometimes be exceedingly fatiguing.

with whatever body process may intervene between drive and performance, but a number of independent studies have related muscle tension level to learning. Most of these studies were carried out some decades ago, antedating Spence's theory and the contemporary interest in anxiety. The experimenters of the 1930's were interested in muscle tension as an independent phenomenon, but since it is a common concomitant of anxiety, their findings are potentially relevant to the present exposition.

Learning and Induced Muscle Tension

In a number of studies the effect of muscle tension on simple learning had been found to follow the Yerkes-Dodson principle. Courts (1942) sums up the early research by noting that "the inverted U-shaped curve appears to be typical of the relationship between learning and degree of experimentally induced tension." An excellent illustration appears in a study by Courts himself (1939). Using a hand dynamometer, he obtained a maximum hand-grip pressure for each of his subjects. They were

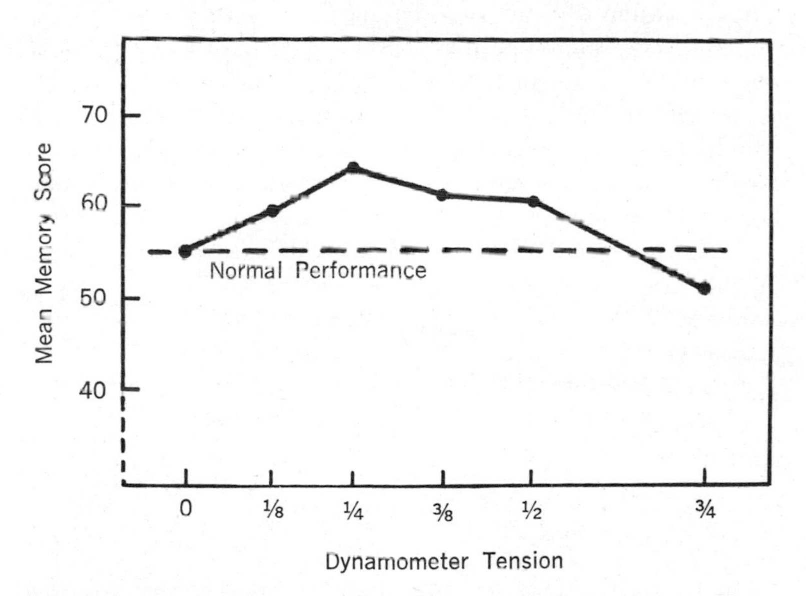

Figure 5. Learning and muscle tension. *Reproduced from Courts (1939) by permission of the American Psychological Association.*

then required to learn lists of nonsense syllables while gripping the dynamometer with varying degrees of pressure, all less than the maximum, beginning with no pressure at all. The fractions of the maximum employed were 1/8, 1/4, 3/8, 1/2, and 3/4. It is assumed, of course, that the degree of induced muscle tension is directly related to the amount of pressure.

The findings are depicted graphically in Figure 5. The curve shows that learning increases from the normal or no-tension situation to a peak of efficiency at 1/4 of the maximum tension. Beyond this point, learning efficiency begins to drop off. When the degree of tension exceeds about 5/8 of the maximum, learning is inhibited as compared with the no-tension situation. This curvilinear relationship parallels the original findings of Yerkes and Dodson with drive level in animals.

Anxiety-Proneness, Induced Tension, and Learning

Because induced muscle tension was always proportionate to an established maximum, we can safely assume that the levels of induced tension did not vary among Courts's subjects. We cannot, however, assume that there was no intersubject variability in the *no-tension* state. In fact, it is more likely that naturally occurring muscle tension did differ among Courts's subjects. Individuals with high predisposition to anxiety would probably manifest more muscle tension in the no-tension state than would those of lesser proneness.

Courts did not distinguish among subjects with respect to muscle tension in the no-tension state, but this variable has been examined in a more recent study (Meyer and Noble, 1958). Subjects categorized as high and low anxious, as measured by the MAS, were required to learn a "verbal maze" consisting simply of a correct sequence of a series of the words "left" and "right." They learned the sequence under two conditions. One was neutral; the other was a muscle tension situation induced by gripping a hand dynamometer with a standard pressure of 10 pounds.

The results were reported in terms of number of errors on the first and last of a series of 30 trials. In the no-tension situation, the high anxious subjects made fewer errors both at the beginning and at the end of the series, but in the tension situation they made more errors at both points. The differences between the high and low anxious groups are not striking. What is remarkable is the almost precise reversal of performance in the two conditions. The data in the two conditions are almost identical if we simply reverse the group averages in either condition.

Overall, it would appear that the degree of induced muscle tension was insufficient to improve performance for both high and low anxious groups. On one hand, the performance of the high anxious group was more efficient in the no-tension situation, presumably because the subjects' chronic muscle tension level was higher. When induced muscle tension was added to the elevated chronic level, the effect became disruptive. On the other hand, the effect was facilitative for the low anxious group, increasing their muscle tension level to that of the high anxious group in the no-tension situation. Thus the findings of Meyer and Noble are actually in accord with the Yerkes-Dodson Law even though they suggest that pre-experimental individual differences can affect experimental results.

Induced Tension and Performance

A recent experiment (Wood and Hokanson, 1965) suggests that the effect of induced muscle tension on an intellectual performance which does not definitely involve learning may be somewhat different than in the type of experiment Courts conducted. Wood and Hokanson essentially duplicated Courts's procedure, but they included performance at the maximum hand-gripping pressure. The criterion task was the Digit Symbol Test. Change in the subject's heart rate as he performed was simultaneously recorded. The findings, which are depicted graphically in Figure 6, are obviously similar to those of Courts and equally obviously in keeping with the Yerkes-Dodson Law. One difference is that performance does not drop below normal even at the maximum induced tension, though such impairment appeared at a level *below* the maximum in the Courts study. A task difficulty factor is clearly suggested.

Figure 6 shows that heart rate is directly and linearly related

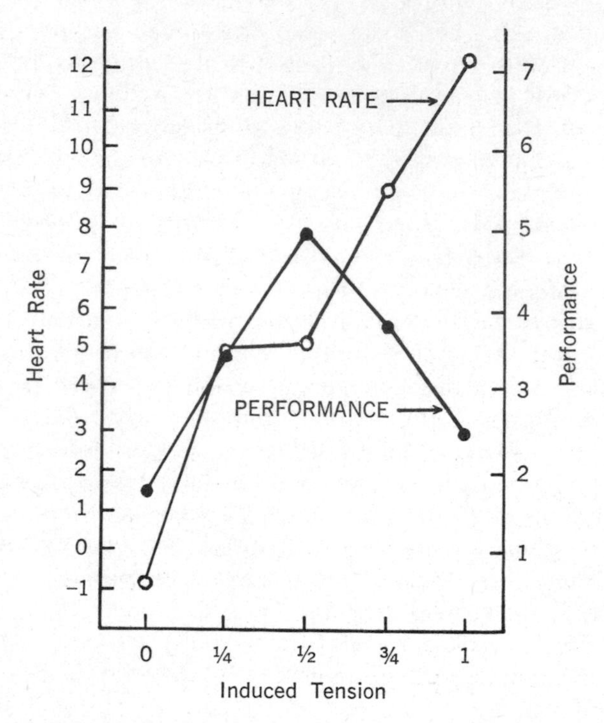

Figure 6. Performance, induced tension, and heart rate. *Reproduced from Wood and Hokanson (1965) by permission of the American Psychological Association.*

to induced tension, a finding which suggests that the subject's physiological state at the time of performance resembles that of general emotional arousal. One possible inference is that a high state of arousal itself, rather than the subjective experience of emotion, facilitates or disrupts performance, a point in keeping with activation theory as advanced by Duffy, Malmo, and others.

Summary

The two theories of the effect of anxiety on learning which have been most successful (that is, have stimulated the most research) were developed by psychologists at the University of Iowa and at Yale. The Iowa position conceives of anxiety as a general, energizing drive. Its effect is to strengthen all available response tendencies in proportion to their strength at the moment of energizing. The response tendencies are ordered in a habit hierarchy depending upon initial strength. When the correct response ranks high in the habit hierarchy, performance at any particular moment is facilitated. This conceptualization applies most directly to simple learning situations. On complex learning tasks, the effect of anxiety is to interfere with learning at first, and to facilitate it eventually, when the correct habit moves up in the hierarchy as a function of practice.

The position of the Yale theorists is that anxiety is largely determined by the nature of the situation, interacting with personal characteristics of the individual. A person develops characteristic ways of reacting to anxiety. These may be task-relevant or task-irrelevant, depending upon the nature of the task and the manner in which the learning situation is perceived by the individual. These factors are of much greater importance than the simplicity or difficulty of the task.

Both theories have some experimental support. For example, studies of simple learning, especially of the one-response type, suggest that anxiety functions as an energizing drive in such situations. Support for the Yale theory comes from investigations which show that anxiety can facilitate performance on certain complex tasks, and that the experimenter, by altering the subject's perception of a complex learning situation, can reduce the interfering effects of anxiety.

The Yerkes-Dodson Law postulates that the relationship between anxiety and learning is curvilinear. Both low and high levels of anxiety do not improve performance. Optimal positive effect is obtained in the middle range.

The Yerkes-Dodson Law also states that the optimal anxiety level will be inversely related to the complexity of the task. Many experimental investigations with human beings indicate that anxiety interferes with performance on complex learning, a finding which indirectly supports the Yerkes-Dodson Law. According to the Iowa theory, the phenomenon is a function of the fact that complex tasks are characterized by many weak response tendencies which compete with the correct one. In such a situation, the energizing effect of anxiety interferes with performance. The explanation of the Yale theorists is that task-irrelevant responses are more likely to occur in complex situations, primarily because of the increased threat of failure.

In addition to task complexity and the nature of the task itself, other factors that have been shown to influence the relationship between anxiety and learning are intelligence, muscular tension, and experimental milieu.

8

ANXIETY AND COGNITIVE PROCESSES

Human existence has many activities besides learning that involve higher-order brain functioning. Clinical practice and general observation suggest that most of these activities are inhibited, retarded, or otherwise disadvantageously affected by strong emotions like anxiety. Unfortunately, it is easier to form an opinion based on clinical examination than it is to design a definitive experiment. Constructs like "creativity" and "reasoning" are difficult to define for experimental purposes. Complex cognitive processes are apt to be influenced by many factors besides anxiety. It is difficult to control these extraneous variables—many of which are as yet unknown—so as to isolate the anxiety effect.

Consequently, experimentation dealing with the relationship between anxiety and complex cognitive processes is in a rudimentary state. A handful of suggestive, though hardly conclusive, findings is presented in this chapter.

Problem-Solving

Most laboratory learning experiments use lists of words or nonsense syllables as the learning task. Rote learning tasks minimize the importance of previous learning, of whatever response tendencies the subject may bring with him to the experimental situation, thus sharpening the focus of the study. Of course, the effects of previous experience can never be completely eliminated. The idea is to keep them from becoming so influential that they obscure relationships between experimental variables or the effects of experimental treatment.

The rote learning task has the advantage of being amenable to easy quantification; one nonsense syllable is very much like another. It is also suitable for trials or blocks of trials. The amount of material in the task, the time factor, if any, and the relative difficulty of the task are easily controlled and manipulated by the experimenter.

On the whole, a list of nonsense syllables is an ideal learning task for the laboratory. Regrettably, rote learning is not of great importance in human life, and what there is of it seldom takes place under the kind of conditions imposed by the researcher. Most people will never have occasion to learn a list of nonsense syllables from a memory drum unless they have the ill luck to run afoul of an experimental psychologist.

The extent to which laboratory findings can be generalized to extralaboratory behavior is uncertain. It *appears* that at least some of them are applicable. Perhaps a better approximation to "real-life" learning can be obtained from studies dealing with more complex intellectual activities. One such activity is called *problem-solving.*

Problem-solving is the label given to "a diverse class of performances which differs . . . only in degree from other classes of learning and performance, the degree of difference depending upon the extent to which problem-solving demands location or integration of previously learned responses" (Duncan, 1959). Included in those "previously learned responses" may be any sort of motoric action, or such higher intellectual process as reasoning or logical analysis, or the application of prior knowledge and experience. In short, the ability to solve a problem depends upon more personal factors than does rote learning.

Anxiety-Proneness and Problem-Solving

The effect of anxiety-proneness on problem-solving ability is illustrated in a study by Harleston (1962). The subjects were given two and one-half minutes to solve each of a series of easy and hard five-letter anagrams ("ablte" is easy; "geerm" is hard). The breakdown into anxiety groups was accomplished by means

Table XIX

Number of Anagrams Solved as a Function of Anxiety-Proneness *

	TYPE OF ANAGRAM		
Anxiety group	*Easy*	*Hard*	*All*
Low	155	118	273
Medium	151	89	240
High	147	88	235

* Data from Harleston (1962).

of a modified form of the TAQ. The numbers of correct solutions of hard and easy anagrams are shown in Table XIX. Overall, there is a linear relationship to anxiety, those of the lowest proneness solving the most anagrams, those of the medium group, the next most, and those of the highest proneness, the smallest number. The difference between the medium and high anxiety-prone groups is trivial, however. Most of the variation lies between these two groups and the low group. Furthermore, all but a small fraction of the intergroup performance discrepancy is a function of the hard anagrams.

One could argue that the effect of anxiety-proneness on problem-solving ability does not follow the Yerkes-Dodson principle. One might also surmise that the task is of sufficient difficulty that performance is measurably disrupted by even a moderate amount of anxiety. Such an inference would be in accord with the original Yerkes-Dodson findings. It cannot, however, be contended that the speed factor interfered with performance in the more anxiety-prone subjects. Although Harleston's subjects required about twice as long, on the average, to solve the hard anagrams, solution times for correctly solved anagrams did not differ among the three anxiety groups. In other words, there is no evidence that the more anxiety-prone subjects were working more slowly.

Naturalistic Stress and Problem-Solving

Fifty years ago, Hamilton (1916) devised an ingenious task, intricate enough to be clearly considered a problem, yet so simple that experimental subjects could be lower animals as well as humans. The experimental situation was an enclosure that had four exit doors all at equal distances from the entrance. On each trial, only one door was unlocked, and the subject was required to discover this open exit. Maximally effective problem-solving behavior called for discovering the experimenter's scheme: the same door was never unlocked on successive tries. Except for this consideration, the open door on any trial was designated on a purely random basis.

After experimenting with various animals, Hamilton found that five kinds of problem solutions occurred often enough to be noted:

Type A. The subject ignores the door that was unlocked on the previous trial and tries each of the other three exits once, in a regular order.

Type B. The subject attempts to open each of the four doors once in a random order. The door that was unlocked on the previous trial may or may not be ignored.

Type C. The subject tries all four doors once in a regular order, clearly including the door opened on the previous trial.

Type D. The subject tries a door, then another door, then returns to try the first door.

Type E. The subject attempts to open the same door several times before trying any other one.

These solution types, from A through E, logically appear to indicate a range of behavior from the most adaptable to the least adaptable, from a behavior that has the highest probability of success, through behaviors with lesser probabilities, to a behavior that has the least probability of success.

The curves of Figure 7 show results obtained with human subjects and with rats; they are not at all surprising. About 60 per cent of the solutions by humans were Type A, the most adaptable; humans exhibited only small percentages of Type D and E solutions, the least adaptable. The problem-solving behavior of rats was almost exactly the reverse. Nearly 50 per cent of the solutions were Type E, with only small proportions of Types A and B.

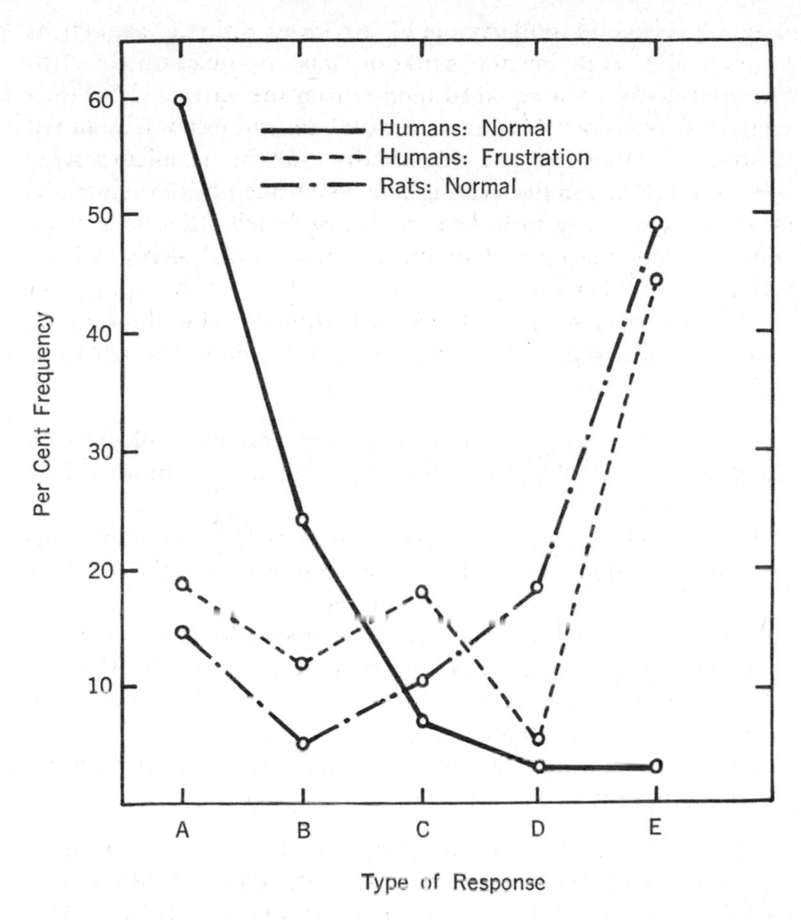

Figure 7. Effect of naturalistic stress on problem-solving. *Reproduced from Underwood (1949) by permission of Appleton-Century-Crofts, Inc.*

Many years later, Patrick (1934a,b) undertook to determine what happens to human problem solving behavior in Hamilton's enclosure under severe stress. Patrick was not sparing with his ammunition. He exposed his subjects to continual electric shock by means of a grid that covered the floor, or directed streams of cold water at them, or blasted their ears with a raucous automobile horn.

The third curve in Figure 7 indicates the effect of these stressful procedures. The problem-solving behavior of the human subjects changed dramatically, and now clearly resembled that of the rat. It is as if the subjects had temporarily been deprived of their characteristic human ability to reason and had become suddenly much given to the use of physical strength in its stead. Underwood (1949) has characterized Type D and E solutions as "bulldozing responses"—that is, attempts to solve the problem by muscular force instead of by use of higher brain centers. Patrick (1934b), in a more metaphorical though equally appropriate expression, called them *rattled-hit-or-miss-childlike* behaviors.

The performance of Patrick's subjects is reminiscent of *panic behavior* as it has been described by Schultz (1964) and various sociological observers. Severe, extreme stress has resulted in a primitivization of human behavior, a feat that appears far beyond the efficacy of standard laboratory stress procedures, which sometimes *improve* performance. One is reminded of Leeper's (1948) point that emotion has a disorganizing effect only in its most intense form.

Incidental Learning

Learning, in the customary sense of the word, entails a direct focus on a stimulus with the explicit purpose of altering the learner's behavior. Investigations and theories of learning assume that such a direct focus is involved. There is another kind of learning that occurs unintentionally. A person reads and rereads a favorite story, or listens many times to a passage of music, and then finds that he can quote from the story or hum bars of the music though he has apparently made no deliberate attempt to learn. Acquisition of this kind is called *incidental learning*.

Incidental learning may be more significant in human life than formal learning. It appears, for example, that when a child is acquiring patterns of behavior, he may do so to a great extent through incidental learning, though it is not easy to determine whether a particular instance of naturally occurring learning is incidental or not. In the experimental laboratory situation, the technique for studying incidental learning consists of presenting simultaneously a formal learning task to which the subject's attention is directed, and background stimuli as the incidental learning task.

The effect of anxiety on incidental learning is suggested by an experiment by Silverman (1954). The focused learning task consisted of moving a lever whenever a line of appropriate length appeared on a screen before the subject. During this performance, a muted voice in the background recited 20 two-syllable words. No attention was directed to this list by the experimenter; learning it was not presented as part of the experimental situation.

One group of subjects was continuously threatened during performance by the possibility of an electric shock administered to the wrist and ankle. Another group performed under neutral conditions. Subsequent measurement disclosed that the unstressed group could recall almost twice as many of the background words as the threatened group. This finding appears clearly to illustrate that anxiety had an interfering effect on incidental learning.

The paradigm experimental design employed by Silverman seems to have few direct analogs outside the laboratory. Naturally occurring incidental learning, as by the child, appears to be a function of imitation of, or identification with, an adult or peer. Although the child may not be trying to learn, he is also not usually faced simultaneously with a focused learning task and the stimuli that are incidentally to be learned. It is thus not clear, no matter how logical the relationship may be, that generalization from results like those of Silverman to the natural situation is warranted.

Verbal Communication

Verbal communication is a form of behavior most typical of the human organism. Some social scientists consider it to be of paramount importance; they attribute many of the major problems that beset human society to difficulties in communication among people. Whether or not the contention of the "semanticists" is valid, verbal communication is undoubtedly a highly significant behavior in many walks of life. It is also a highly complex phenomenon. Many factors are likely to be involved in determining the effectiveness or lack of effectiveness of communication: intelligence, education, and vocabulary of the communicator, nature of the subject matter, and awareness of the comprehension level of the audience, to mention a few. Not many of these potential influences have been investigated experimentally, but a few experiments have dealt with the effect of anxiety on communication.

Anxiety in the Communicator

Gynther (1957) attempted to determine the effect of anxiety-proneness and stress on the ability to communicate. She identified high and low anxious groups by means of the Welsh A Factor Scale and objectively measured their ability to communicate verbally in a neutral and in a stress situation. Stress was induced by means of instructions calculated to arouse both test anxiety and evaluation apprehension.

The task required each subject to answer eleven questions about himself. The questions were somewhat vague and presumably difficult to answer. Responses were tape-recorded and analyzed by a rating method that provided a statistically reliable index of "communicative efficiency" (CE). CE is based on a breakdown of each response into units; these units were then characterized by expert judges according to the degree to which each was relevant to the stimulus question.

Gynther found that the stress condition reduced CE for both groups of subjects. In both conditions, the low anxious group communicated significantly more effectively, demonstrating about 17 per cent more communicative efficiency than the high anxious group.

Gynther concludes:

> This experiment demonstrates a phenomenon that is repeatedly observed in everyday contacts between people. Impressions and evaluations of a person, whether in a business, social, or professional setting, are influenced by one's ability to communicate one's ideas. This study shows that the lack of fluency in an interview situation is in part a function of the individual's degree of anxiety. . . .

Studies of speech patterning furnish an explanation of the disruption of communication in the anxious individual. Kasl and Mahl (1965) have found that stressed individuals show significant increases in such indicators of "flustered" speech as repetition, stuttering, omissions, incomplete sentences, and correcting the form or content of an expression in the midst of making it. Geer (1966) found that people who express great anxiety about public speaking speak more slowly before an audience and have longer and more frequent periods of silence in their presentations. These speech phenomena seem much like typical instances of task-irrelevant reactions that serve to reduce the comprehensibility of verbal messages and thereby render the communicator less effective.

Message Anxiety

Gynther's experiment, like that of Feshbach and Singer (1957) which is outlined in the next chapter, suggests that communication may be adversely affected when the content itself evokes anxiety, either in the communicator or in the audience. Communicative efficiency may be partly a function of the degree of "message anxiety," as Nunnally puts it.

Nunnally (1961) prepared two similar explanations of electroshock treatment of psychiatric patients. The explanations presented essentially identical information, but they differed in affective tone. One form was intended to evoke anxiety in readers; the other was neutral. For example, in the neutral form, the text stated, "A psychiatrist and several attendants prepare him (that is, the patient) for the treatment." In the form intended to evoke anxiety, the same fact is presented as, "The patient is carried into a room and strapped into position on a bed." Similarly, "a weak electrical current" in the neutral form becomes "a powerful electric current" in the stress form. "Actually less painful than many routine medical treatments" is rephrased as "a painful type of electrical treatment which is more agonizing than other medical treatments."

The explanations were presented in written form to groups of subjects, who were asked to rate the degree to which each passage was understandable and simple, or mysterious and complicated.

On the average, the form invested with message anxiety was rated significantly lower on the "understandability factor" than its companion piece. The logical inference is that the arousing of anxiety by the verbal material itself reduces its comprehensibility, at least as subjectively reported by the reader.

Mode of Responding

A possible explanation of the interfering effects of anxiety on learning involves the concept of stimulus generalization. Remember that Dollard and Miller (1950) suggest that one consequence of strong anxiety is that the individual tends to respond anxiously to stimuli that are similar to an original anxiety-provoking stimulus. He seems to have lost some of his ability to discriminate among stimuli. Perhaps the anxious individual is less able in general to discriminate among similar objects in the environment. This perceptual defect would tend to impoverish his repertory of responses. For example, suppose that there are 10 stimuli each requiring a different response. The anxious individual cannot distinguish among some of them, so that he actually perceives only five different types of stimuli among the 10. He would therefore learn only five responses and would respond incorrectly to five stimuli. This attrition of repertory is sometimes called *response stereotypy.*

A highly suggestive experiment involving response stereotypy in perception was carried out by Eriksen and Wechsler (1955). They presented their subjects with a series of 11 squares ranging in size from 20 to 50 millimeters square. The task was to determine the size of the stimulus square using assigned numbers from one to 11 in order of magnitude. Each square was presented for five seconds during which interval the subjects responded with the number which they believed designated the size of the square.

One group of subjects performed under neutral conditions. A second group received a random series of 25 electric shocks during the course of 14 presentations of the series of 11 stimuli.

There are two important considerations in this study. First, the task is a relatively difficult one; each square differed from the squares adjacent to it in the ordered sequence by only three millimeters per side, a small difference. Secondly, it is known that when people are required to use a series of numbers in a purely random fashion they tend to use certain numbers more frequently than others. Number preferences are idiosyncratic. Now, Eriksen and Wechsler point out, "If we consider these number preferences or biases as reflecting unequal habit strengths among number responses, the presence of anxiety should act to enhance these preferences or biases."

That is precisely what happened in their study. The strengthening of preferences can be seen most clearly in the fact that the stressed group resorted significantly more often to their two most preferred response numbers. Of the 154 responses, the average anxious subject used his two favorite numbers more than 46 times, compared to an average of 41 times for the nonanxious subjects.

This study suggests that anxiety reduces the number of responses that the individual employs. It also gives some support to Spence's idea that anxiety gives relatively more strength to those responses that originally had greater habit strength.

There is one joker in the Eriksen-Wechsler experiment. The response stereotypy induced by anxiety did *not* interfere with accuracy of identification of the stimuli. In this respect the neutral group performed no better than the anxious subjects, perhaps because of the difficulty of the task. When discrimination is inherently difficult under optimal circumstances, the effect of response stereotypy is not as likely to be pronounced. Moreover, the actual degree of stereotypy induced by anxiety was evidently not very great. Perhaps it would have to be more pronounced in order to affect performance detrimentally.

Intelligence Test Performance

The construct *intelligence* is defined in the clinic or the laboratory by a standard test and a consequent score. All intelligence tests are based on the same principle; the subject is presented with an opportunity to demonstrate his capacities by performing on a number of different intellectual tasks. These include measures of verbal and arithmetical reasoning, abstract thinking, rote memory, vocabulary usage, and so forth.

Clinical psychologists generally believe that intelligence test scores are adversely affected by emotional states like anxiety. Hadley (1958) remarks typically:

> Emotional factors such as general depression, anger, or resentfulness, fear, sheepishness, or a feeling of shame, shyness, embarrassment, general nervous excitement, the lack of confidence, and combinations of these or other factors may all contribute to the kind and level of performance.

A convincing experimental demonstration of the effect of anxiety on intelligence test performance is not as easy to design as it might seem. Such an experiment would require that the same test be administered to subjects in a neutral state and again during a period of anxiety. As with many tasks, there is likely to be a practice effect, a carry-over from the first administration of the test to the second. This might very well obscure or distort the anxiety effect. A study by Diethelm and Jones (1947) indicates that the performance of psychiatric patients on intelligence tests improves after acute anxiety has subsided. Some of this improvement may have been due to practice effect.

A number of investigations show that scores on the Manifest Anxiety Scale and other instruments that measure general predisposition to anxiety are unrelated to intelligence test scores. Such test anxiety measures as the TAQ generally show small to moderate negative correlations with intelligence test scores, a fact which suggests that test anxiety may have a detrimental effect on performance. A cause-and-effect relationship is logical, but it is not demonstrated by the fact of relationship alone. For example, individuals of lower intelligence may possibly be made more anxious by tests.

A plausible explanation of the negative relationship between test anxiety and intelligence test scores involves speed of performance. It is fairly well established that anxiety commonly has the effect of slowing performance on complex tasks. Some intelligence tests and parts of tests are timed; others are not. In some cases test items are recorded as failed if performance is not completed within a specified time limit. In other instances, score bonuses are awarded for correct responses given within a time limit. A score on the widely used Wechsler Adult Intelligence Scale can be increased by more than 10 IQ points through time bonuses.

A little study by Siegman (1956) suggests the effect of anxiety on intelligence tests performance as a function of speed instructions. Table XX shows the average scores obtained on the timed

Table XX

Effect of Anxiety on Timed and Untimed Measures of Intelligence *

	AVERAGE SCORE ON		
Group	*Timed subtests*	*Untimed subtests*	*All subtests*
High anxious	10.1	11.5	10.7
Low anxious	11.7	10.9	11.4

* Data from Siegman (1956).

and untimed subtests of the WAIS by groups of subjects who scored high and low on the MAS. The high anxious subjects perform more effectively on the untimed subtests, and less effectively on the timed subtests, than the low anxious group. The effects tend to cancel out, so that the net effect on the total score is minimal. This affords an explanation of why MAS scores are usually found to be unrelated to total intelligence test scores. It also explains the occasionally reported low negative relationship with IQ scores when the entire test is timed—as, for example, the American Council on Education Psychological Examination (Matarazzo, *et al.*, 1954).

The results also suggest that anxiety functions as an energizing drive à la Spence when the task is untimed, but that it evokes task-irrelevant reactions, as in the Yale theory, when speed enhances performance.

Summary

Experimental investigations suggest that anxiety detrimentally affects such cognitive processes as problem-solving, incidental learning, ability to communicate, and performance on standard intelligence tests. Under extreme stress, human problem-solving behavior falls from its lofty level and resembles the performance of infrahuman mammals. The effect of anxiety on intelligence test performance appears to be a function of a time factor. Anxiety has a detrimental effect on subtests which have time limits, but it does not disrupt those on which speed of performance is inconsequential.

Comprehensibility of a communicated message is unfavorably influenced when the content itself is anxiety-producing. Thus it appears that the ability to communicate is at least partly a function of the nature of the message.

Anxiety appears also to bring about response stereotypy, at least in certain situations. This finding is in accord with Spence's theory of the differential effect of anxiety on the habit hierarchy. Apparently, response stereotypy does not invariably exercise a negative effect on performance. The consequences of anxiety-induced response stereotypy appear to depend on other factors, one of which is probably task complexity.

9

ANXIETY AND PERSONALITY

Personality is the broadest construct employed by behavioral scientists. It is usually considered to encompass all aspects of the individual except anthropometric, physiological, and intellectual attributes. These are thought to affect personality, but they are not regarded directly as part of it.

Personality is conceptualized as composed of units or elements which influence the individual's behavior so that it is relatively stable and consistent across circumstances, and is therefore predictable. These elements have been called "generalized habits," "determining tendencies," "sentiments," and so forth. *Trait,* though not the most recently adopted unit designation, is probably still most widely favored.

Traits are characterized by such vernacular adjectives as "passive," "sociable," "dominant," and the like. Some theorists have attempted to organize traits into *personality types.* The best known typology is C. G. Jung's extrovert-introvert-ambivert triad. Typologies are still sometimes advocated by theorists with a philosophical orientation, but they have been abandoned by behavioral science. They are too broad and vague to be of any real value to a science of personality. The variegations of human behavior are too great to be meaningfully organized into any simple system of types.

A number of methodological difficulties are involved in the use of traits, or any other unit, to describe human personality. A detailed discussion is beyond the scope of this chapter, but the problems can be summarized simply by pointing out that a trait is a construct. When a person is described as "sociable," we mean that he manifests certain behaviors—that is, he consistently seeks the company of others, appears to enjoy himself when he interacts with them, and is less content, or even tense, when he is alone. These behaviors could just as reasonably be subsumed under a trait label like "friendly" or "gregarious." Or they might be conceptualized as the antipode of a trait called "unsociable" or "unfriendly."

The important point is that the trait itself, whatever it may be called, has no independent existence apart from procedures and devices that are used to measure it. One must take care not to confuse the scientific meaning of a trait with the lexicographer's definition of the adjective. To be sure, the scientist selects a particular trait name in order to exploit some of its vernacular meaning, but the trait is actually defined by measurement procedures, not by the dictionary.

Is There an "Anxious Personality"?

Anxiety-proneness or predisposition is a personality trait no different, conceptually, from other traits. One might reasonably wonder whether trait anxiety is related to other traits. Does the person with high proneness to experience anxiety have other traits that are distinguishable from those of his less anxious fellows? Is there a constellation of particular traits which is associated with high anxiety-proneness, and which might perhaps be called the *anxious personality?*

Many investigations have been designed to cast light on this question. With rare exceptions, findings are equivocal, ambiguous, or conflicting. The results within a single study may indicate that the high anxious subject has more "rigidity" as measured by one instrument, less according to another instrument, and the same amount as the low anxious subject on a third measuring device. One investigation shows that anxious individuals are higher in trait *X*, another experiment finds that they are lower, and still another suggests that there is no difference.

Experimenters are usually concerned with averages; all the statements in the previous paragraph are understood to be qualified by the implicit expression, "on the average." But an average is not the only way of describing a distribution of scores obtained from a group of subjects. Distributions yielding identical averages may still be quite different. Assuming that distributions are perfectly symmetrical, an average score of 50 describes equally well distributions with score ranges of 0–100, 25–75 and 45–55. The fact that two groups of subjects have identical average scores on a measuring instrument does not mean that they are precisely alike with respect to the trait being measured. The *variability* of scores may be considerably different.

One effect of a high anxiety level, either trait or state, is to increase the variability of response among the members of a group even though the average score may not be affected. The increment in variability of performance on learning and intellectual tasks is sharply illustrated in studies by Mandler and Sarason (1952) and Sarason (1957), and in a number of the earlier investigations reviewed by Lazarus and his associates (1952). In the Sarason (1957) experiment, the high anxious subjects showed an increased variability of nearly 60 per cent in the stressed state as compared with the neutral state, and were two and one-half times as variable in their performance as the low anxious group.

Schwab and Iverson (1964) reported that an anxiety-prone sample was almost *nine times* as variable in recognition time of a perceptual distortion as a low anxious group. Both groups showed small increments in variability of performance when stressed; this amounted to 33 per cent for the low anxious group.

The most parsimonious explanation of these findings is that stress improves the performances of some members of an experimental sample and interferes with it in others. Assuming that the two effects are equivalent, the average performance is unaffected. The stress effect would manifest itself only in an increase in the variability of the distribution of scores. If more subjects are energized to perform, the group average may then show an increase. If most performances are disrupted, the average will go down. In either event, however, the increase in variability is still likely to be manifested.

It is doubtful whether performance on simple intellectual and perceptual tasks is ever a valid measure of personality. But responses to the Rorschach ink-blots are consensually accepted by psychologists as measures of personality, though it is not always certain exactly what aspect is being measured. Westrope (1953) has reported greater variability in the responses of a high anxious group on five Rorschach measures. Applezweig (1954) found that candidates for submarine service in the Navy were 70 per cent more variable on an alleged Rorschach rigidity factor shortly before experiencing a stressful training experience than they were a week after completing the experience.

Feshbach and Singer (1957) were interested in the effect of threatening communications on expressed race prejudice. The communications to which independent groups of subjects were exposed dealt with the stressful aspects of marriage, mental illness, fire, flood, and atomic war. All threatened groups manifested an increase in the variability of race prejudice as compared with an unstressed control group, although only two of the five threats produced the expected average increase in prejudice.

Increased variability of scores is likely to be overlooked or not even reported by the experimenter. He is usually interested in average differences. A difference in variability is seldom amenable to any simple interpretation. When the anxiety-prone group is found to have a greater average score on trait *X*, the interpretation is straightforward. But what does it mean when this group is significantly more variable in its scores, though averages may or may not differ?

Returning for a moment to the discussion of defenses against anxiety, we may consider the individual whose primary defense mechanism is repression. When anxiety is high, for whatever reason, he becomes increasingly withdrawn and inhibited as his defenses rigidify and the scope of their functioning becomes more extensive. Under the same conditions, an individual whose major mechanism is regression is likely to make more demands on others for support and satisfaction of needs, thereby interacting with them to a greater extent. In other words, the behavioral effect of high anxiety is exactly opposite in these two individuals because they employ different primary defense mechanisms. Similarly, an individual with obsessive-compulsive defenses becomes increasingly rigid and stereotyped, whereas a person whose defenses are already seriously weakened may become completely disorganized.

Many theorists have proposed that anxiety and hostility are related emotions, but the correlation has never been solidly verified by experimental study. Again, this may be because of interindividual differences in defenses. Individuals who are prone to employ projection as a defense may manifest increasing hostility as anxiety level increases. Those who characteristically use avoidance or regression, or perhaps other mechanisms, become less hostile as anxiety rises.

Differences among individuals in the primary defense mechanism employed constitute a reasonable, theoretical explanation of why high anxiety-proneness or stressful conditions increase variability of performance or trait measurement in any group of individuals, though the central tendency is not necessarily affected.

Defense mechanisms and traits are theoretically considered to be closely linked. Freud regarded most adult traits as the result of fixations occurring in the early years of life, but research has generally failed to demonstrate the interrelationships necessary to support this belief (see Sears, 1943). The prevalent view of the relationship between defenses and traits is a consequence of the theory proposed by the analyst Wilhelm Reich. According to Reich (1949), traits result largely from the use of particular defense mechanisms. For example, the trait of neatness is an inevitable consequence of the use of compulsivity as a defense; introversion is a consequence of repression, and so forth. Reich coined the term *character armor* to describe the alliance of defenses and traits to guard against awareness of anxiety.

The concept of character armor was never worked out carefully. Reich was no scientist; his theorizings are vague, confusing, and often illogical. Yet, to clinical practitioners of various disciplines the idea of character armor seems to make sense. The practitioner infers the existence of a particular defense from the patient's behavior. This same behavior is also used as the basis for ascribing a trait. Thus defenses and traits are viewed as

Table XXI

Theoretical Relationships Between Defense Mechanisms and Personality Traits

Defense mechanism	*Traits*
Denial	Stubborn, self-assertive, unimaginative
Projection	Critical, intolerant, hostile
Regression	Dependent, demanding, irresponsible
Compulsivity	Rigid, orderly, narrow, ruminative
Repression	Inhibited, withdrawn, guarded

linked. The trait is a label assigned to manifest behavior; the defense is a construct of a higher order which seeks to explain the behavior.

Table XXI shows the theoretical associations between some traits and defense mechanisms. Or, if you prefer, the traits are the labels for behaviors from which the existence of the defenses is inferred. The table is strictly a speculative analysis, not to be confused with an empirically derived set of relationships.

The concept of the defense mechanism-trait alliance has the virtue of explaining, at least on a theoretical level, why many investigations of the relationship between anxiety and personality are negative or ambiguous, and why anxiety so often acts to increase the variability of behavior within a group of individuals, without necessarily affecting the central tendency of the behavior.

Anxiety and Personality Styles

The available experimental evidence does not support the concept of an "anxious personality" identified in terms of traits other than anxiety-proneness itself. The trait (or one of the synonyms for "trait") is not the only unit with which personality has been described. Such constructs as emotions, needs, sentiments, values, and attitudes are also thought of as components of personality. Sometimes these are viewed as traits, sometimes not. Certain attributes not commonly regarded as traits definitely fall into the category of personality factors. We might think of them as *styles* of personality.

Theoretically, personality style and trait are loosely differentiated according to the broadness of influence on behavior. Both trait and style are usually defined narrowly for experimental purposes, but style is considered to exercise a far-reaching influence on the individual's life and functioning. It also seems that styles are unrelated to defense mechanisms, or at least not as closely related as traits.

Perhaps the distinction is merely a matter of semantic convention or personal choice, in which case, of course, quibbling about it is pointless. Let us rather examine some data concerning relationships between anxiety-proneness and what will here be called personality styles.

Self-Esteem

An individual with a high predisposition to anxiety is one who is more easily threatened than his fellows. Such a person is likely to have a relatively poor opinion of himself because he is easily threatened. The logic of the relationship is most clearly seen in achievement or test anxiety. Anxiety is high because the individual doubts his ability to achieve, to perform successfully on the task or test. The relationship need have nothing to do with the individual's actual abilities, only with his perception of them. Thus we might say that low self-esteem is an important cause of high anxiety-proneness.

A relationship reported by Rosenberg (1962) is hence not surprising. Rosenberg measured self-esteem in more than five thousand junior and senior high school students by means of a questionnaire comprising 10 items like "On the whole, I am satisfied with myself," and "I feel I do not have much to be proud of." A somewhat crude measure of anxiety was obtained by means of self-reports of incidents of physical symptoms associated with anxiety. Rosenberg found a definite, inverse relationship between the self-esteem and the anxiety measures, a finding which indicates that a high level of anxiety was associated with a low level of self-esteem.

A similar finding has been reported by Suinn and Hill (1964), who used a questionnaire measure of "self-acceptance" similar in content to the self-esteem scale used by Rosenberg. In a sample of college students Suinn and Hill found substantial, negative correlations between the self-acceptance measure and both the MAS and the TAQ. The magnitude of the correlation coefficients (−.68 and −.58) suggests that the relationship between self-esteem and anxiety-proneness is marked and pervasive.

Guilt-Proneness

We may recall that guilt, according to Freud, is another form of anxiety—moral anxiety, a transmuted fear of being punished because of moral transgression. Because of his defenses, primarily repression occurring relatively early in life, the individual experiences this fear in the form of guilt feelings rather than as a fear of punishment. The connection is neatly phrased by Horney (1937):

> . . . if guilt feelings are carefully examined and are tested for genuineness, it becomes apparent that much of what looks like feelings of guilt is the expression either of anxiety or of a defense against it. . . . In our culture it is considered nobler . . . to refrain from something because of conscience rather than because of a fear of getting caught. Many a husband who pretends to be faithful because of his conscience is in reality merely afraid of his wife. Because of the great amount of anxiety in neuroses, the neurotic is inclined more often than the normal individual to cover up anxiety with guilt feelings.

Freud's moral anxiety and Horney's "fear of being found out" are manifested in the same way. The common-sense psychiatrist would say that guilt is one of the feelings that can generate anxiety. Thus guilt-proneness is either a special form of anxiety-proneness, or it is closely linked to it. For this reason, and possibly for other reasons as well, experimentation has not been much occupied with guilt as a construct apart from anxiety.

One of the few attempts to distinguish between anxiety-proneness and guilt-proneness was made recently by Lowe (1964). As we have seen, the items in Taylor's Manifest Anxiety Scale were selected from the MMPI pool on the basis of clinicians' judgments. Lowe performed the identical operation for guilt feelings, using four clinical psychologists as judges. They agreed on 44 items of the MMPI total of 550. Only six of these were also included in the 50 picked by Taylor's judges. As Lowe points out, "This suggests strongly, of course, that the judges of each scale were, in fact, guided in their selection of items by quite distinctive psychological constructs."

In several groups of normal persons and psychiatric patients, the correlation between the MAS and Lowe's guilt scale averaged .75. This coefficient approaches the reliability of either scale, a fact which suggests that the guilt scale could actually be used as an alternate form of the MAS.

The absence of overlap in item content indicates that the conceptualization of guilt-proneness as a construct apart from anxiety-proneness is reasonable. The extremely high correlation between the scales must be interpreted to mean that anxiety and guilt, regarded as separate constructs, are highly related. We may infer that individuals with high anxiety-proneness are given to stronger guilt feelings or to more easily provoked guilt feelings than are people with low anxiety-proneness. An alternate interpretation is that anxiety and guilt are really not separate constructs, that guilt is simply another form of anxiety, as Freud postulated.

Hypnotizability

For many decades it was generally believed that emotionally disturbed people, those who would be characterized, as a group, by relatively high anxiety levels, were more susceptible to hypnosis than better adjusted individuals. Only in recent years has this been shown to be a misconception. The tide of scientific opinion is now turning in the opposite direction. Recent research definitely suggests that psychiatric patients are *less* susceptible to hypnosis than normal people.

The findings concerning anxiety and hypnotizability are even more clear-cut within the normal group itself. Hilgard (1965) reports that almost three-quarters of the most susceptible hypnotic subjects were rated by interviewers as "normal-outgoing" and less than 25 per cent as "troubled-withdrawn." In a study by Levitt, Brady, and Lubin (1963) a group of female subjects who were found to resist hypnosis obtained a mean score on the IPAT Anxiety Scale of 32. A group which was otherwise comparable, but which was extremely susceptible to hypnosis, had a mean score of only 22.

The relationship is especially interesting because hypnotizability is unrelated to personality traits in general, at least traits in the usual sense of the construct. Other personality styles, attitudes, and past experience are currently considered as possible influences on hypnotic susceptibility, but no definite relationships with these factors have as yet been established. In the end, it may be demonstrated that the degree of predisposition to anxiety is the major determinant of hypnotizability.

Curiosity

Simple logic indicates that an individual who is highly predisposed to anxiety will be threatened by unknown and unfamiliar circumstances and thus will prefer a well-explored milieu even if it is mundane and uninteresting. Such behavior suggests a generalized avoidance defense, what the clinician calls "restricting the scope of operations in order to avoid anxiety." It seems to be a popular defense mechanism. It follows that anxious people will be less motivated by *curiosity,* will not evince as much interest in exploring new arenas and in having new experiences. This restrictive tendency may even be reflected in relatively trivial circumstances. For example, McReynolds and his associates (1961) observed and rated the exploratory behavior of a group of sixth-grade children who were given an opportunity to examine a number of small objects like a miniature flashlight. An "object curiosity score" was found to be negatively related to teachers' estimates of psychological adjustment.

Penney and McCann (1964) advanced the investigation of curiosity by defining it more clearly as a personality style. They constructed a "reactive curiosity scale" for children, consisting of items like, "It's fun to see inside the big buildings downtown," "I like to learn about people who live in other countries," and "I like a place better the more I am around it." Scores on this scale were found to be negatively related to scores on the Children's Manifest Anxiety Scale in intermediate-grade elementary school children (Penney, 1965).

Sensation-Seeking

Recent research developments have led behavioral scientists to the theoretical position that the human organism requires an optimal level of general sensory and emotional stimulation in order to maintain psychological homeostasis. Too little stimulation (sensory deprivation) or too much stimulation (sensory overload) both lead to emotional disruption and disorganized behavior.

Like other human attributes, the optimal level of stimulation is most likely to be variable among people, depending upon a large number of causative factors. Predisposition to anxiety may very well be one of these factors.

The potentiality of the relationship becomes clearer if we attempt to translate the construct of optimal stimulation level into behavioral terms. "Stimulation" has the connotation of interest in the sensual, in excitement, in the novel, strange, and unpredictable. These would be the pursuits of the individual with a high optimal stimulation level. The person with a low level seeks the moderate, regular, predictable, and familiar, apparently using general avoidance as a defense.

This line of thinking led Zuckerman and his co-workers (1964) to design a "sensation-seeking" inventory as an operational definition of optimal stimulation level. Scores on this forced-choice scale, which included 34 items, were found to have a moderate negative correlation of −.32 with scores on the general form of the Affect Adjective Check List.

Apparently, optimal stimulation level, or sensation-seeking (which is perhaps a more plausible construct designation), is somewhat reduced by anxiety predisposition, most probably because of the stressful flavor of novelty, sensuality, and the unpredictable. The anxious individual requires less stimulation to maintain emotional balance, is perhaps less tolerant of stimulation in general.

This finding is conjunctive with the work on curiosity. In fact, the Penney-McCann and Zuckerman scales are somewhat overlapping in item content. To some extent, sensation-seeking in the adult is analogous to curiosity in the child. The differences between them, as reflected in the two scales, are largely a function of the child's more restricted behavioral repertory, general functioning, and experience.

Daydreaming

Imagination or *conscious fantasy,* the capacity to experience sensations, perceptions, and emotions that are stimulated from within the organism, appears to be uniquely human. Conscious fantasy, a widespread phenomenon, has both positive and negative aspects. It may be employed to anticipate pleasure, to review past gratification, to design something practical, or to plan for the future. It can yield pleasurable fantasies of success and achievement; fantasy achievement may reflect a realistic motivation, or it may concern itself with heights of life that are in actuality inaccessible to the imaginer. Imagination can also torture the individual with unavoidable fear, shame, or guilt.

Daydreaming—the vernacular designation for conscious fantasy—is found at all age levels, though it is most common in childhood. The correlation with age suggests another relationship; the more a person can actually achieve, the less will he daydream. This suggests further that daydreaming may be a substitute, at least at times, for other forms of behavior.

The negative relationship between anxiety and sensation-seeking indicates that the anxiety-prone person has a reduced scope of functioning in his milieu. He might, therefore, be more inclined to engage in fantasy activity as a substitute for behavior that is restricted because of anxiety. If this is, in fact, the case, we should find that anxiety-proneness is positively related to the incidence or extent of daydreaming behavior.

The few available studies unanimously indicate that anxiety-proneness and the frequency of daydreams are positively correlated. The relationship is emphasized by the fact that four different anxiety measures have furnished the positive correlations. Reiter (1963) used the MAS; Singer and Schonbar (1961) employed Welsh's A factor; and Singer and Rowe (1962) used the IPAT Scale and the Alpert-Haber AAT. The correlation coefficients ranged from .25 for the AAT to .50 for the IPAT.

Summing up the findings, Singer (1966) states:

> The evidence from a number of studies . . . indicates that daydreaming frequency does correlate positively at moderately high levels with questionnaire measures of anxiety. . . . This would suggest that persons reporting more frequent daydreams also describe themselves as more anxious, sensitive, and fearful.

The use of conscious fantasy as a compensatory process is suggested by substantial positive correlations between anxiety-proneness and the needs for achievement and self-aggrandizement, as these needs are reflected in fantasy itself (Singer and Schonbar, 1961). The anxiety-prone individual is more likely than the low anxious person to have daydreams in which he accomplishes notable feats or attains material possessions or high status.

The evidence appears to suggest a constellation of styles which might constitute the "anxious personality." The typically anxiety-prone individual has poor self-esteem, is much given to guilt, daydreams more than his fellows, and is less curious, sensation-seeking, and amenable to hypnosis. These findings, however, are derived from investigations which are independent of each other. It would be incautious to conclude that the various styles actually are aggregated in a constellation. Conceivably, one subgroup of anxiety-prone individuals is responsible for the negative correlation with self-esteem, another for the positive correlation with daydreaming, and so forth. In a particular individual anxiety may be found in association with one or more styles, but not with other styles, though these latter may be correlated with proneness in other people.

Hilgard (1964) provides an excellent illustration of these differing correlations. His investigations disclosed that hypnotic susceptibility was positively correlated with sensation-seeking behavior in *some* good hypnotic subjects. This would be expected, for both these factors have been shown to be negatively correlated with anxiety-proneness. Hypnotic susceptibility and fantasizing were positively correlated in a *different* group of good hypnotic subjects. This would *not* be expected, for fantasy is positively related to anxiety-proneness.[1]

According to this line of reasoning, there is probably no one "anxious personality," but there may be several different "anxious personalities," each comprising different styles or traits. Such a hypothesis can be truly examined only in multivariate experiments in which the interrelationships among anxiety and a number of personality factors are investigated simultaneously.

Summary

If personality is conceptualized in terms of traits or discrete, descriptive units, then little evidence supports the existence of a typical "anxious personality." This can be explained by postulating that traits are a result of the employment of particular defense mechanisms. The individual who is under temporary stress, or who has a high predisposition to anxiety, manifests an accentuation of the "character armor" he uses to defend against anxiety. The nature of the defense determines the manifest reaction to anxiety. Individuals with different defense mechanisms may therefore show directly opposite reactions to stress. The fact that one of the measured effects of the induction of anxiety is an increase in the variability of behavior supports this position.

Research suggests that anxiety-proneness is related to certain broader personality tendencies, which may be thought of as styles. Researchers have found that anxious individuals tend to have low self-esteem, are more prone to feelings of guilt, have less curiosity and less sensation-seeking behavior, daydream more often, and are more resistant to hypnosis. The evidence does *not* indicate that these styles form a constellation which characterizes the anxious person. Most probably, there are several different "anxious personalities," each comprising different styles, depending largely on developmental influences.

[1] Hilgard suggests that these "alternative routes into hypnosis" are a function of background and developmental factors.

10

THE ANXIETIES OF EVERYDAY LIFE

Sigmund Freud ended his incredible career in disenchanted pessimism about the future of mankind. Happiness as a limitless experience, an "oceanic" feeling, is a goal sought in vain by man, he concluded. The pursuit of pleasure is an illusion. One does not really seek pleasure; one only strives to avoid pain and tension.

The towering figure of psychoanalysis summarized his disillusionment in a bitter monograph called *Civilization and Its Discontents* (1930). In it, he wrote, "Life as we find it is too hard for us; it entails too much pain, too many disappointments, impossible tasks."

If Freud were alive today, he would probably be an existentialist, one of the philosophers who espouse the view that man's fundamental problem is that he exists at all. The sapient *homo,* the contemporary psychoanalyst Erich Fromm (1947) affirms, " . . . is the only animal for whom his own existence is a problem which he has to solve and from which he cannot escape."

Life is certainly not a placid stream for anyone. The process of living is one of continual coping with circumstances and events that test the defenses against anxiety; it demands constant coping efforts by the individual. Many of these stresses are relatively minor, permitting adequate adjustment without undue strain. But then there are severe stress situations whose reality defies the power of defense mechanisms and which raise the anxiety level noticeably. Menninger (1963) sums up the point with consummate succinctness:

> The unexpected is always happening. Emergencies are constantly arising. The "mis"-behavior of other individuals, the occurrence of dis-

ruptive events, the change in certain situations—deaths, births, accidents—all sorts of things happen which may strain the capacity of the individual for easy accommodation. His comfort, his gratifications, perhaps even his growth or safety are threatened.

The stresses of ordinary daily living are the phenomena with which the behavioral scientist is actually vitally concerned in his long-range effort to predict and control human behavior and to improve society. Yet very little information about these phenomena has come from direct, scientific investigation. Most of our knowledge about anxiety comes from the experimental laboratory and the clinician's office. The methodological problems of scientific study in natural milieus have thus far proven too much for researchers to overcome.

Nevertheless, this book would be incomplete if it entirely ignored the anxiety-evoking events which people face in the course of existence.[1] Some of these stresses, like fear of disease, are widespread. Others—social isolation or social overstimulation, for example—occur less frequently, but they are prospects for all of us, especially as national and international tensions increase.

The volume of research on everyday stress is small, compared, say, with the number of published accounts of laboratory studies of the effects of anxiety on learning. This chapter will necessarily be brief and sketchy.

Illness

Most people know that a *hypochondriac* is a person who is overly concerned about his physical health. Anxiety is reflected in a preoccupation with body functions, in various physical complaints, some of which may be chronic, and in an incapacity to be reassured that one's ills are minor or that symptoms are exaggerated.

Hypochondriasis, once a standard diagnostic category, has now

[1] Perusing any sophisticated book of case histories of psychotherapy patients (e.g., Goldstein and Palmer, 1963), one cannot help but be struck by the significant incidence of such events as disease, accident, injury, death, divorce, and pregnancy in the etiology of emotional illness.

fallen into disuse, though it is still sometimes employed to describe a symptom. The *Diagnostic and Statistical Manual* of the American Psychiatric Association (1952) does not list it, though the text makes incidental use of such expressions as "hypochondriacal preoccupation." Hypochondriasis has been discarded as a primary diagnosis because minor physical symptoms and concern about physical health are very common among psychiatric patients, but they seldom constitute a primary symptom. Descriptively, the clinician might still use hypochondriasis as a diagnosis with an occasional patient. Dynamically, health concerns constitute an important medium through which many people express anxiety.

Apprehension about physical disease is common among normal people, those who show no signs of mental or emotional illness. What might be called *illness anxiety* may be nonspecifically related to contracting a serious illness or infirmity, or it may be expressed as concern about pain, treatment, temporary or permanent disability, financial loss, separation from family, personality changes, and death. The focus may be the self or others, especially members of the immediate family. Fifty-two per cent of the normal women surveyed by Robbins (1962) directly expressed some degree of fear that they might contract cancer, the disease which appears to be currently most feared in the community. An additional 26 per cent admitted to indirect anxiety; the disease was "a source of real concern" to them.

An analysis of data obtained with Robbins' Medical Attitude Inventory, a true-false measure of illness anxiety, indicates that among normal people there is also considerable fear of heart disease, mental illness, and polio.[2] Illness anxiety, as measured by the MAI, correlates .32 with the Manifest Anxiety Scale, indicating that anxiety-prone individuals are more likely to fear illness, just as they are more likely to have other specific fears.

Educational level is a factor in illness anxiety. Robbins found that respondents with a high school education or less manifested

[2] Robbins' survey preceded the widespread use of effective vaccines, which has practically wiped out polio. It is improbable that as much as one-third to one-half of a current sample of respondents would express anxiety about this disease.

significantly greater anxiety than those with advanced education. Only 51 per cent of the college graduates in a large sample interviewed by Levine (1962) feared cancer a great deal, as compared with 61 per cent of those with 11 or fewer years of education. These findings suggest that knowledge about a disease, or diseases in general, may serve as a prophylactic against fear, or that illness anxiety is partly a result of misinformation or lack of information. On the other hand, Levine's respondents who claimed to know "a lot" about a disease tended to be more apprehensive about it than those who disclaimed specific knowledge. We should, of course, hesitate to accept as valid the layman's unverified contention that he knows "a lot" about a technical matter. If the statements of Levine's subjects are credited, a different hypothesis would be required to explain the negative correlation between illness anxiety and educational attainment. We might then speculate that knowledge about disease is unrelated to educational level among laymen, and that the better educated individual is able to make more effective use of denial as a defense mechanism.

On Robbins' MAI, women scored higher than men, married women higher than single women (but the reverse for men), and parents higher than those without children. These findings suggest that a person's anxiety about disease may focus not only on the self but also on a loved one or an intimate, and that mothers usually assume the primary responsibility for family health.

It is noteworthy that illness anxiety is unrelated to prophylactic measures against illness, such as obtaining influenza vaccination or frequency of visits to health clinics. This may reflect the use of avoidance and denial as defenses against illness anxiety. Or it may mean that self-report is a poor measure of illness anxiety.

Illness anxiety is often an aspect of anxiety-proneness in general, but it has a more realistic basis in fact than many of the fears of anxious people. Serious diseases are contracted by people continually, and they do result in harm and death. The reality orientation of illness anxiety appears in Levine's (1962) findings. People tend *not* to fear diseases that do not threaten them imminently. Old people do not fear polio; the young do not fear arthritis. Sixty-five per cent of those who believed that cancer afflicts many people expressed fear of it, compared with only 42 per cent of those who believed that it affects few. In Freud's terms, fear of illness may be either neurotic anxiety or reality anxiety.

Surgery

A surgical procedure is a fearful prospect for most people. Indeed, it is the very quintessence of circumstances that evoke anxiety. As Janis (1958) points out,

> From a psychological standpoint, a major surgical operation constitutes a stress situation which resembles many other types of catastrophes and disasters in that the "victim" faces a combination of three major forms of imminent danger—the possibility of suffering acute pain, of undergoing serious body damage, and of dying.

Rothenberg (1966) estimates that surgery is performed on *twelve million* people in the United States each year. This enormous incidence could be a significant source of anxiety in the community, a major contributor to the stresses of everyday living.

Janis (1958) conducted an intensive investigation of the psychological effects of surgery. His findings, based on self-reports by patients, indicate that more than 75 per cent expressed a moderate to high degree of preoperative anxiety. The percentage of patients expressing fear increased as the hour for the surgery approached, reaching its peak in the operating room. Up to this point, differences in reactions to major and minor surgeries, and, in fact, to routine dental treatment, are minor. As the curves of Figure 8 show, differentiation occurred in postoperative anxiety, which dropped off more sharply for the minor surgeries.

One of Janis' most significant findings concerns the relationship between the preoperative self-report of anxiety and postoperative behavior. Compared with those who manifested either high or low preoperative anxiety, patients who displayed a moderate amount of preoperative anxiety developed fewer of such postoperative emotional symptoms as acute anxiety, depression,

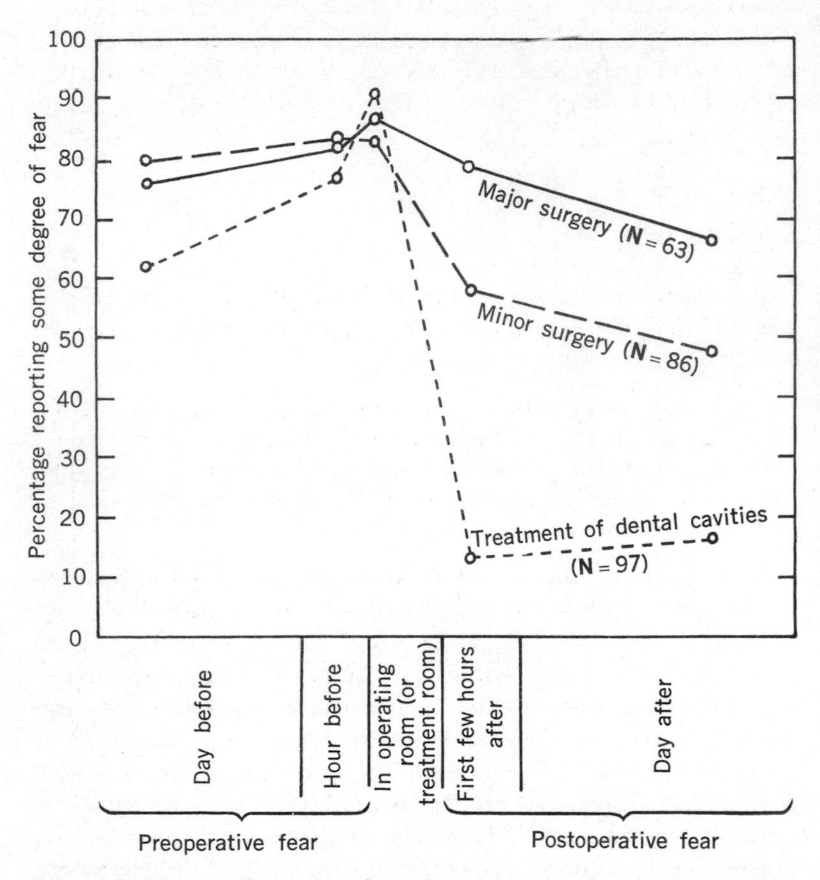

Figure 8. Temporal course of anxiety in various groups of surgery patients. *Reproduced from Janis (1958) by permission of John Wiley & Sons, Inc.*

and hostility. Figure 9 shows the relationship between the level of preoperative fear and the appearance of postoperative emotional symptoms.

The reader will immediately observe that the curve in Figure 9 markedly resembles the Yerkes-Dodson curve, the typical inverted U. Low and high preoperative anxiety levels are antecedent to more disturbed postoperative adjustments. More

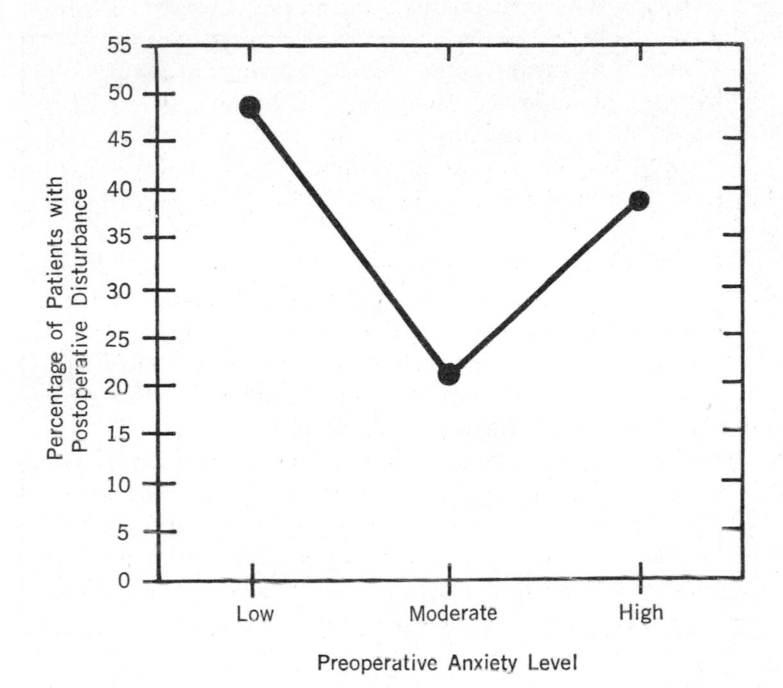

Figure 9. Postoperative emotional disturbance as a function of preoperative anxiety level. *Data from Janis (1958).*

satisfactory adjustments are made by those with moderate preoperative anxiety.

Janis' explanation of the curvilinearity, derived from a qualitative analysis of interview data, seems eminently sensible. Individuals with low anticipatory fear make extensive and somewhat unrealistic use of denial as a defense.

When actual suffering occurs, it comes as a somewhat shocking surprise and is frequently interpreted as meaning that someone has failed to treat them properly. The usual pains, discomforts, and unpleasant postoperative treatments tend to be regarded as unnecessary accidents caused by the hospital staff. Thus, instead of regarding their suffering as an unavoidable consequence of surgery, they are inclined to place the blame upon danger-control personnel, who are now apperceived as being inept, unprotective, or malevolent.

The person with high preoperative anxiety appears, according to Janis, to have "a chronic psychoneurotic predisposition," having suffered from various acute anxiety reactions in the past. The high postoperative anxiety level seems to be related to fear that some permanent injury has been incurred or that something went wrong in the surgical procedure. Even authority figures, Janis points out, find it extremely difficult to reassure these patients.

Patients with a moderate degree of preoperative anxiety appear to be those who are basically emotionally stable and manifest a rational orientation to the realities of the situation. They trust the authority figures involved with them, and they behave as if the most reasonable approach is to do whatever they are told and to believe the information given them.

Janis' investigation suggests that the Yerkes-Dodson principle has a meaningful analog in the relationship between stress in real life and emotional adjustment to it. The ability to perceive and to tolerate *some* anxiety when faced by an actual threat is the healthiest adjustment. Either to completely minimize or to exaggerate the threat leads to less wholesome adaptations.

Dental Treatment

The underlying cause of illness anxiety varies with the specific pathology (Robbins, 1962). Cancer is feared primarily because it may be incurable and lead to death. Chronic disability is the primary etiological factor in fear of heart disease; tuberculosis is feared because it leads to separation of the patient from the family, and so forth.

The actual treatment of the illness or disability is ordinarily not an important cause of illness anxiety. There is an outstanding exception to this finding—dental troubles. Fear of the dentist's chair is extensively reflected in folklore, fiction, and comedy. The research evidence suggests that it is no joking matter. Forty-six per cent of the people in Robbins' sample were worried about dental problems. This is a substantial number, exceeded only by the percentage fearing cancer. But only 2 per cent were diffusely anxious about their teeth, whereas 89 per cent were specifically fearful of *dental treatment*.

Figure 8 (page 172) indicates that fear of the dentist's drill occurs as frequently as preoperative anxiety about such major surgeries as appendectomy and tumor removal. In fact, the anxiety level of the dental patient in the dentist's office is indistinguishable from that of the patient on the surgical table. Patients facing tooth extractions behave as anxiously as do those anticipating any other surgical process. Seventy-five per cent report some degree of anxiety in the hour prior to the extraction, and many are still anxious in the postoperative phase (Janis, 1958).

Robbins (1962) found that certain items on the MAI identified a "dental anxiety factor." Analysis of findings indicated that dental anxiety is unrelated to educational level or to general illness anxiety. It is found equally in the well-educated and the minimally educated, in those who are anxious about disease in general and in those who are not.

Anxiety about dental treatment inclines people to avoid the dentist. Kegeles (1963) found that among those who were fearful of dental treatment 49 per cent made "preventively oriented" visits to the dentist, compared with 65 per cent of those who were not anxious. Naturally, if a person shuns diagnostic dental procedures, he cannot be informed that he requires the feared treatment. This is a good illustration of avoidance and denial defenses functioning to the detriment of the individual.

Death

The human being is very probably the only living organism capable of foreseeing its own eventual demise as a consequence of natural causes. An animal may conceivably fear death when it is immediately impending. Death anxiety in the human need have no relationship to threatening circumstances and may appear at an early age.

Most people are aware that existence will eventually end, and it may be argued that fear of death is common, that it is an anxiety of some importance in human life. Some psychoanalytic theorists have postulated that *thanatophobia*[3] is the underlying fear of all fears, that many other anxieties are merely its "dissembling guises," as Feifel (1965) calls them.

Fear of death, according to Feifel, is a fear of "total annihilation and loss of identity." But the condition of death, as Masserman (1955) points out, has no basis in personal experience and is hence beyond imagination and conceptualization. No one can actually imagine what it would be like not to exist at all, to lose the unique consciousness that is the self, to be unconscious forever. Thus, literal expressions of thanatophobia do not occur frequently; one does not know exactly what to fear. The dread of the unimaginable loss of the self must be expressed as anxiety about the myriad of circumstances that may lead to death—disease, accidents, natural disasters, and so forth. These are its "dissembling guises."

An alternative hypothesis is offered by Diggory and Rothman (1961). They contend that a person fears death "because it eliminates his opportunity to pursue goals important to his self-esteem." They surveyed a large sample of individuals of various ages in an effort to determine the underlying causes of thanatophobia. Maximum agreement was obtained from the subjects on statements dealing with death as an end to "purposive activity," such as "I could no longer have any experiences," and "All my plans and projects would come to an end." The survey results, which tended to be fairly stable across age groupings from 15 to 55, seemed to support the experimenters' hypothesis.

Despite the potential significance of death anxiety, behavioral science does not know very much about it. Wahl (1959) complains that psychiatric and psychoanalytic literature does not even provide a good description of it. The handful of available research evidence suggests that death anxiety occurs in adolescents (Alexander and Adlerstein, 1958), and that after childhood it is unrelated to age (Feifel and Heller, 1961; Rhudick and Dibner, 1961). The young adult expresses as much fear as the aged person; octogenarians express no more fear than those aged 65. Thanatophobia is "not necessarily more with the dying than

[3] The word is used here simply as a convenient synonym for anxiety about dying, not in the classical sense of a phobia.

with the living." Indeed, the reaction of a person who becomes aware that he has a terminal illness is one of profound depression rather than of anxiety (Glaser and Strauss, 1965). Perhaps this reflects the increasing use of denial defenses as one's demise approaches.

The use of denial makes it somewhat difficult to estimate the prevalence of thanatophobia. The tendency for elderly people to make greater use of this defense might also serve to obscure a correlation between death anxiety and age. For example, Swenson (1959) found that only 10 per cent of individuals over 60 admitted fear of death, but 44 per cent were "distinctly evasive," indicating that they preferred not to think about it. In a similar group, Jeffers and his associates (1961) reported that only 10 per cent frankly answered "yes" to the question, "Are you afraid to die?" However, only 35 per cent were able to give an unqualified "no" response to the question.

The available evidence also indicates that thanatophobia is unrelated to sex and educational attainment (Rhudick and Dibner, 1961) but is related to emotional stability (Feifel and Heller, 1961; Rhudick and Dibner, 1961), possibly as a consequence of the breakdown of denial defenses among the maladjusted.

Religious attitudes are commonly believed to provide a bulwark against fear of death. However, no research evidence supports this viewpoint. Kalish (1963), for example, found that fear of death is unrelated to adherence to a religion, or to the type of religion, or to belief in life after death or in God.

The potential significance of death anxiety for human existence, although great, remains largely uninvestigated. Perhaps, as the few investigators in this area wryly charge, scientists ignore death as an experimental area because dealing with it threatens their own denial defenses.

The Social Psychology of Anxiety

The natural milieus in which most of us spend most of our lives usually contain other human beings. The psychologist's experimental laboratory, in which the subject sits alone memorizing nonsense syllables, is, as a paradigm of a life situation, less common. Solitary performance permits study of the individual's emotional state, or other personal factors, apart from the confounding and often confusing influences of social interaction and interpersonal relationships. Although a single, personal variable is more visible in the laboratory experiment, the degree to which findings can be generalized to extra-laboratory fields, especially those in which the individual usually participates with others, is open to question. To be sure, the isolated situation is likely to be more obscuring when the study is concerned with attitudes, opinions, and other cognitive phenomena that are definitely known to be heavily influenced by social factors. But even emotions are not immune from social influence. Objectively measured pain tolerance has been shown to be significantly higher when subjects were tested in pairs than when they were tested alone (Seidman, *et al.*, 1957). Bovard (1959) concludes, after reviewing a number of studies, that the presence of others reduces stress responses and thereby exerts a "protective effect" on the stressed organism. Clinical examination suggests that people are more or less prone to express anxiety, or to react anxiously, in the presence of other people.

Increased emphasis on the conquest of space in the last decade has directed the attention of behavioral scientists to the social psychology of emotion. The astronauts of the future will be subjected to prolonged periods of restricted, unvarying sensory stimulation and social environment. Will the abnormal milieu of the space traveler have disadvantageous psychological consequences? The emotional reactions of astronauts are being studied, but space travel is as yet too limited to provide definitive answers. For the moment, predictions must be based on data obtained from analogous circumstances.

Reduced Environmental Stimulation

Environmental conditions that reduce stimulation of the organism can be classified in several ways. Reduction of direct stimulation to the senses is called *sensory deprivation* or *sensory restriction. Total* sensory deprivation invariably involves *social isolation,* the complete absence of other people in the environment. Social isolation per se is a form of partial sensory restriction. Repetitive, monotonous sensory stimulation is also a form of sensory deprivation. A narrow, unvarying social milieu leads to *social restriction,* a limited form of social isolation. In such circumstances the physical structure of the milieu is unchanging and always includes the same few people.

Being reared in social isolation or restriction markedly affects the sensory and intellectual development of mammalian organisms. Intelligence, learning ability, and exploratory behavior are retarded later in life. Organisms that are normally nurtured by their progenitors during the early stages of life require this attention not only to survive but also to develop normal sensory and cognitive capacities. The human being, who of all animals spends the longest period of time being nurtured, is especially susceptible to the detrimental effects of this kind of deprivation. Children who have spent their infancy in orphanages, without the relatively continual sensory stimulation ordinarily provided by the mother, are frequently functionally mentally retarded in later childhood.

Defective development of the intellect and senses is a function of sensory deprivation, rather than of the social isolation that leads to it. Sensory deprivation no longer affects the senses once they are developed, but it may have significant emotional and psychological effects. Sensory deprivation or restriction disturbs psychological equilibrium in many people. This finding has been reported in many laboratory studies (see the reviews by Kubzansky, 1961, and Schultz, 1965).

The customary design in studies of sensory deprivation is to place the individual in a fixed position in a totally dark room. Acoustical earmuffs block any sounds, even those which the subject himself may make. Arms and hands are confined to prevent tactile self-stimulation.

Under such circumstances, normal individuals report not only the expected boredom and restlessness but also distorted fears and anxieties of unusual proportions, even panic attacks that cause them to voluntarily flee the experimental setting. Significant increases in self-reported anxiety have been obtained on such measures of situational anxiety as the Affect Adjective Check List and the Subjective Stress Scale. Sometimes the fears become so unrealistic that they approach delusion or are associated with hallucinatory experiences. There is considerable variation in the capacity of individuals to resist the pathological effects of isolation. Those with higher predispositon to anxiety, those who are more impulsive, and those who have a greater need for sensation, as measured by Zuckerman's sensation-seeking scale, react with greater anxiety, but few people are completely unaffected.

Total sensory deprivation necessarily involves a socially isolated environment, but the individual may be socially isolated without being totally deprived of sensory stimulation. Most experimental studies of reduced environmental stimulation do not discriminate between the effects of sensory deprivation that includes social isolation and the effects of social isolation alone. This discrimination was attempted in two recent investigations by Zuckerman, Persky, and their co-workers (Zuckerman, *et al.*, 1966; Persky, *et al.*, 1966). All subjects underwent both 8-hour and 24-hour periods of complete sensory deprivation, and similar periods of social isolation that did not include auditory or visual restriction. In the social isolation conditions, music was continuously piped into the room and pictures were periodically placed in a special holder so that the subject could look at them, or the subject was provided with radio and television sets. Most subjects made continual use of one or the other source of sensory stimulation.

A large number of physiological and psychological measurements were made before, during, and after the reduced stimulation sessions. The findings suggest the following conclusions:

1. Both sensory deprivation and social isolation alone caused a considerable upsurge of anxiety in the subjects.
2. In the social isolation condition, anxiety was reflected largely in physiological reactions.
3. Subjective feelings of anxiety, especially the occasional report of bizarre sensations like hallucination, were reported most often in the sensory deprivation condition.

There are a few investigations of social restriction in natural and naturalistic settings (see Schultz, 1965). Notable among these is a study of the effects of isolation in small groups at stations in Antarctica, conducted by the Navy's Medical Neuropsychiatric Research Unit (for example, Gunderson, 1963). Some stations had as few as 15 men, and some had as many as a hundred. The incidence of negative emotional reactions and physical symptoms associated with anxiety was somewhat greater in the smaller stations, but these manifestations occurred with considerable frequency among personnel at all stations. They included free-floating anxiety, nervousness and shakiness, feelings of uneasiness, tension, and a wide variety of such minor physical symptoms as heart palpitations, nausea, polyurination, and insomnia. As Schultz points out,

> True, the presence of other people in the small group isolation situation may provide meaningful and varied stimulation *for a time,* but prolonged confinement can minimize even this source of varied sensory input. The other people in the situation are, after all, almost as constant and unchanging (after repeated exposure to them) as the physical stimulation available.

Of course, personnel at the Antarctica stations also faced danger, cold, and other hardships. But Mullin (1960) has reported interview evidence from the Antarctic stations which suggests that these circumstances were not nearly as stressful as the "sameness" of the environment.

A number of theories have been advanced to account for the malignant effects of social isolation and sensory deprivation. Most are distinguished by the level or terms in which the explanation is formulated and are really complementary. They postulate the existence of a central brain mechanism, probably in the reticular system, which impels the individual to seek and maintain some level of stimulus variation (see Malmo, 1957). This level, which varies among individuals, must be maintained in order to sustain an optimal general arousal level. When the arousal level falls too low, the functioning of the organism shows gross disruption, for the individual is deprived of perceptual cues which he uses to impose structure on his environment, in accordance with his past experience. Total deprivation of these cues leads to a chaotic and therefore stressful circumstance within which the individual finds it difficult to structure reality or to formulate expectancies of future occurrences. A secondary, anxiety-producing effect is that absence of contact with reality results in a weakening of superego control, with a consequent upsurge of what the psychoanalyst calls "primary process thinking,"—that is, an awareness of one's socially unacceptable sexual and hostile impulses.

Sensory Overload

The human nervous system appears to require a continual, meaningful input from the environment in order to function at an optimal level. If the senses are suddenly blocked or are subjected to continuous monotonous or insignificant stimulation, the individual is likely to develop psychopathological reactions. Much of the requisite stimulation comes from the presence of other people. It would follow from activation theory and from studies of social isolation that *excessive* social stimulation, in the form of the presence of large numbers of people in the environment, might also have disruptive effects.

Feelings of vague uneasiness and discomfort in the midst of a crowd or in a crowded place are reported fairly frequently, though *ochlophobia* as an acute, psychopathological state is rare. But clinical practitioners have observed that it is not unusual for an acute anxiety state to have its onset in a crowded place. Recent experimental evidence (Welch, 1964) suggests that infrahuman mammals who have lived for a time in crowded cages show consequent marked changes in size and functioning of the adrenal glands, changes which presumably reflect the effects of excessive emotional stimulation. The stressful effects of a crowd or of overcrowding—the high level of stimulation provided by many people milling about, talking, laughing, and so forth—represents sensory overload, the antipode of sensory deprivation.

As we saw in Chapter Six, Malmo conceives of anxiety as an instance of sensory overload, though, of course, there is no indication that the phenomenon is invariably a result of excessive social stimulation. The behavior of Patrick's (1934a) subjects, noted in Chapter Eight, is an instance of serious disruption in normal behavior apparently induced by sensory overload. The "hit-or-miss-rattled" reaction to stress exemplifies the disorganizing effect of intense stress described by Leeper (1948). This extreme reaction is sometimes called *panic.*

Panic Behavior:
A Form of Sensory Overload

"Panic" is ordinarily used to describe the behavior of a group, though an occasional theorist prefers to reserve it for individual behavior and to call the group reaction *rout.* Panic, when applied to a group, is uncontrollable flight that is nonadaptive for the physical survival of the group or group members, leads to the destruction of the group as an entity, and is an immediate consequence of acute fear (Schultz, 1964).

The nonrational (as opposed to irrational) quality of panic behavior is emphasized by such social theorists as Quarantelli (1954). Panic is nonrational in the sense that panicky people do not consider any method other than flight for terminating the stress situation. But flight is ordinarily an adaptive solution; it does not become nonadaptive until cooperative behavior in the group breaks down.

> Cooperative behavior is required for the common good but has very different consequences for the individual depending upon the behavior of others. Thus, at a theater fire, if everyone leaves in an orderly manner, everyone is safe, and an individual waiting for his turn is not sacrificing his interests. But, if the cooperative pattern of behavior is disturbed, the usual advice, "Keep your head, don't push, wait for your turn, and you will be safe," ceases to be valid. If the exits are blocked, the person following this advice is likely to be burned to death. In other words, if everybody cooperates, there is no conflict between the needs of the individual and those of the group. However, the situation changes completely as soon as a minority of people cease to cooperate. . . . Cooperative behavior at a theater fire is likely to deteriorate progressively as soon as an initial disturbance occurs. If a few individuals begin to push, the others are apt to recognize that their interests are threatened; they can expect to win through . . . only by pressing their personal advantages at the group's expense. Many of

them react accordingly, a vicious circle is set up, and the disturbance spreads . . . (Mintz, 1951).

Mintz's explanation is plausible as far as it goes. The question is, why does *anyone* lose sight of the necessity for maintaining cooperative behavior and thereby precipitate the panic? And why should the behavior of a few group members cause many to suddenly lose sight of the fact that optimal conditions of escape still require cooperation?

An explanation in terms of sensory overload has been proposed by Schultz (1964):

> Perhaps, then, in an unorganized group in a theater fire there exist different thresholds of sensory stimulation for the individual members of the audience. When the visual, auditory, and tactile stimulation—such as sight of smoke, higher noise level, and jostling with neighbors—surpasses this "threshold" level, the individual is no longer capable of efficiently coping with the situation and displays some form of non-rational behavior.

Those who do not initially panic are assailed by an increased sensory stimulation brought on by the behavior of those few whose thresholds are low. Thus, more individuals are subjected to sensory overload and fall prey to panic behavior. As panic behavior mounts in the group, so does the extent of sensory overload; eventually it overtakes all or most of the members of the group, resulting in a full-blown panic.

Summary

Little is known about the serious stress situations that people continually face during their lives. Scientific study of stress in the natural milieu is beset by methodological problems which have thus far proven largely insurmountable. A small number of investigations suggest that the occurrence or anticipation of such events as illness, dental treatment, surgery, and death are anxiety-evoking for many people. When a stressful event like surgery actually constitutes a serious threat to the integrity of the individual, the evidence suggests that the relationship between anticipatory anxiety and consequent readjustment is curiously parallel to the Yerkes-Dodson principle. Individuals who exaggerate the threat, or who unrealistically deny anxiety, manifest post-traumatic upset more frequently than those who admit to moderate anticipatory fear.

Fear of disease is widespread, and currently focuses on cancer. The primary motivation for illness anxiety varies with the specific entity. Anxiety about dental treatment rivals fear of major surgery and serious illness. There appears to be no relationship between illness anxiety and voluntary prophylactic measures against disease, except in the case of dental troubles.

Anxiety about death occurs at all ages and is a central concept in some psychoanalytic views. Its incidence is difficult to determine because denial is apparently used commonly as a defense against death anxiety. The evidence suggests that thanatophobia is unrelated to sex, age, or educational level, but that it is related to general emotional adjustment and illness anxiety.

Sensory deprivation and social isolation tend to create anxiety in the individual. The most recent available evidence suggests that anxious reactions in socially limited settings are reflected primarily in physiological systems. Subjective feelings of anxiety are reported more commonly in sensory deprivation situations.

Panic behavior, an extreme form of acute anxiety, may be explained as an instance of sensory overload or excessive sensory stimulation.

Sensory deprivation and sensory overload are the extremes of a continuum whose middle ground is optimal sensory stimulation. Both extremes lead to anxiety and disruption of behavior. The individual is able to function normally only when stimulation is within the optimal range. At this point, another application of the Yerkes-Dodson principle should be obvious.

11

ANXIETY: A BRIEF OVERVIEW

Methodological Problems

The utility of a theory is a function of the fundament of established facts upon which it is built. As has been noted, experimentation in the behavioral sciences is still in a rather rudimentary stage, and the accumulated body of knowledge in most areas is small. The hypothetical constructs with which behavioral science deals are as yet only promissory notes; we are unable to handle them in the fashion which true scientific rigor dictates. As a matter of everyday experience, the existence of anxiety is undeniable. As a scientific construct, so few findings are established beyond any question that the ground remains unsure. We have not yet advanced past the stage of prescientific occupation with semantic distinctions among such words as anxiety, fear, and stress.

The Absence of a Consensual Definition

From its beginning the study of human anxiety has been handicapped by the absence of a consensual operational definition of the construct. The multiplicity of definitions makes for confusion and difficulty in understanding conflicting experimental findings. When the results of two investigations, similar except for the construct definition, are in conflict, there is always the possibility that the conflict is a consequence of the differences in definition.

Occasionally a particular definition, like Taylor's Manifest Anxiety Scale, appears promising and becomes popular. Early positive findings (an invariable phenomenon) encourage other researchers to employ the definition. Disenchantment, brought on by negative results, seems inevitably to follow, though it is sometimes slow in overtaking the research effort.

The success of the Manifest Anxiety Scale, judged in terms of the frequency of its employment in experiments, has been partly a function of the method of its construction. Clinical researchers are likely to be favorably inclined toward an instrument originally derived through the judgment of clinicians, and experimentalists are impressed by the idea that the device is intended to measure an experimentally based concept like drive.

The MAS has proven to be surprisingly useful, considering that it is simply constructed and that it was never intended to be a measure of trait anxiety in the clinical sense. It is merely a set of MMPI items which is known to be practically indistinguishable from some of the formal MMPI scales themselves. It is overweighted with items dealing with physical symptomatology, and it requires the respondent to make rather complex judgments about his perennial and average states. Despite its usefulness, it has not turned out to be the ultimate definition that science requires for the accumulation of knowledge and the development of sound theory.

The introduction of the MAS spurred research in anxiety, as Levy's (1961) survey shows. Its eventual failure as a criterion measure now appears to have inclined behavioral science to cast a jaundiced eye on the inventory approach to the measurement of anxiety. In the search for an ultimate criterion of anxiety, researchers are slowly turning toward physiological indices. The general finding so far has been that such measures are not consistently related to inventory scores and to other psychological criteria. Increased attention to physiological measurement is in itself encouraging, but such a change of focus could be unfortunate if it were to preclude extensive work with some of the recently developed inventories. The STAI, for example, is a promising development and warrants extensive use in future research on anxiety.

The Problem of the Physiology of Anxiety

Investigation of the physiological bases of emotional behavior has been perennially handicapped by a traditional isolation of disciplines. Physiologists and biochemists deal with their own subject matter in a highly sophisticated fashion, but, when left to their own devices, they handle the accompanying behavioral aspects crudely. Psychologists deal capably with behavior and emotion, but they are insufficiently versed in physiology and biochemistry. Progress in research requires a union of investigators from biological and behavioral disciplines. Recent years have seen a slow increase in the number of such joint endeavors, but they still represent only a small fraction of the total research effort.

A continuing and thorny problem is that most studies which simultaneously involve physiological and behavioral measures are carried out with animal subjects. The physiological make-up of infrahuman mammals and of humans is similar enough that ordinarily one can safely generalize from the former to the latter with respect to chemical toxicity. Psychoactive medications that cause liver damage in human patients will generally injure rats as well. The characteristic fear reaction in a rat—cowering, urination, and defecation—is no more than an exaggeration of the pattern of autonomic reactivity found in human beings. But there always seems to be a limit beyond which generalization from the lower organism to man breaks down. For example, Bishop and his co-workers (1964) found striking differences in the intracranial self-stimulation behavior of rats and of a schizophrenic patient. The behavior of animals engaging in self-stimulation is markedly and immediately affected by such factors as changes in the intensity of the current and the rate of reinforcement. Bar-pressing behavior to receive stimulation occurs much more rapidly when the animal receives the desirable current each time the bar is pressed, as compared to when it receives stimulation every five or ten bar-presses. A comparable drop in the frequency of the behavior occurs when the current is reduced below the optimal intensity. When the current is turned off entirely, the animal promptly ceases bar-pressing. None of these factors affected the bar-pressing behavior of the human subject. It was maintained at a constant high level regardless of the reinforcement schedule or the intensity of the current.

Consequently, Bishop suggests that the human subject's verbal reports of pleasurable sensations are likely to be "grossly unreliable and probably should not be accepted as valid." Equally likely, however, is that this particular form of behavior, under these particular circumstances, is characteristically different for humans and for rats. Generalization from rat to human behavior is, perhaps, unwarranted.

The enormous variability of autonomic response among human beings is rarely encountered among lower organisms. A finding that is established beyond any possible question is that among people there is no *one* pattern of autonomic reactivity to stress. The greater homogeneity of response among animals is thus likely to be misleading at times.

Although experimentation with animals is, and probably always will be, of inestimable value to behavioral science, it would seem that conclusive findings concerning man must, in every instance, be based on research with human subjects. Until refinement and further development of measuring techniques permits extensive, safe human experimentation, dark spots will remain in the accumulated store of knowledge.

Single-Factor Versus Multifactor Studies

A learned historian once noted that the most dangerous concept ever introduced in politics was the idea that the solution to any problem involving human beings is simple. As a corollary it can be stated that human motivation is almost always complex and that human behavior is complexly motivated. Yet a surprisingly large number of behavioral science investigations involve a single independent variable and a single dependent variable. Clarity of presentation and amenability to interpretation appear to be the reasons why single-factor experiments remain common. A single correlation coefficient has optimal visibility and is grasped, interpreted, and assimilated without undue difficulty. A finding that high anxiety disrupts learning presents no problems. If the experimenter simultaneously seeks to investigate the effects of other variables, such as type of material to be learned, the learning situation, and characteristics of the learner, the results are likely to be confusing and difficult to understand, let alone to interpret. Multifactor studies seldom yield unambiguous data. The reader—and often the experimenter as well—finds himself lost in a welter of statistical analyses pointing in every direction at once.

Consider, as an illustration, the following interpretation of the findings of an investigation involving anxiety, social class, sex, intelligence, and academic achievement measured in several different ways (Phillips, 1962).

> Sex differences in level of anxiety were obtained, males having lower anxiety scores than females; and differences in the achievement of subjects with high and low anxiety were found, with high anxiety being associated with lower achievement. However, the significance of these areas of agreement is diminished by the finding that both the level of anxiety and relationship to school achievement depended upon the interaction of sex and social class.
>
> As the first indication of this interaction, sex differences and level of anxiety occurred *only* in the lower social class, where females have significantly higher anxiety scores than males. In addition to this, it should be noted that middle-class and lower-class males differed less in anxiety scores than middle-class and lower-class females.
>
> As a further indication of the interaction of sex and social class, lower-class males with high anxiety had higher intelligence scores than lower-class males with low anxiety, although middle-class males with high anxiety did not differ significantly in intelligence from middle-class males with low anxiety. Furthermore, in both social class levels females with high anxiety had lower intelligence than females with low anxiety.
>
> Finally, the interaction between sex and social class was evident in relationships between anxiety and school achievement. In general, anxiety as a debilitating factor was more evident in relation to teacher grades than in relation to achievement tests, with the achievement of lower-class males being less affected than the achievement of other adolescents.

The experimenter is evidently struggling manfully—and with questionable success—to extract some cohesiveness and sensibility from a distressingly complicated set of findings.

The problem with the multifactor study is that significant interactions between variables seem to arise accidently. Sampling techniques in the behavioral sciences are seldom adequate; rarely does an investigator employ an actual random sample. The fates which cast a certain, small subgroup of particularly influential subjects into one or another experimental sample may, in a particular experiment, exercise a sufficiently strong influence to bias an experimental outcome. The perplexed researcher usually is at a loss to determine which interactions are truly meaningful and which are fortuitous. One explanation of his perplexity is that there are no theories which are really multifactor. We hypothesize that sufficiently strong anxiety disrupts learning, but our theory construction has not yet advanced to the point of incorporating into the cause and effect relationship the influences of such factors as age, sex, and the situation. A sound theory would suggest to the experimenter which relationships are meaningful and which have arisen by accident.

Human behavior is usually determined by a complex constellation within which a number of factors interact to produce behavior at any given moment. In the single-factor experiment, the investigator attempts to control extraneous variables so that the relationship between *X* and *Y* can emerge in vivid purity. Unfortunately, most often we do not know which factors need to be neutralized. This kind of knowledge becomes available primarily through the cumbersome multifactor studies.

Thus the psychological study of emotion is in a bind. The nature of human motivation demands a multifactor research approach; owing to an absence of theory, multifactor studies generally yield confusing and ambiguous results; the development of theory requires multifactor investigation; the control of extraneous variables in the single-factor studies also requires knowledge obtained from multifactor experiments; and so forth.

The cycle evidently must be broken at some point. Possibly the most promising focus is on the improvement of sampling techniques and the formulation of large-scale experiments that span regions of the country and different strata of society. In order to be effectively implemented, such research undoubtedly needs some kind of governmental direction leading to the establishment of a nation-wide research operation.

The Origin of Anxiety

In a very broad sense, behavioral science has identified the fountainhead of human anxiety. Theories and evidence agree that anxiety is an inevitable by-product of the process by which a person learns to become a member of a society. Every culture, no matter how underdeveloped or primitive it may be, imposes restrictions on the behavior of its members; without such limitations it could not hope to survive as an institution. No society tolerates indiscriminate and immediate gratification of the needs, desires, and impulses of its members. The human being is born with a limitless flexibility to adopt any set of values, to conform to any dictated patterns of behavior. He must learn not only to control impulses but also to discern the channels through which his society permits him to express impulses. The fact that the human being can experience fear permits this learning to take place. In the process, anxiety arises. All basic anxiety is thus what Whiting and Child (1953) call "socialization anxiety."

Anxiety-proneness is the conglomerate result of a natural human capacity and the need for social conformity. Behavioral science has not been able to progress very far beyond this diffuse conclusion. The conditions under which anxiety serves the purposes of socialization or eventually interferes with them are not yet known with certainty. Child-raising practices and adult personality patterns or styles have not yet been connected in a reliably predictive manner.

Investigation of the source and specific development of human anxiety is badly handicapped by technical difficulties. Sustained, accurate observation and measurement of human psychosocial development is possible only in principle, not in fact. The behavioral scientist cannot manipulate continuous influences on the child in his natural milieu, as he can with laboratory animals. He cannot construct and control an environment in which children are actually reared in order to determine the effect of various factors or their absence.

Deprived of direct approaches to observation and measurement, the researcher resorts to data obtained from parents and teachers, from the child himself at a given moment, or from adults in retrospect. Not only are these data gross and relatively unreliable; they are also, we have every reason to suspect, somewhat distorted by personal and mnemonic influences. Findings based on such data are generally regarded as unsatisfactory by the rigorous scientist, either for theory construction or for the prediction and control of behavior.

Not surprisingly, theories of the development of anxiety-proneness have emerged largely from the clinician's office and the animal laboratory. As a method of collecting scientific data, the former is woefully deficient. This contention need not be labored; the fallibility of unsupported human observation of other human beings is all too well known to behavioral science. Furthermore, some of the theoretical positions of psychoanalysis are by their nature unverifiable. One cannot, for example, test the Freudian hypothesis that the initial phase of primary anxiety occurs at birth. The significance of an infant's behavior can be inferred but never truly comprehended. If a baby stops crying when a nipple is put into his mouth, this may suggest that the cry is a consequence of hunger or perhaps of some other discomfort. Physiological measurement may disclose a state of arousal, but the experience of anxiety in the preverbal organism cannot be verified.

Theories originating in clinical practice are at least derived from the study of human beings. Experimentally based theories, although more systematic and methodologically sound, are based largely on research with infrahuman mammals. The experimental psychologist, with his greater devotion to scientific principle, is more keenly aware than the psychoanalyst of the lacunae in his theoretical formulations. He knows that laboratory research, though it has been able to deal fairly successfully with basic drives in animals, has limited applicability to the development of complex human motivation. Learning theory is more a model than an explanatory statement. It is a logical structure that follows from evidence derived from experiments with lower organisms. Whether the principles that have been isolated do, in fact, apply to human learned drives like anxiety remains a matter of speculation.

The rueful summary of Miller and Dollard (1950) is still appropriate: We do not yet have a science of child-raising. Until such a discipline is developed, we will continue to have more vagueness, conflict, and sheer speculation than useful findings and sound theory.

The Concept of Anxiety

The most current views of anxiety as a construct distinguish between trait anxiety, a predisposition to respond anxiously in a variety of situations, and a state, or transient condition, of emotional arousal (Cattell and Scheier, 1961; Spielberger, 1966; Lazarus, 1966). In this conception, the degree of state reaction is a function of trait level. Individuals who are highly prone to anxiety should react more strongly to stressful circumstances, though there may be exceptions depending on the individual's personal experiences.

The hypothesized correlation is implicit in such early theories about anxiety as the psychoanalytic, and in a great deal of experimental study. Whether "high anxious" refers to trait or state anxiety is often unclear. All but a few of the inventories measure trait anxiety, but they are frequently employed in experiments in which the investigator apparently intends to measure state anxiety. The trait-state relationship as a general statement appears inescapable, but the correlation may vary considerably depending upon the stress that evokes the state. Where a measure of state anxiety is required, findings of experiments that employ a conventional inventory may be affected by the failure to make a clear distinction.

Experimenters seeking a measure of state anxiety are looking with increasing frequency at physiological systems. A change in breathing rate, in systolic blood pressure, or in a blood level is unquestionably a state reaction. Investigation has so far not succeeded in establishing the hypothesized trait-state correlation when the former is defined by an inventory and the latter by physiological measurement. Subjective reports of state anxiety are more often found to be related to physiological reactivity, but even these findings are variable and inconsistent.

There are several possible explanations of the failure to establish the trait-state correlation. Research has been handicapped by the absence of psychological measures of anxiety that are based on, and empirically reflect, the trait-state correlation. For example, useful tests of intelligence were constructed by deliberately fitting the instruments to a theoretical model in which the average intelligence quotient is 100 and the distribution of IQ's has a given range and shape. Successful application of intelligence test scores is accepted as sound evidence that the theoretical model is correct.

Empirical evaluation of the trait-state relationship requires instruments that have been deliberately constructed with this hypothesis as a model. Such measures were not available before the development of the STAI. Preliminary data presented by Spielberger and Gorsuch (1966) indicate that the STAI can provide data in keeping with the trait-state hypothesis. Experimentation with this inventory, and perhaps with the AACL, may eventually yield some definitive answers.

An explanation of the absence of relationship between trait anxiety and physiological measures lies in the concept of emotion as a state of general, physiological arousal. If physiological reaction to stress is nonspecific, then increased blood pressure or pulse rate may reflect a state of anger or general excitement or even pleasure, rather than of anxiety, in some individuals. This would serve to obscure the trait-state correlation that exists among those subjects who are experiencing anxiety in response to the stress stimulus.

General arousal theory maintains that an emotional state is specific only at the level of subjective experience. Perhaps the emotional response of some people is found *only* at the subjective level or *only* at the physiological level, but not at both. In order to discover relationships among phenomena, researchers would have to distinguish these two types from those who react at both levels.

Anxiety as a State of General Arousal

The concept of emotion as a state of nonspecific, physiological arousal or activation was originally proposed in a clear and convincing fashion by Cannon. With the identification of the two adrenomedullary hormones, adrenaline and noradrenaline—a distinction that was not available to Cannon—came an upsurge of interest in their potential differential significance for emotional states. On one hand, the evidence that adrenaline mediates fear states, whereas noradrenaline is more critically involved in anger and rage, is tenuous at best. On the other hand, that specific physiological correlates of particular emotional states cannot be reliably identified supports the general arousal and activation theories of emotion. The evidence of the ingenious Schachter experiments and of the studies from Levi's laboratory in Sweden are more striking than any testimony that can be marshaled by the proponents of specific physiological patterns.

Additional evidence for the theory of general arousal is provided by the analogous studies of arousal and performance. According to all variants of arousal theory, the relationship between activation and performance should follow the Yerkes-Dodson principle, with maximally effective behavior occurring at the midpoint, rather than at the minimum or maximum level of arousal. The studies of muscular tension and learning illustrate the relationship with clarity. The testimony for activation theory stands out sharply; muscle tension is definitely a characteristic of all aroused states and is unique to no one of them.

Korchin (1962), in his defense of activation theory, points out that "despite general agreement that increased activation and performance are related in an inverted-U function, there are relatively few studies which bear directly on this assumption, at least under experimental conditions." He suggests that "the term anxiety might best be reserved for the mid to high portion of the activation continuum, rather than be used to cover the entire spectrum. . . ." Following this argument, we arrive at a plausible explanation of the relative paucity of experimental demonstrations of the inverted-U relationship. The problems involved in stressing laboratory subjects might easily lead to the speculation that anxiety—conceived as an extreme arousal reaction—is seldom actually produced in the laboratory. Experimenters deal almost exclusively with the low and middle ranges of the state. The relationship obtained, therefore, would show only one half of the expected U. The antipodal half has been obtained only in an occasional experiment, such as those by Patrick (1934a) and Stennett (1957). It is easily obtained in experiments in which the arousal level can be systematically varied from very low to very high, as in the muscular tension studies and in animal experiments of which the old Yerkes and Dodson (1908) experiment is the acknowledged forerunner. To be sure, many human experiments have compared stressed and unstressed performances, but construction of a ditonic curve requires more than two points. It is neither practical, ethical, nor, perhaps, legal to deliberately subject a human to the extremes of stress that seem to be necessary in order to provide the complete U-shaped data.

Perhaps the most telling evidence in support of the Yerkes-Dodson principle and general arousal theory comes from natural and naturalistic studies. One thinks of Janis' surgery patients and the disruptive consequences of sensory deprivation at one extreme and of sensory overload at the other. These phenomena are more striking than the laboratory experiments with their artificial contexts and methodological shortcomings.

Spence's concept of anxiety as a general, energizing drive is consonant with activation theory, within limits. Spence views anxiety as a force that motivates the individual to perform, but his theory does not extend to a level of drive that disrupts performance. Spence's theory may reflect the scarcity of laboratory data illustrating the interfering effects of high anxiety levels.

The evidence for emotion as a state of general arousal is almost convincing. But a nagging doubt remains. If the states of arousal are indistinguishable physiologically, why should two adrenal hormones, or perhaps more, be involved in mediating physiological activation? Nothing in nature is without purpose. There must be a reason for the coexistence of adrenaline and noradrenaline. Until the specific roles played by various adrenal hormones in emotion are known, general arousal theory will probably not be completely accepted.

Intracranial Stimulation as Psychotherapy

Studies of the effects of direct electrical stimulation of limbic system areas, such as the work of Olds and of Brady, and more specifically the studies of Heath and his co-workers with human subjects, have a major, significant implication for treatment of mental illness. Heath (1964a) rightfully calls attention to this possible—and exciting—consequence of his work.

> Psychodynamic theory should suggest applications of this therapeutic modality to correction of clinical disorders. . . . According to our theory, behavioral patterns are established on the basis of reward (pleasure) and punishment (pain). The self-operating behavioral mechanism of adults is established in early years as a result of relations with other people, usually parents or parental surrogates, who provided reward or punishment. Adaptive or normal behavior results when the person learns, through these early relations, to avoid realistic danger (pain) in the interest of self and society and to approach benefits (pleasure) in the same interests. The neurotic or maladapted person, in contrast, acquires faulty learning habits through his early interpersonal relations, so that painful emergency emotions develop with situations that should be pleasurable or neutral. This is the nucleus of maladaptive or neurotic behavior. . . . If this dynamic formulation of normal and neurotic behavior is correct, then elimination of unwarranted, inappropriate fear or rage in the neurotic person through introduction of pleasure with stimuli to the brain should be therapeutic. Theoretically, the neurotic person's inappropriate fear of a nonhazardous situation would be replaced instantly with a pleasurable feeling, and the reparative patterns which represent the neurotic maneuvers would disappear.

In other words, psychotherapy would consist of a conditioning process within which previously stressful objects and situations are presented simultaneously with appropriate stimulation of limbic system pleasure sites by the therapist. This conditioning process would, in theory, reverse a naturally occurring process through which the stimulus had become stressful.

Of course, use of the permanently implanted electrode is not practical for general psychotherapy, as Heath points out. The establishment of the cerebral pleasure sites may, however, provide an incentive to researchers to develop either an implantation or a surface stimulation method that is generally applicable to humans, or a chemical agent that will have comparable effects. Such a development would constitute a dramatic, major breakthrough in the treatment of the emotionally ill.

The Social Value of Anxiety

The mental health professional regards anxiety as a painful, debilitating, even catastrophic condition that cries for alleviation. Anxiety as a malignancy is a limited concept. It considers the emotion only in the extreme intensity in which it disrupts behavior. Moderately intense anxiety, however, energizes the organism and improves performance. White (1952) suggests that moderate forms of anxiety not only are used to shape behavior in the child, but also may serve "as a very definite incentive in the normal process of growing up." Psychological maturation is fostered by the drive to overcome the anxieties of childhood.

Some defenses against anxiety, like compulsivity and counterbehavior, seem to be constructive as long as they do not get out of hand. It is perhaps plausible that much human striving, much of the endless doing that we call progress, is in one way or another a consequence of anxiety. Stein (1964) summarizes evidence which indicates that learning in rats is seriously retarded if accompanied by stimulation of the limbic system pleasure sites. On purely logical grounds, hedonism and social progress are antithetical. We may conjecture that the advance of human society over the ages is, at least in part, a consequence of the human organism's capacity to experience anxiety. This view, which was expressed by such nineteenth-century philosophers as Kierkegaard, is summed up by Berthold (1963):

> But within all this they see an "anxiety to. . . ." They read the signs as tokens of a desire to better one's lot and imply that without anxiety there would be no impetus to learning or improvement. Knowledge, in

this connection, is the transformation of anxiety into fear—the identification of *what* is "wrong." But anxiety is the mother of the drive to know.

A few theorists have carried the philosophical speculation even further, suggesting that anxiety, or emotional maladjustment in the general sense, produces creativity. Even if we could define creativity for experimental purposes, the hypothesis is untestable. There have been, and are, geniuses who seemed extraordinarily well adjusted, and some who appeared equivalently mentally disturbed. What someone might have been if the circumstances of his life had been different is an unanswerable question. We can only wonder vainly what De Quincey or Poe or Van Gogh would have produced if he had been emotionally better balanced.

Thus anxiety is a Janus-headed creature that can impel man to self-improvement, achievement, and competence, or can distort and impoverish his existence and that of his fellows. The distinction appears to be a sheer matter of degree, of intensity, as it is with many other phenomena of human life. The urgent need is to acquire the knowledge to utilize anxiety constructively, to be its master and not its slave.

REFERENCES

Aiken, L. R. Stress and anxiety as homomorphisms, *Psychological record,* 11 (1961), 365–372.

Alexander, I. E., and Adlerstein, A. M. Affective responses to the concept of death in a population of children and adolescents, *Journal of genetic psychology,* 63 (1958), 167–177.

Alpert, R., and Haber, R. N. Anxiety in academic achievement situations, *Journal of abnormal and social psychology,* 61 (1960), 207–215.

American Psychiatric Association. *Diagnostic and statistical manual: mental disorders.* Washington, D.C., 1952.

Applezweig, D. C. Some determinants of behavioral rigidity, *Journal of abnormal and social psychology,* 49 (1954), 224–228.

Basowitz, H., Persky, H., Korchin, S. J., and Grinker, R. R. *Anxiety and stress.* New York, McGraw-Hill, 1955.

Beam, J. C. Serial learning and conditioning under real-life stress, *Journal of abnormal and social psychology,* 51 (1955), 543–551.

Bendig, A. W. The development of a short form of the manifest anxiety scale, *Journal of consulting psychology,* 20 (1956), 384.

Berkun, M. M., Bialek, H. M., Kern, R. P., and Yagi, K. Experimental studies of psychological stress in man, *Psychological monographs,* 76 (1962), no. 15, whole no. 534.

Berthold, F. Anxious longing. In S. Hiltner and K. Menninger, eds., *Constructive aspects of anxiety.* New York, Abingdon, 1963.

Bindra, D., Paterson, A. L., and Strzelecki, J. On the relation between anxiety and conditioning. *Canadian journal of psychology,* 9 (1955), 1–6.

Bishop, M. P., Elder, S. T., and Heath, R. G. Attempted control of operant behavior in man with intracranial self-stimulation. In R. G. Heath, ed., *The role of pleasure in behavior.* New York, Hoeber, 1964.

Bovard, E. W. The effects of social stimuli on the response to stress, *Psychological review,* 66 (1959), 267–277.

Brady, J. V. The paleocortex and behavioral motivation. In H. F. Harlow and C. N. Woolsey, eds., *Biological and biochemical bases of behavior.* Madison, University of Wisconsin Press, 1958.

Breggin, P, R. The psychophysiology of anxiety, *Journal of nervous and mental disease,* 139 (1964), 558–568.

Buss, A. H. *The psychology of aggression.* New York, Wiley, 1961.

Campbell, D. T., Miller, N., Lubetsky, J., and O'Connell, E. J. Varieties of projection in trait attribution, *Psychological monographs,* 78 (1964), whole no. 592.

Cannon, W. B. *Bodily changes in pain, hunger, fear, and rage.* Boston, Charles T. Branford, 1929; new edn., New York, Harper and Row, 1963.

Castaneda, A., McCandless, B. R., and Palermo, D. S. The children's form of the manifest anxiety scale, *Child development,* 27 (1956), 317–326.

Cattell, R. B., and Scheier, I. H. The nature of anxiety: a review of thirteen multivariate analyses comprising 814 variables, *Psychological reports,* 4 (1958), 351–388.

Cattell, R. B., and Scheier, I. H. *The meaning and measurement of neuroticism and anxiety.* New York, Ronald, 1961.

Christie, R., and Budnitzky, S. A short forced-choice anxiety scale. *Journal of consulting psychology,* 21 (1957), 501.

Courts, F. A. Relations between experimentally induced tension and memorization, *Journal of experimental psychology,* 25 (1939), 235–256.

Courts, F. A. Relationships between muscular tension and performance, *Psychological bulletin,* 39 (1942), 347–367.

Dahlstrom, W. G., and Welsh, G. S. *An MMPI handbook: a guide to use in clinical practice and research.* Minneapolis, University of Minnesota Press, 1960.

Davids, A., and Eriksen, C. W. The relation of manifest anxiety to association productivity and intellectual attainment, *Journal of consulting psychology,* 19 (1955), 219–222.

Dickson, C. *Fear is the same.* New York, William Morrow, 1956.

Diethelm, O., and Jones, M. R. Influence of anxiety on attention, learning, retention, and thinking, *Archives of neurology and psychiatry,* 58 (1947), 325–336.

Diggory, J. C., and Rothman, D. Z. Values destroyed by death, *Journal of abnormal and social psychology,* 63 (1961), 205–210.

Dollard, J., and Miller, N. E. *Personality and psychotherapy*, New York, McGraw-Hill, 1950.

Duffy, E. The conceptual categories of psychology: a suggestion for revision, *Psychological review*, 48 (1941), 177–203.

Duffy, E. *Activation and behavior*. New York, Wiley, 1962.

Dunbar, F. *Mind and body: psychosomatic medicine*. New York, Random House, 1947.

Duncan, C. P. Recent research on human problem solving, *Psychological bulletin*, 56 (1959), 397–429.

Endler, N. S., Hunt, J. M., and Rosenstein, A. J. An S-R inventory of anxiousness, *Psychological monographs*, 76 (1962), no. 17, whole no. 536.

English, H. B., and English, A. C. *A comprehensive dictionary of psychological and psychoanalytical terms*. New York, Longmans, Green, 1958.

Eriksen, C. W., and Davids, A. The meaning and clinical validity of the Taylor anxiety scale and the hysteria-psychasthenia scale from the MMPI, *Journal of abnormal and social psychology*, 50 (1955), 135–137.

Eriksen, C. W., and Wechsler, H. Some effects of experimentally induced anxiety upon discrimination behavior, *Journal of abnormal and social psychology*, 51 (1955), 458–463.

Feifel, H. The problem of death, *Catholic psychological record*, 3 (1965), 18–22.

Feifel, H., and Heller, J. Normalcy, illness, and death, *Proceedings of the Third World Congress of Psychiatry*. Toronto, University of Toronto Press, 1961, pp. 1252–1256.

Feldstein, A. Schizochemistry, *Psychiatric opinion*, Fall 1965, pp. 17–21, 24–25.

Feshbach, S., and Singer, R. The effects of personal and shared threats upon social prejudice, *Journal of abnormal and social psychology*, 54 (1957), 411–416.

Fox, H. M., Gifford, S., Murawski, B. J., Rizzo, N. D., and Kudarauskas, E. N. Some methods of observing humans under stress, *Psychiatric research reports 7*, American Psychiatric Association, 1957, pp. 14–26.

Freeman, M. J. The development of a test for the measurement of anxiety: a study of its reliability and validity, *Psychological monographs*, 67 (1953), no. 3, whole no. 353.

Freud, S. *Civilization and its discontents.* New York, J. Cape and H. Smith, 1930.

Freud, S. *The problem of anxiety.* New York, Norton, 1936. Originally published in 1923 in German, under the title *Inhibition, symptom, and anxiety.*

Friedman, I. Phenomenal, ideal, and projected conceptions of the self, *Journal of abnormal and social psychology,* 51 (1955), 611–615.

Fromm, E. *Man for himself.* New York, Rinehart, 1947.

Geer, J. H. The development of a scale to measure fear, *Behaviour research and therapy,* 3 (1965), 45–53.

Geer, J. H. Effect of fear arousal upon task performance and verbal behavior, *Journal of abnormal and social psychology,* 71 (1966), 119–123.

Glaser, B. G., and Strauss, A. L. *Awareness of dying.* Chicago, Aldine, 1965.

Goldstein, M. J., and Palmer, J. O. *The experience of anxiety.* New York, Oxford University Press, 1963.

Grinker, R. R., Sabshin, M., Hamburg, D. A., Board, F. A., Basowitz, H., Korchin, S. J., Persky, H., and Chevalier, J. A. The use of an anxiety-producing interview and its meaning to the subject, *Archives of neurology and psychiatry,* 77 (1957), 406–419.

Gunderson, E. K. Emotional symptoms in extremely isolated groups, *Archives of general psychiatry,* 9 (1963), 362–368.

Gynther, R. A. The effects of anxiety and of situational stress on communicative efficiency, *Journal of abnormal and social psychology,* 54 (1957), 274–276.

Hadley, J. M. *Clinical and counseling psychology.* New York, Knopf, 1958.

Hall, C. S. *A primer of freudian psychology.* Cleveland, World Publishing Co., 1954.

Hall, G. S. A synthetic genetic study of fear, *American journal of psychology,* 25 (1914), 149–200.

Hamilton, G. V. A study of perseverance reactions in primates and rodents, *Behavior monographs,* 3 (1916), serial no. 13.

Harleston, B. W. Test anxiety and performance in problem-solving situations, *Journal of personality,* 30 (1962), 557–573.

Heath, R. G., ed. *The role of pleasure in behavior.* New York, Hoeber, 1964a.

Heath, R. G. Pleasure response of human subjects to direct stimulation of the brain: physiologic and psychodynamic considerations. In R. G. Heath, ed., *The role of pleasure in behavior.* New York, Hoeber, 1964b.

Heineman, C. E. A forced-choice form of the Taylor anxiety scale, *Journal of consulting psychology,* 17 (1953), 447–454.

Hilgard, E. R. *Hypnotic susceptibility.* New York, Harcourt, Brace and World, 1965.

Hilgard, E. R. The motivational relevance of hypnosis. In D. Levine, ed., *Nebraska Symposium on Motivation.* Lincoln, Neb., University of Nebraska Press, 1964.

Hilgard, E. R., Jones, L. V., and Kaplan, S. J. Conditioned discrimination as related to anxiety, *Journal of experimental psychology,* 52 (1951), 94–99.

Hoch, P. H., and Zubin, J., eds. *Anxiety.* New York, Grune and Stratton, 1950.

Horney, K. *The neurotic personality of our time.* New York, Norton, 1937.

Hull, C. L. *Principles of behavior.* New York, Appleton-Century-Crofts., 1943.

Janis, I. L. *Psychological stress.* New York, Wiley, 1958.

Jeffers, F. C., Nichols, C. R., and Eisdorfer, C. Attitudes of older persons toward death: a preliminary study, *Journal of gerontology,* 16 (1961), 53–56.

Kalish, R. S. Some variables in death attitudes, *Journal of social psychology,* 59 (1963), 137–145.

Kamin, L. J., and Clark, J. W. The Taylor scale and reaction time, *Journal of abnormal and social psychology,* 54 (1957), 262–263.

Kasl, S. V., and Mahl, G. F. The relationship of disturbances and hesitations in spontaneous speech to anxiety, *Journal of personality and social psychology,* 1 (1965), 125–133.

Kegeles, S. S. Some motives for seeking preventive dental care, *Journal of the american dental association,* 7 (1963), 90 98.

Kerle, R. H., and Bialek, H. M. The construction, validation, and application of a subjective stress scale. Staff Memorandum, U.S. Army Leadership Human Research Unit, Monterey, Cal., 1958.

Kety, S. Biochemical theory of schizophrenia, *International journal of psychiatry,* 1 (1965), 409–430.

Korchin, S. J. Anxiety and cognition. In C. Scheerer, ed., *Cognition: theory, research, promise.* New York, Harper and Row, 1964.

Korchin, S. J., and Levine, S. Anxiety and verbal learning, *Journal of abnormal and social psychology,* 54 (1957), 234–240.

Kubzansky, P. E. The effects of reduced environmental stimulation on human behavior: a review. In A. D. Biderman and H. Zimmer, eds., *The manipulation of human behavior.* New York, Wiley, 1961.

Lazarus, R. S. *Psychological stress and the coping process.* New York, McGraw-Hill, 1966.

Lazarus, R. S., Deese, J., and Osler, S. F. The effects of psychological stress upon performance, *Psychological bulletin,* 49 (1952), 293–317.

Leeper, R. W. A motivational theory of emotion to replace "emotion as disorganized response," *Psychological review,* 55 (1948), 5–21.

Levi, L. The urinary output of adrenalin and noradrenalin during different experimentally induced pleasant and unpleasant states. Paper presented at the Annual Conference of the Society for Psychosomatic Research, London, 1963.

Levine, G. N. Anxiety about illness: psychological and social bases, *Journal of health and human behavior,* 3 (1962), 30–34.

Levitt, E. E. *Clinical research design and analysis in the behavioral sciences.* Springfield, Ill., C. C. Thomas, 1961.

Levitt, E. E. Scientific evaluation of the "lie detector," *Iowa law review,* 40 (1955), 440–458.

Levitt, E. E., Brady, J. P., and Lubin, B. Correlates of hypnotizability in young women: anxiety and dependency, *Journal of personality,* 31 (1963), 52–57.

Levitt, E. E., Persky, H., Brady, J. P., and Fitzgerald, J. A. The effect of hydrocortisone infusion on hypnotically induced anxiety, *Psychosomatic medicine,* 25 (1963), 158–161.

Levitt, E. E., Persky, H., Brady, J. P., Fitzgerald, J., and den Breeijen, A. Evidence for hypnotically induced amnesia as an analog of repression, *Journal of nervous and mental disease,* 133 (1961), 218–221.

Levy, L. H. Anxiety and behavior scientists' behavior, *American psychologist,* 16 (1961), 66–68.

Levy, N. A short form of the children's manifest anxiety scale, *Child development,* 29 (1958), 153–154.

Lindsley, D. B. Emotion. In S. S. Stevens, ed., *Handbook of experimental psychology*. New York, Wiley, 1951.

Lowe, M. C. The equivalence of guilt and anxiety as psychological constructs, *Journal of consulting psychology*, 28 (1964), 553–554.

McReynolds, P. A restricted conceptualization of human anxiety and motivation, *Psychological reports*, 2 (1956), 293–312.

McReynolds, P., Acker, M., and Pietila, C. Relation of object curiosity to psychological adjustment in children, *Child development*, 32 (1961), 393–400.

McReynolds, P., and Acker, M. Presentation of different forms of the Assimilation Scale (mimeographed). Palo Alto, Cal. Veterans Administration Hospital, 1966.

McReynolds, P., and Acker, M. On the assessment of anxiety: II, By a self-report inventory, *Psychological reports*, 19 (1966), 231–237.

Malmo, R. B. Experimental approach to symptom mechanisms in psychiatric patients, *Psychiatric research reports* 7, American Psychiatric Association, 1957, pp. 33–49.

Malmo, R. B. Activation: a neuropsychological dimension, *Psychological review*, 66 (1959), 367–386.

Mandler, G., and Cowen, J. E. Test anxiety questionnaires, *Journal of consulting psychology*, 22 (1958), 228–229.

Mandler, G., and Sarason, S. B. A study of anxiety and learning, *Journal of abnormal and social psychology*, 47 (1952), 166–173.

Martin, B. The assessment of anxiety by physiological behavioral measures, *Psychological bulletin*, 58 (1961), 234–255.

Masserman, J. H. Emotional reactions to death and suicide. In S. Liebman, ed., *Stress situations*. Philadelphia, Lippincott, 1955.

Matarazzo, J. D., Ulett, G. A., and Saslow, G. Human maze performance as a function of increasing levels of anxiety, *Journal of general psychology*, 53 (1955), 79–95.

Matarazzo, J. D., Ulett, G. A., Guze, S. B., and Saslow, G. The relationship between anxiety level and several measures of anxiety, *Journal of consulting psychology*, 18 (1954), 201–205.

Mednick, S. A. Generalization as a function of manifest anxiety and adaptation to psychological experiments, *Journal of consulting psychology*, 21 (1957), 491–494.

Menninger, K., with Mayman, M., and Pruyser, P. *The vital balance: the life process in mental health and illness*. New York, Viking, 1963.

Meyer, D. R., and Noble, M. E. Summation of manifest anxiety and muscular tension, *Journal of experimental psychology,* 55 (1958), 599–602.

Mintz, A. Non-adaptive group behavior, *Journal of abnormal and social psychology,* 46 (1951), 150–159.

Modlin, H. C. A study of the Minnesota multiphasic personality inventory in clinical practice, *American journal of psychiatry,* 103 (1947), 758–769.

Monroe, R. R. A psychiatrist looks at medical hypnosis, *Journal of the Louisiana State Medical Society,* 112 (1960), 148–154.

Montague, E. K. The role of anxiety in serial rote learning, *Journal of experimental psychology,* 45 (1953), 91–95.

Mullin, C. S. Some psychological aspects of isolated antarctic living, *American journal of psychiatry,* 117 (1960), 323–325.

Murray, H. A. *Explorations in personality.* New York, Oxford University Press, 1938.

Nunnally, J. C. *Popular conceptions of mental health.* New York, Holt, Rinehart and Winston, 1961.

Olds, J., and Milner, T. Positive reinforcement produced by electrical stimulation of septal area and other regions of rat brain, *Journal of comparative and physiological psychology,* 47 (1954), 419–427.

Patrick, J. R. Studies in rational behavior and emotional excitement. I: Rational behavior in human subjects, *Journal of comparative psychology,* 18 (1934a), 1–22.

Patrick, J. R. Studies in rational behavior and emotional excitement. II: The effect of emotional excitement on rational behavior in human subjects, *Journal of comparative psychology,* 18 (1934b), 153–195.

Paul, G. L., and Eriksen, C. W. Effects of test anxiety on "real-life" examinations, *Journal of personality,* 32 (1964), 480–494.

Penney, R. K., and McCann, B. The children's reactive curiosity scale, *Psychological reports,* 15 (1964), 323–334.

Penney, R. K. Reactive curiosity and manifest anxiety in children, *Child development,* 36 (1965), 697–702.

Perkins, C. W. The effect of muscle relaxation and suggested therapeutic benefit on the reduction of anxiety. Unpublished doctoral dissertation, University of Illinois, 1966.

Persky, H. Adrenocortical function during anxiety. In R. Roessler and N. S. Greenfield, eds., *Physiological correlates of psychological disorder.* Madison, University of Wisconsin Press, 1962.

Persky, H., Zuckerman, M., Basu, G. K., and Thornton, D. Psychoendocrine effects of perceptual and social isolation, *Archives of general psychiatry,* 15 (1966), 499–505.

Phillips, B. N. Sex, social class, and anxiety as sources of variation in school achievement, *Journal of educational psychology,* 53 (1962), 316–322.

Purcell, C. K., Drevdahl, J., and Purcell, K. The relationship between attitude-IQ discrepancy and anxiety, *Journal of clinical psychology,* 8 (1952), 82–85.

Quarantelli, E. The nature and conditions of panic, *American journal of sociology,* 60 (1954), 267–275.

Reich, W. *Character-analysis.* 3rd ed. New York, Farrar, Straus and Cudahy, 1949.

Reiter, H. H. Some personality correlates of the Page fantasy scale, *Perceptual and motor skills,* 16 (1963), 747–748.

Rhudick, P. J., and Dibner, A. S. Age, personality, and health correlates of death concerns in normal aged individuals, *Journal of gerontology,* 16 (1961), 44–49.

Robbins, P. R. Some explorations into the nature of anxieties relating to illness, *Genetic psychology monographs,* 66 (1962), 91–141.

Rosenberg, M. The association between self-esteem and anxiety. *Journal of psychiatric research,* 1 (1962), 135–151.

Rosenberg, M. J. When dissonance fails: on eliminating evaluation apprehension from attitude measurement, *Journal of personality and social psychology,* 1 (1965), 28–42.

Rosenthal, R. *Experimenter effects in behavioral research.* New York, Appleton-Century-Crofts, 1966.

Rosenthal, R., Persinger, G. W., Kline, L. V., and Mulry, R. C. The role of the research assistant in the mediation of experimenter bias, *Journal of personality,* 31 (1963), 313–335.

Rothenberg, R. E. *Understanding surgery.* New York, Pocket Books, 1966.

Ruebush, B. K. Anxiety. In H. W. Stevenson, J. Kagan, and C. Spiker, eds., *Child psychology: The sixty-second yearbook of the National Society for the Study of Education.* Chicago, University of Chicago Press, 1963.

Ruebush, B. K. Interfering and facilitating effects of test anxiety. *Journal of abnormal and social psychology,* 60 (1960), 205–212.

Sarason, I. G. Effect of anxiety and two kinds of motivating instructions on verbal learning, *Journal of abnormal and social psychology,* 54 (1957), 166–171.

Sarason, I. G. Effects on verbal learning of anxiety, reassurance, and meaningfulness of material, *Journal of experimental psychology,* 56 (1958), 472–477.

Sarason, I. G. Intellectual and personality correlates of test anxiety, *Journal of abnormal and social psychology,* 59 (1959), 272–275.

Sarason, I. G. Empirical findings and theoretical problems in the use of anxiety scales, *Psychological bulletin,* 57 (1960), 403–415.

Sarason, S. B., Davidson, K. S., Lighthall, F. F., Waite, R. R., and Ruebush, B. K. *Anxiety in elementary school children.* New York, Wiley, 1960.

Sarason, S. B., and Gordon, E. M. The test anxiety questionnaire: scoring norms, *Journal of abnormal and social psychology,* 48 (1953), 447–448.

Sarason, S. B., and Mandler, G. Some correlates of test anxiety, *Journal of abnormal and social psychology,* 47 (1952), 810–817.

Schachter, S. The interaction of cognitive and physiological determinants of emotional states. In P. H. Leiderman and D. Shapiro, eds., *Psychobiological approaches to social behavior.* Stanford, Cal., Stanford University Press, 1964.

Schachter, S., and Singer, J. Cognitive, social and physiological determinants of emotional states, *Psychological review,* 69 (1962), 379–399.

Schachter, S., and Wheeler, L. Epinephrine, chlorpromazine, and amusement, *Journal of abnormal and social psychology,* 65 (1962), 121–128.

Schlesinger, A. J., Jr. *The vital center.* New York, Houghton-Mifflin, 1948.

Schultz, D. P. *Panic behavior.* New York, Random House, 1964.

Schultz, D. P. *Sensory restriction.* New York, Academic Press, 1965.

Schwab, J. R., and Iverson, M. A. Resistance of high-anxious subjects under ego threat to perception of figural distortion, *Journal of consulting psychology,* 28 (1964), 191–198.

Sears, R. R. Experimental studies of projection. I: Attribution of traits, *Journal of social psychology,* 7 (1936), 151–163.

Sears, R. R. A survey of objective studies of psychoanalytic concepts, *Social Science Research Council bulletin 51* (1943).

Seidman, D., Bensen, S. B., Miller, I., and Meeland, T. Influence of a partner on tolerance for a self-administered electric shock, *Journal of abnormal and social psychology,* 54 (1957), 210–212.

Selye, H. *The stress of life.* New York, McGraw-Hill, 1956.

Siegman, A. W. The effect of manifest anxiety on a concept formation task, a nondirected learning task, and on timed and untimed intelligence tests, *Journal of consulting psychology,* 20 (1956), 176–178.

Silverman, R. E. Anxiety and the mode of response, *Journal of abnormal and social psychology,* 49 (1954), 538–542.

Singer, J. L. *Daydreaming: an introduction to the experimental study of inner experience.* New York, Random House, 1966.

Singer, J. L., and Schonbar, R. A. Correlates of daydreaming: a dimension of self-awareness, *Journal of consulting psychology,* 25 (1961), 1–6.

Singer, J. L., and Rowe, R. An experimental study of some relationships between daydreaming and anxiety, *Journal of consulting psychology,* 26 (1962), 446–454.

Spence, K. W. *Behavior theory and learning.* Englewood Cliffs, N.J., Prentice-Hall, 1960.

Spence, K. W. Anxiety (drive) level and performance in eyelid conditioning, *Psychological bulletin,* 61 (1964), 129–139.

Spielberger, C. D. The effects of manifest anxiety on the academic achievement of college students, *Mental hygiene,* 46 (1962), 420–426.

Spielberger, C. D., and Katzenmeyer, W. G. Manifest anxiety, intelligence, and college grades, *Journal of consulting psychology,* 23 (1959), 278.

Spielberger, C. D. Theory and research on anxiety. In C. D. Spielberger, ed., *Anxiety and behavior.* New York, Academic Press, 1966.

Spielberger, C. D., and Gorsuch, R. L. Mediating process in verbal conditioning. Report of United States Public Health Service Grants MH 7229, MH 7446, and HD 947. September, 1966.

Stein, L. Reciprocal action of reward and punishment mechanisms. In R. G. Heath, ed., *The role of pleasure in behavior.* New York, Hoeber, 1964.

Stennett, R. G. The relationship of performance level to level of arousal, *Journal of experimental psychology,* 54 (1957), 54–61.

Stern, J. A., and McDonald, D. G. Physiological correlates of mental disease, *Annual review of psychology,* 16 (1965), 225–264.

Suinn, R. M., and Hill, H. Influence of anxiety on the relationship between self-acceptance and acceptance of others, *Journal of consulting psychology,* 28 (1964), 116–119.

Swenson, W. M. Attitudes toward death among the aged, *Minnesota medicine,* 42 (1959), 399–402.

Taylor, J. A. The relationship of anxiety to the conditioned eyelid response, *Journal of experimental psychology,* 41 (1951), 81–92.

Taylor, J. A. A personality scale of manifest anxiety, *Journal of abnormal and social psychology,* 48 (1953), 285–290.

Thompson, C. *Psychoanalysis: evolution and development.* New York, Hermitage House, 1950.

Tyler, E. A. The process of humanizing physiological man, *Family process,* 3 (1964), 280–301.

Tyler, E. A. Psychiatry—inherited or acquired knowledge?, *Journal of medical education,* 35 (1960), 689–695.

Underwood, B. J. *Experimental psychology.* New York, Appleton-Century-Crofts, 1949.

Wahl, C. W. The fear of death. In H. Feifel, ed., *The meaning of death.* New York, McGraw-Hill, 1959.

Walk, R. D. Self ratings of fear in a fear-invoking situation, *Journal of abnormal and social psychology,* 52 (1956), 171–178.

Walker, R. E., and Spence, J. T. Relationship between digit span and anxiety, *Journal of consulting psychology,* 28 (1964), 220–223.

Webster's New Collegiate Dictionary. Springfield, Mass., Merriam, 1956.

Weiner, S., Dorman, D., Persky, H., Stach, T. W., Norton, J., and Levitt, E. E. Effect of increasing the plasma hydrocortisone level on anxiety, *Psychosomatic medicine,* 25 (1963), 69–77.

Welch, B. L. Psychophysiological response to the mean level of environmental stimulation: a theory of environmental integration, *Symposium on medical aspects of stress in the military climate.* Washington, D.C., Walter Reed Army Institute of Research, 1964.

Welsh, G. S. An anxiety index and an internalization ratio for the MMPI, *Journal of consulting psychology,* 16 (1952), 65–72.

Wenar, C. Reaction time as a function of manifest anxiety and stimulus intensity, *Journal of abnormal and social psychology,* 49 (1954), 335–340.

Westrope, M. R., Relations among Rorschach indices, manifest anxiety, and performance under stress, *Journal of abnormal and social psychology,* 48 (1953), 515–524.

White, R. W. *Lives in progress: a study of the natural growth of personality.* New York, Dryden, 1952.

Whiting, J. W. M., and Child, I. L. *Child training and personality.* New Haven, Yale University Press, 1953.

Winkel, G. H., and Sarason, I. G. Subject, experimenter, and situational variables in research on anxiety, *Journal of abnormal and social psychology,* 68 (1964), 601–608.

Wood, C. G., and Hokanson, J. E. Effects of induced muscular tension on performance and the inverted U function, *Journal of personality and social psychology,* 1 (1965), 506–510.

Yerkes, R. M., and Dodson, J. D. The relation of strength of stimulus to rapidity of habit-formation, *Journal of comparative neurology and psychology,* 18 (1908), 459–482.

Zuckerman, M. The development of an affect adjective check list for the measurement of anxiety, *Journal of consulting psychology,* 24 (1960), 457–462.

Zuckerman, M., Kolin, E. A., Price, L., and Zoob, I. Development of a sensation-seeking scale, *Journal of consulting psychology,* 28 (1964), 477–482.

Zuckerman, M., Persky, H., Hopkins, T. R., Murtaugh, T., Basu, G. K., and Schilling, M. Comparison of stress effects of perceptual and social isolation, *Archives of general psychiatry,* 14 (1966), 356–365.

SELECTED SUGGESTIONS FOR ADVANCED READING

Blum, G. S. *Psychoanalytic theories of personality.* New York, McGraw-Hill, 1953.

Cannon, W. B. *Bodily changes in pain, hunger, fear and rage.* New York, Harper and Row, 1963.

Cofer, C. N., and Appley, M. H. *Motivation: theory and research.* New York, Wiley, 1964.

Duffy, E. *Activation and behavior.* New York, Wiley, 1962.

Lazarus, R. S. *Psychological stress and the coping process.* New York, McGraw-Hill, 1966.

May, R. *The meaning of anxiety.* New York, Ronald, 1950.

Ochs, S. *Elements of neurophysiology.* New York, Wiley, 1965. Chapter 24.

Sarason, I. G., ed. *Contemporary research in personality.* Princeton, N.J., Van Nostrand, 1962. Section VII.

Spielberger, C. D., ed. *Anxiety and behavior.* New York, Academic Press, 1966.

INDEX

A Factor Scale, 62, 66, 146, 165
Achievement Anxiety Test, 75–76, 165
Acker, M., 66, 67
Acquiescence set, 59
Adler, A., 116*n*
Adlerstein, A. M., 176
Adrenal glands, 182, 198
  cortex, 97–99
  medulla, 97–99, 101
Adrenaline (epinephrine), 97–98, 101, 102, 196, 197
Affect Adjective Check List, 67–69, 71, 163, 180, 195
Aggression, 24, 41, 157, 172, 182, 198
Aiken, L. R., 12
Alexander, I. E., 176
Algophobia, 9
Alpert, R., 75
Ambivalence, 32
ACE, 151
Amnesia, hypnotically induced, 39–40
Anticipation method, 110
Anxiety
  achievement, 116
  acute, defined, 13–14
  chronic, defined, 13–14
  concept of, 1, 194–195
  about death, 1, 175–177
  definitions of, 5–7
  about dental treatment, 174–175
  as drive, 27, 112–114, 115, 117. *See also* Iowa theory; Theory, Spence
  endocrinology of, 97–103
  experiment, 85–88
  experimental relief from, 130–132
  experimenter's, 89
  free-floating, 8, 9, 41, 63, 181
  as general arousal, 100–103. *See also* General arousal theory
  about illness, 168–171
  kinds of, 13–15
  message, 147–148
  moral, 19, 22, 160
  neurotic, 19, 22, 171
  physiological measures of, 56–57, 194–195
  physiological research on, 105–107
    problems of, 106–107, 187–189
  postoperative, 171–174
  preoperative, 171–174
  primary, 21, 23, 24, 25, 33
  reality, 19, 171
  secondary, 25, 33
  situational, 115. *See also* Yale theory: Mandler-Sarason theory

social psychology of, 177–184
social value of, 199–200
socialization, 192
as state, 15, 71, 72, 83, 194–195
about surgery, 171–174, 197
test, 72, 116
as trait, 15, 71–72, 154, 194–195
See also Effects of anxiety; Inventories, anxiety; Methodology; Theory
Anxiety Index, 62
Anxiety research, problems of, 186–195
definition, 186–187
design, 189–191
on origins, 192–194
on physiology, 187–189
Applezweig, D. C., 156
Assimilation Scales, 66–67
Assimilation theory, 66–67
Autonomic reactions, 56–57, 91–92, 93, 95, 188, 189
Avoidance, 36–37, 38, 52, 162, 170, 175

Bard, P., 93
Basowitz, H., 128, 129
Beam, J. C., 129
Bendig, A. W., 61
Berkun, M. M., 69
Berthold, F., 199
Bialek, H. M., 69
Bindra, D., 123
Bishop, M. P., 95, 188, 189
Bovard, E. W., 178
Brady, J. V., 94, 95, 100, 162, 198
Brain
anti-anxiety area of, 94–95
hypothalamus, 93, 94
limbic system, 93–95
paleocortex, 93
pleasure sites, 94–95, 198–199
reticular formation, 96, 181
self-stimulation of, 94–95, 188, 198–199
thalamus, 93
Breggin, P. R., 98, 99, 100
Budnitzky, S., 62
Buss, A. H., 99

Campbell, D. T., 42
Cannon, W. B., 93, 97, 100, 196
Cannon-Bard theory, 93
Castaneda, A., 62
Cattell, R. B., 14, 56, 63, 64, 194
Character armor, 157
Child, I. L., 192
Christie, R., 62
Clark, J. W., 84, 85
Claustrophobia, 9, 46
Communication, verbal, 145–148
Communicative efficiency, 146–147
Compulsivity, 25, 49–50, 51, 199
Conditioning, defined, 111
Conflict, 30–32
Construct, defined, 5
Coping mechanisms, 50–53
list of, 53
Corneal reflex, 111, 112–113, 123
Counterbehavior, 47–49, 199
Counterphobia, 48, 85
Courts, F. A., 133, 134, 135
Cowan, J. E., 74, 75
Cue, 27, 29, 181
Curiosity, 162–163, 165
Curiosity scale, 162–163

Dahlstrom, W. G., 62
Davids, A., 63, 124
Daydreaming, 53, 164–165
Death, anxiety about, 1, 175–177

Defense mechanisms, 13, 18*n*, 22, 25, 34–50, 105, 167
avoidance, 36–37, 38, 52, 162, 170, 175
compulsivity, 25, 49–50, 51, 157, 199
counterbehavior, 47–49, 199
reaction formation, 47
counterphobia, 48, 85
denial, 25, 37–38, 52, 56, 69, 170, 173, 175, 177
fixation, 44, 157
obsessive-compulsive, 50, 157
projection, 41–43, 47, 71
regression, 43–45, 156
repression, 25, 38–41, 69, 156, 157, 160
somatization, 45–47
and traits, 156–158
Denial, 25, 37–38, 52, 56, 69, 170, 173, 175, 177
Dental treatment, anxiety about, 174–175
Dependency needs, 24, 33
Dibner, A. S., 176, 177
Diethelm, O., 150
Diggory, J. C., 176
Dodson, J. D., 117, 118, 134
Dollard, J., 26, 27, 30, 32, 112, 148, 194
Drive, 26–27. *See also* Anxiety as drive
Duffy, E., 100, 102, 103, 107, 136
Dunbar, F., 46
Duncan, C. P., 140

Effects of anxiety
on intelligence test performance, 149–151
on learning
complex, 120–122, 124–126, 150
incidental, 144–145
and instructions, 130–132
and intelligence, 127–128
multi-correct response, 123–124
and natural stress, 128–130
and nature of task, 126–127
one-response, 113, 123
simple, 124–126
on mode of responding, 148–149
on problem-solving, 139–144
on variability of measurement, 155–158
on verbal communication, 145–148
Ego, 19–22, 23
Emotion, neurophysiology of, 91–97
"Empirical," defined, 3
Endler, N. S., 64, 74
English, A. C., 6
English, H. B., 6
Epinephrine. *See* Adrenaline
Eriksen, C. W., 63, 124, 132, 148, 149
Evaluation apprehension, 88
Existentialism, 167
Experiment anxiety, 85–88
Experimenter's anxiety, 89
Eye-blink reflex, 111, 112–113, 123

Fear Survey Schedule, 66
Fear undifferentiated from anxiety, 8–11
Feifel, H., 176, 177
Feldstein, A., 106
Feshbach, S., 147, 156
"Fight or flight" reaction, 97
Fitzgerald, J. A., 100

Fixation, 44, 157
Forced-choice item, 60
Fox, H. M., 105
Freeman, M. J., 70
Freud, S., 1, 9, 18–25, 26, 32, 34, 35, 39, 41, 44, 45, 46, 47, 53, 105, 116*n*, 157, 160, 161, 167, 171
Freudian theory, 1, 9, 18–22, 23, 35, 194
Friedman, I., 42
Fromm, E., 23, 167
Frustration, 21, 24

Galvanic skin reflex, 56*n*
Geer, J. H., 66, 147
General adaptation syndrome, 100, 104–105
General Anxiety Scale for Children, 75
General arousal theory, 100–103, 195–198
Generalization gradient, 28
Glaser, B. G., 177
Goldstein, M. J., 168*n*
Gordon, E. M., 74
Gorsuch, R. L., 71, 72, 195
Grinker, R. R., 80
Guilt-proneness, 160–161, 165
Guilt-proneness scale, 161
Gunderson, E. K., 181
Gynther, R. A., 146, 147

Haber, R. N., 75
Habit, 113, 114
Habit hierarchy, 113–114, 149
Hadley, J. M., 150
Hall, C. S., 1
Hall, G. S., 9
Hamilton, G. V., 141, 142, 143
Harleston, B. W., 140, 141
Harmavoidance, 116*n*
Heath, R. G., 95, 198, 199
Heineman, C. E., 61, 62, 86
Heller, J., 176, 177
Hilgard, E. R., 123, 161, 165, 166*n*
Hill, H., 160
Hoch, P. H., 1
Hokanson, J. E., 135
Homeostasis, 34, 36, 53
Horney, K., 23, 48, 101*n*, 160
Hull, C. L., 26*n*, 112
Hydrocortisone, plasma, 40, 99–100, 104
Hypnosis, 40, 46, 161–162, 165, 166
Hypnotizability, 161–162, 165, 166
Hypochondriasis, 168–169
Hypothalamus, 93, 94
Hysteria, 45, 46

Id, 19–22, 23, 26
Ideal concept of self, 41, 42
Illness, anxiety about, 168–171
Infavoidance, 116*n*
IPAT Anxiety Scale, 63–64, 81, 83*n*, 162, 165
Intelligence, and tests of, 77, 127–128, 149–151, 190, 195
Inventories, anxiety, 58–77
  A Factor Scale, 62, 66, 146, 165
  Achievement Anxiety Test, 75–76, 165
  Affect Adjective Check List, 67–69, 71, 163, 180, 195
  Anxiety Index, 62
  Assimilation Scales, 66–67
  Fear Survey Schedule, 66
  General Anxiety Scale for Children, 75

IPAT Anxiety Scale, 63–64, 81, 83*n*, 162, 165
Manifest Anxiety Scale, 60–62, 63, 66, 67, 71, 82, 83*n*, 85, 89, 114, 120, 123, 124, 125, 128, 134, 150, 151, 160, 161, 165, 169, 186–187
children's form of, 62, 163
forced-choice form of, 61, 62, 86
short form of, 61, 62
Manifest Anxiety Test, 70–71
MMPI item scales, 62–63
State-Trait Anxiety Inventory, 71–72, 187, 195
S-R Inventory of Anxiousness, 64–66, 71, 85
short form of, 65
Subjective Stress Scale, 69–70, 71, 180
Test Anxiety Questionnaire, 72–75, 132, 141, 150, 160
Test Anxiety Scale, 74, 130
children's form of, 75
Inventory, defined, 58
Inverted-U curve, 117, 120, 133, 172, 196–197. *See also* Yerkes-Dodson Law
Iowa theory, 60, 112–114, 132, 197
Iverson, M. A., 81, 88, 155

James, W., 92, 100
James-Lange theory, 92–93
Janis, I. L., 38, 171, 173, 174, 175, 197
Jeffers, F. C., 177
Jones, M. R., 150
Jung, C. G., 153

Kalish, R. S., 177
Kamin, L. J., 84, 85
Kardiner, A., 23
Kasl, S. V., 147
Katzenmeyer, W. G., 128
Kegeles, S. S., 175
Kerle, R. H., 69
Kety, S., 106
Kierkegaard, S., 199
Korchin, S. J., 125, 126, 196
Kubzansky, P. E., 179

Lange, C., 93
Lazarus, R. S., 12, 14, 155, 194
Learning
complex, 114, 120–122, 124–126, 150
defined, 108–110
incidental, 144–145
measurement of, 110–112
multi-correct response, 123, 124
and muscle tension, 119–120, 132–136, 196
one-response, 113, 122, 123
rote, 139, 140
simple, 114, 124–126
verbal, 110
Learning theory, 26–32, 112
Leeper, R. W., 144, 183
Levi, L., 101, 196
Levine, G. N., 125, 126, 170
Levitt, E. E., 6, 40, 56, 100, 162
Levy, L. H., 60, 187
Levy, N. A., 62
Lie scale, 60
Limbic system, 93–95
Lindsley, D. B., 96
Lowe, M. C., 161
Lubin, B., 162

McCandless, B. R., 62
McCann, B., 162, 164
McDonald, D. G., 106

McLean, P. D., 93
McReynolds, P., 66, 67, 162
Mahl, G. F., 147
Malmo, R. B., 96, 100, 107, 136, 181, 182
Mandler, G., 60, 72, 74, 75, 115, 116*n*, 125, 126, 130, 155
Mandler-Sarason theory, 114–116, 132
Manifest Anxiety Scale, 60–62, 63, 66, 67, 71, 82, 83*n*, 85, 89, 114, 120, 123, 124, 125, 128, 134, 150, 151, 160, 161, 165, 169, 186–187
Manifest Anxiety Test, 70–71
Martin, B., 98, 99, 100
Masserman, J. H., 176
Matarazzo, J. D., 120, 151
Medical Attitude Inventory, 169, 170, 175
Mednick, S. A., 84, 86, 87, 88
Memory drum, 110, 130, 140
Menninger, K., 48, 49, 51, 52. 167
Message anxiety, 147–148
Methodology in anxiety experiments, 77–89
  experimental design, 82–84, 189–191
  extraneous personal factors in
    evaluation apprehension, 88
    experiment anxiety, 85–88
    experimenter's anxiety, 89
  sampling variations, 84–85, 191
  sources of anxiety
    artificial stress as, 78–82, 83, 88
      validity of, 79–82
    natural and naturalistic conditions as, 77–78, 88
Meyer, D. R., 134, 135
Miller, N., 26, 27, 30, 32, 112, 148, 194
Milner, T., 94
MMPI, 60, 161
MMPI item scales, 62, 63
Mintz, A., 184
Modlin, H. C., 62
Monroe, R. R., 46
Montague, E. K., 124, 125
Mullin, C. S., 181
Murray, H. A., 116*n*

Neo-Freudian theory, 23–25, 48, 50–51, 101, 160
Nervous system
  parasympathetic, 91–92
  sympathetic, 56, 91–92, 97
Noble, M. E., 134, 135
Nonsense syllables, 110, 124, 129–130, 134, 140, 178
Noradrenaline (norepinephrine), 97–98, 101, 196, 197
Nunnally, J. C., 147

Obsessive-compulsive (defense), 50, 157
Ochlophobia, 182
Olds, J., 94, 198

Pain, 27, 33, 46, 78, 167, 171, 173, 178, 198, 199
Paired associates, 110, 113
Paleocortex, 93
Palermo, D. S., 62
Palmer, J. O., 168*n*
Panic, 144, 179, 183–184
Papez, J. W., 93
Papez-McLean theory, 93–94
Patrick, J. R., 143, 144, 182, 197
Paul, G. L., 132
Peccatophobia, 9

Penney, R. K., 162, 163, 164
Perkins, C. W., 65
Persky, H., 99, 100, 180
Personality, 1, 153–158
  anxious, 154–158, 165–166
  composition of, 153–154
Personality styles, 158–166
  curiosity, 162–163, 165
  daydreaming, 53, 164–165
  guilt-proneness, 160–161, 165
  hypnotizability, 161–162, 165, 166
  self-esteem, 48, 159–160, 165
  sensation-seeking, 163–164, 165
Phillips, B. N., 190
Phobia, 9–10, 36, 50
  algophobia, 9
  claustrophobia, 9, 46
  ochlophobia, 182
  peccatophobia, 9
  taphophobia, 9
  thanataphobia, 176, 177
Polygraph, 56
Primary process thinking, 182
Problem-solving, 139–144
Projection, 41–43, 47, 71
Projective techniques, 57–58
Purcell, C. K., 62

Quarantelli, E., 183

Reaction formation, 47
Reactive curiosity scale, 162–163
Reflex, salivary, 123
Regression, 43–45, 156
Reich, W., 157
Reinforcement, 26, 188
Reiter, H. H., 165
Repression, 25, 38–41, 69, 156, 160
Response set, 58–59
Response stereotypy, 29, 148–149
Reticular activating system, 96, 181
Reticular formation, 96, 181
Rhudick, P. J., 176, 177
Robbins, P. R., 169, 174, 175
Rorschach test, 57, 156
Rosenberg, M., 159, 160
Rosenberg, M. J., 88
Rosenthal, R., 89
Rothenberg, R. E., 171
Rothman, D. Z., 176
Rowe, R., 75, 165
Ruebush, B. K., 6, 126, 127

Sarason, I. G., 74, 83, 89, 130, 132, 155
Sarason, S. B., 1, 60, 72, 74, 75, 115, 116, 125, 126, 130, 155
Schachter, S., 101, 102, 103, 196
Scheier, I. H., 14, 56, 63, 64, 194
"Schizochemist," 106
Schizophrenia, 104, 105, 106, 188
  hebephrenic, 44
  paranoid, 42, 47
Schlesinger, A. J., Jr., 1
Schonbar, R. A., 165
Schultz, D. P., 144, 179, 181, 183, 184
Schwab, J. R., 81, 88, 155
Sears, R. R., 42, 157
Seidman, D., 178
Self-concept, 41, 42
Self-esteem, 48, 159–160, 165
Self-stimulation, intracranial, 94–95
  as psychotherapy, 198–199
Selye, H., 11, 100, 104
Sensation-seeking, 163–164, 165
Sensation-seeking scale, 163, 180
Sensory deprivation, 163, 178–182, 197

Sensory overload, 163, 182–184, 197
Siegman, A. W., 151
Silverman, R. E., 145
Singer, J. L., 75, 102, 147, 156, 165
Social desirability, 59–60, 71
Social isolation, 168, 179–180, 181, 182
Social psychology of anxiety
  panic, 144, 179, 183–184
  reduced environmental stimulation, 178–182
  sensory overload, 163, 182–184, 197
Social restriction, 179, 181
Somatization, 45–47
Spence, K. W., 60, 80, 88, 112, 113, 114, 122, 123, 132, 149, 151, 197
Spielberger, C. D., 14, 15, 71, 72, 128, 194, 195
State-Trait Anxiety Inventory, 71–72, 187, 195
Stein, L., 199
Stennett, R. G., 119, 120, 197
Stern, J. A., 106
Stimulation, optimal level of, 96, 163, 181
Stimulus generalization, 9, 27–30, 86–87, 148–149
S-R Inventory of Anxiousness, 64–66, 71, 85
Strauss, A. L., 177
Stress, 11–12, 13
  artificial, 78–82, 83, 88
  defined, 12
  everyday, 51, 167–168, 171
  natural and naturalistic, 77–78, 88
  techniques for inducing, 78–79
Subjective Stress Scale, 69–70, 71, 180
Suinn, R. M., 160
Sullivan, H. S., 23
Superego, 19–22, 23, 182
Surgery, anxiety about, 171–174, 197
Swenson, W. M., 177

Taphophobia, 9
Task-irrelevant reaction, 115, 122, 126, 147, 151
Task-relevant reaction, 115, 126
Taylor, J. A., 60, 123, 161
Tension, 12–13, 51–52, 181
  defined, 13
  muscle, 119–120, 132–136, 196
Test anxiety, 72, 116
Test Anxiety Questionnaire, 72–75, 132, 141, 150, 160
Test Anxiety Scale, 74, 75, 130
Tests, psychological
  ACE, 151
  guilt-proneness scale, 161
  Medical Attitude Inventory, 169, 170
    dental anxiety factor on, 175
  MMPI, 60, 161
  reactive curiosity scale, 162–163
  Rorschach, 57, 156
  sensation-seeking scale, 163, 180
  Wechsler Adult Intelligence Scale, 80, 111, 150
    Digit Span Subtest, 80
    Digit Symbol Subtest, 111, 135
Thalamus, 93
Thanataphobia, 176, 177
Theory
  activation, *see* Theory, general arousal
  assimilation, 66–67

Cannon-Bard, 93
of effect of anxiety on learning
Iowa, 60, 112–114, 132, 197
Yale, 114–116, 132
Freudian, 1, 9, 18–22, 23, 35, 194
general arousal, 100–103, 136, 195–198
James-Lange, 92–93
learning, 26–32, 112
Mandler-Sarason, 114–116, 132
Neo-Freudian, 23–25, 48, 50–51, 101, 160
of origins of anxiety
Freudian, 18–22, 193
learning, 26–32, 193–194
Neo-Freudian, 23–25
Papez-McLean, 93–94
purpose of, 17–18
Spence, 60, 112–114, 132, 197
Thompson, C., 23
Tyler, E. A., 44, 45, 46

Underwood, B. J., 144
U-shaped curve, 117, 119. *See also* Yerkes-Dodson Law

Variable
dependent, 82, 86, 189
independent, 82, 83, 109
intervening, 13

Wahl, C. W., 176
Walk, R. D., 129
Walker, R. E., 80, 88
Webster, 5
Wechsler, H., 148, 149
Wechsler Adult Intelligence Scale, 80, 111, 135, 150
Weiner, S., 100
Welch, B. L., 182
Welsh, G. S., 62
Wenar, C., 84, 85
Westrope, M. R., 156
Wheeler, L., 101
White, R. W., 35, 199
Whiting, J. W. M., 192
Winkel, G. H., 89
Wood, C. G., 135

Yale theory, 114–116, 132
Yerkes, R. M., 117, 118, 134
Yerkes-Dodson Law, 87, 116–120, 132, 133, 135, 141, 172, 174, 196–197. *See also* Inverted-U curve; U-shaped curve

Zubin, J., 1
Zuckerman, M., 67, 163, 164, 180